The MENA Region and COVID-19

Focusing on the Middle East and North Africa (MENA) region, which comprises some of the world's richest countries next to some of the poorest, this book offers excellent insights into the discriminatory consequences of the COVID-19 pandemic.

With a geographic focus on the MENA region, the multidisciplinary case studies collected in this edited volume reveal that the coronavirus's impact patterns are a question of two variables: governance performance and socioeconomic potency. Given the global, unprecedented, complex and systemic nature of COVID-19 – and its long-term implications for societies, governments, international organisations, citizens and corporations – this volume entails a relevance to regions undergoing similar dynamics. Analyses in the book, therefore, have implications for the comparative study of the pandemic and its impact on societies around the globe. Understanding related dynamics and implications, and making use of lessons learned, are a pathway to deal with future similar crises.

Questions covered in the volume are relevant to geopolitics, social challenges and the relations between political leaders and citizens as beings embedded in various strategies of communication. The volume will appeal to scholars of international politics, political science, risk or crisis governance, economics and sociology, human rights and security, political communication and public health.

Zeina Hobaika is a biochemist, holder of a PhD in Structure, Function and Proteins Engineering from Denis Diderot University and an Executive Diploma in Management and Conduct of Strategic Projects from Sciences Po in Paris. Today, she is an associate professor and serves as the head of department of Life and Earth Sciences-Biochemistry, at the Faculty of Sciences at Saint Joseph University of Beirut. She is also head of the Macromolecules Structure and Interactions Research Team. Her main research interests cover rational drug design to contribute to fighting diseases such as AIDS, cancer and Alzheimer's. Another major project she is working on consists of the management and valorisation of agro-industrial byproducts and waste, for a sustainable future. She has been selected for various national and international prizes and awards. In 2017, she became a member of the prestigious Arab–German Young Academy of Sciences and Humanities (AGYA). Last, with a large publication record and one patent, Zeina is involved in a variety of projects with the public and private sector.

Lena-Maria Möller is a visiting professor of Islamic law at the University of Münster and an affiliated research fellow at the Max Planck Institute for Comparative and International Private Law in Hamburg. Holding an MA in Middle East Studies and a PhD in Law (both from the University of Hamburg), her research and teaching interests concern contemporary Middle Eastern and Islamic law, with a particular focus on Muslim family law and the Gulf Cooperation Council (GCC) states, as well as comparative and private international law, and, most recently, law and popular culture in the Middle East. Lena-Maria Möller is a member and former co-president of the Arab–German Young Academy of Sciences and Humanities (AGYA) and serves as Associate Editor of the *Arab Law Quarterly*.

Jan Claudius Völkel is Academic Dean at IES Abroad Freiburg and associate researcher at the Arnold Bergstraesser Institute, University of Freiburg, focusing on contemporary sociopolitical developments in the Middle East and North Africa. He was a DAAD (German Academic Exchange Service) long-term lecturer in Euro-Mediterranean Studies at Cairo University, Faculty of Economics and Political Science (2013–17) and Marie Skłodowska-Curie Fellow at the Vrije Universiteit Brussel, Institute for European Studies with a research project on 'The Role of National Parliaments in the Arab Transformation Processes' (2017–19). In addition, he is the regional coordinator for the Middle East and North Africa at the Bertelsmann Transformation Index (BTI) and alumnus of the Arab–German Young Academy of Sciences and Humanities (AGYA). He has published widely in *Mediterranean Politics*, *Middle East Critique*, *Middle East Law and Governance*, *The Journal of North African Studies*, *European Foreign Affairs Review* and *Comparative Migration Studies*.

Routledge Studies in Middle Eastern Society

This series seeks to examine the various developments and changes in contemporary Middle East society. From a variety of disciplinary approaches it includes books on issues such as globalisation, the impact of economic, religious and political change on people's lives, the family and gender relations in the region.

3. **A Political Economy of Arab Education**
   Policies and Comparative Perspectives
   Mohamed Alaa Abdel-Moneim

4. **Syrian Refugee Children in the Middle East and Europe**
   Integrating the Young and Exiled
   Edited by Michelle Pace and Somdeep Sen

5. **Post-Conflict Transition in Lebanon**
   The Disappeared of the Civil War
   Lyna Comaty

6. **Leisure and Cultural Change in Israeli Society**
   Edited by Tali Hayosh, Elie Cohen-Gewerc, Gilad Padva

7. **Iranian Immigration to Israel**
   History and Voices, in the Shadow of Kings
   Ali L. Ezzatyar

8. **The MENA Region and COVID-19**
   Impact, Implications and Prospects
   Edited by Zeina Hobaika, Lena-Maria Möller and Jan Claudius Völkel

9. **Female Youth in Contemporary Egypt**
   Post-Islamism and a New Politics of Visibility
   Dina Hosni

For more information about this series, please visit: www.routledge.com/middleeaststudies/series/MESOC

The MENA Region and COVID-19

Impact, Implications and Prospects

Edited by
Zeina Hobaika, Lena-Maria Möller and
Jan Claudius Völkel

First published 2022
by Routledge
4 Park Square, Milton Park, Abingdon, Oxon OX14 4RN

and by Routledge
605 Third Avenue, New York, NY 10158

Routledge is an imprint of the Taylor & Francis Group, an informa business

© 2022 selection and editorial matter, Zeina Hobaika, Lena-Maria Möller and Jan Claudius Völkel; individual chapters, the contributors

The right of Zeina Hobaika, Lena-Maria Möller and Jan Claudius Völkel to be identified as the authors of the editorial material, and of the authors for their individual chapters, has been asserted in accordance with sections 77 and 78 of the Copyright, Designs and Patents Act 1988.

The Open Access version of this book, available at www.taylorfrancis.com, has been made available under a Creative Commons Attribution-Non Commercial-No Derivatives 4.0 licence.

Trademark notice: Product or corporate names may be trademarks or registered trademarks, and are used only for identification and explanation without intent to infringe.

British Library Cataloguing-in-Publication Data
A catalogue record for this book is available from the British Library

Library of Congress Cataloging-in-Publication Data
A catalog record has been requested for this book

ISBN: 978-1-032-14581-5 (hbk)
ISBN: 978-1-032-14586-0 (pbk)
ISBN: 978-1-003-24004-4 (ebk)

DOI: 10.4324/9781003240044

Typeset in Times New Roman
by Newgen Publishing UK

Contents

List of contributors	ix
Disclaimer	xv
Acknowledgements	xvi
List of abbreviations	xviii

1 Introduction: The MENA region and COVID-19 – concept and content of this book   1
ZEINA HOBAIKA, LENA-MARIA MÖLLER AND JAN CLAUDIUS VÖLKEL

PART I
Geopolitical implications   17

2 The COVID-19 temptation? Sino–Gulf relations and autocratic linkages in times of a global pandemic   19
THOMAS DEMMELHUBER, JULIA GUROL AND TOBIAS ZUMBRÄGEL

3 The reverse impact of politics on the COVID-19 response: how Hezbollah determined the choices of the Lebanese government   36
NASSIM ABIGHANEM

PART II
Communication strategies   53

4 'American Corona' vs. 'The Chinese virus': blaming and othering in Arab media   55
CAROLA RICHTER, ABDULRAHMAN AL-SHAMI, SOHEIR OSMAN, SAHAR KHALIFA SALIM AND SAMUEL MUNDUA

5 Securitisation dynamics and COVID-19 politics in
   Morocco: old wine in new bottles? 72
   GIULIA CIMINI AND BEATRIZ TOMÉ ALONSO

6 Status-seeking in times of a global pandemic: the United
   Arab Emirates' foreign policy during COVID-19 88
   ALEXANDER LOHSE

PART III
Social response 105

7 Religion and pandemic: state, Islam and society in
   Saudi Arabia and Iran during the coronavirus crisis 107
   NOËL VAN DEN HEUVEL AND ULRIKE FREITAG

8 'On the horns of a dilemma': human traffickers, the
   COVID-19 pandemic and victims of trafficking in
   Khartoum 125
   MANARA BABIKER HASSAN

9 A paradoxical management of COVID-19 in
   Lebanon: challenges and lessons learnt 141
   MICHÈLE KOSREMELLI ASMAR AND
   JOUMANA STEPHAN YERETZIAN

10 Digital learning under COVID-19: challenges and
   opportunities – the Lebanese case 156
   FADI EL HAGE AND FOUAD YEHYA

11 Conclusions: The MENA region and COVID-19 –
   lessons for the future 171
   ZEINA HOBAIKA, LENA-MARIA MÖLLER AND
   JAN CLAUDIUS VÖLKEL

Index 176

Contributors

Nassim AbiGhanem is a senior PhD student in International Relations at the Central European University in Vienna. Nassim received his MA in International Politics from the University of Manchester, focusing on US foreign policy in Lebanon. Nassim's research interest is in non-governmental political organisations, civil society organisations and informal political social networks. Nassim also is a teaching fellow at the Global History Lab at Princeton University. Outside academia, Nassim is the country consultant for Lebanon at the European Endowment for Democracy (EED) and Lebanon country expert at the Bertelsmann Transformation Index (BTI). Nassim publishes written commentary analysis for Lebanese and international outlets, as well as TV stations.

Beatriz Tomé Alonso is an assistant professor in the Department of International Studies at Universidad Loyola Andalucía (Seville) and associate research fellow at the Study Group on Arab and Muslim Societies (GRESAM) at Universidad de Castilla La Mancha. Her research focuses on Islamist movements in the Maghreb, especially Morocco, the interlink between international, regional and domestic arenas, international actors' foreign policies towards the Middle East and North Africa states and responses to these from domestic actors. She has published in *The Journal of North African Studies* and *Contemporary Politics*, among others.

Abdulrahman al-Shami is Associate Professor of Broadcast Journalism at Qatar University. In his research, he focuses on new media and social change, as well as on satellite channels. He is the co-founder of AREACORE, the Arab-European Association of Media and Communication Researchers, and a board member of AUSACE, the Arab-US Association of Communication Educators.

Michèle Kosremelli Asmar is an associate professor and director of the Higher Institute of Public Health at Saint Joseph University of Beirut, where she has been working for the last twenty years. She holds a PhD in Management (health concentration) from Paris Dauphine University and a master's degree in Health Administration from the University of

Montreal, as well as a post-graduate degree in Institutional Management-Health Care from Concordia University, Montreal. She has coordinated the MBAIP-Health Management programme offered in collaboration with Paris Dauphine University and IAE-Paris I Pantheon Sorbonne over the past fifteen years. Her research and teaching focus on public health, interprofessional collaboration and coordination, disability and inclusion health management, quality and accreditation, technology and health, healthcare, human resources, health economics, health systems. She has consulted on health systems and reforms in Lebanon, France and Canada as well as the Middle East and North Africa region. She is the author of several articles and book chapters as well as a member of scientific organisations and committees. Michèle is also the president of the non-governmental organisation Include, which promotes the inclusion of children, youth and adults with special needs in Lebanese society.

Giulia Cimini is a post-doctoral researcher at the Department of Political and Social Sciences, University of Bologna, with a fellowship supported by the Gerda Henkel Foundation. She was previously a teaching assistant of politics at the University of Naples L'Orientale, Visiting Fellow at the University of St Andrews, and at the Centre Jacques Berque in Rabat. Her current research interests include Maghrebi political parties and security dynamics. She has published in *Contemporary Politics*, *The Journal of North African Studies*, *Middle Eastern Studies* and *Contemporary Arab Affairs*, among others.

Thomas Demmelhuber is Professor of Middle East Politics and Society at the Friedrich-Alexander-University of Erlangen-Nürnberg. Before, he was Assistant Professor for Political Science at the University of Hildesheim (2012–15). His dissertation on EU–Egyptian relations was awarded the German Middle East Studies Association's prize for best PhD in Middle Eastern studies. His research focuses on state, power and politics in the Middle East from a comparative perspective. Thomas has edited numerous books, e.g. *The Routledge Handbook on European Neighbourhood Policy* (2018, with Tobias Schumacher and Andreas Marchetti) and *Authoritarian Gravity Centres: A Cross-Regional Study of Authoritarian Promotion and Diffusion* (2020, with Marianne Kneuer).

Fadi El Hage is the Delegate of the Rector for Professional Development and Continuing Education at the Saint Joseph University of Beirut (USJ). He is the chairholder of the Chair of 'Fondation Diane' for Education on Eco-Citizenship and Sustainable Development. Before, he was head of research, head of studies, vice-dean and dean of the Faculty of Education at USJ. He is also the vice-president of the Association for the Development of Education Assessment Methodologies (ADMEE) and the national delegate of the United Nations Educational, Scientific and Cultural Organization (UNESCO) Chair 'Global Health and Education'. He is an associate researcher at the Laboratoire Interdisciplinaire de Recherche en Didactique, Éducation et Formation (LIRDEF) at the University of Montpellier and a lecturer and researcher at the Faculty of Education at USJ.

Ulrike Freitag is a historian of the modern Middle East and director of Leibniz-Zentrum Moderner Orient in conjunction with a professorship at Freie Universität Berlin (since 2002). Her main research interest is the history of the Arabian Peninsula from a translocal perspective, with a particular focus on urban and intellectual history. Her latest book is *A History of Jeddah. The Gate to Mecca in the Nineteenth and Twentieth Centuries* (2020).

Julia Gurol is a post-doctoral researcher and lecturer at the Chair for International Relations at the University of Freiburg. She is also an associate fellow at the Center for Applied Research in Partnership with the Orient (CARPO). Her research focuses on transregional authoritarian practices, Chinese foreign and security policy as well as global governance in the Global South. Her regional focus is on China and the Middle East, in particular the Gulf region. Julia Gurol is currently co-leading a research project on autocratic collaboration in Sino-Gulf relations in the context of the global pandemic, funded by the Volkswagen-Stiftung.

Manara Babiker Hassan is currently working on her research proposal about securitisation of migration to obtain a PhD in Political Science. She earned an MSc degree in International Relations from the University of Khartoum, Department of Political Science, with a thesis on Ethiopian refugees in Sudan. From the same university she also holds a BSc degree in Economics and Social Science and two post-graduate diplomas in Development and Planning Studies and International Law of Human Rights.

Noël van den Heuvel is a scholar of Middle Eastern studies and works at the Leibniz-Zentrum Moderner Orient. Currently his main research focuses on education and state-building in Saudi Arabia before 1979.

Zeina Hobaika is a biochemist, holder of a PhD in Structure, Function and Proteins Engineering from Denis Diderot University and an Executive Diploma in Management and Conduct of Strategic Projects from Sciences Po in Paris. Today, she is an associate professor and serves as the head of department of Life and Earth Sciences-Biochemistry, at the Faculty of Sciences at Saint Joseph University of Beirut. She is also the head of the Macromolecules Structure and Interactions Research Team. Her main research interests cover rational drug design to contribute to fighting diseases such as AIDS, cancer and Alzheimer's. Another major project she is working on consists of the management and valorisation of agro-industrial byproducts and waste, for a sustainable future. She has been selected for various national and international prizes and awards. In 2017, she became a member of the prestigious Arab–German Young Academy of Sciences and Humanities (AGYA). Last, with a large publication record and one patent, Zeina is involved in a variety of projects with the public and private sector.

Alexander Lohse is a PhD candidate and research fellow in the Department of Near and Middle Eastern Politics at the Center for Near and Middle Eastern Studies, as well as a lecturer in International Relations at the Institute for Political Science at Philipps-University Marburg. He is currently working on his PhD project on status-seeking strategies in the United Arab Emirates' foreign policy. His research interests include the foreign policies of the Arab Gulf states and Islamist movements in the Arab world and their role in regional politics.

Lena-Maria Möller is a visiting professor of Islamic law at the University of Münster and an affiliated research fellow at the Max Planck Institute for Comparative and International Private Law in Hamburg. Holding an MA in Middle East Studies and a PhD in Law (both from the University of Hamburg), her research and teaching interests concern contemporary Middle Eastern and Islamic law, with a particular focus on Muslim family law and the Gulf Cooperation Council (GCC) states, as well as comparative and private international law, and, most recently, law and popular culture in the Middle East. Lena-Maria Möller is a member and former co-president of the Arab–German Young Academy of Sciences and Humanities (AGYA) and serves as Associate Editor of the *Arab Law Quarterly* (Brill).

Samuel Mundua is a PhD candidate of Communication Science specialising in Strategic Media Management at the University of South Africa (UNISA). He is also a senior lecturer of Media Studies at Bayan College in Muscat, which is affiliated with Purdue University Northwest. He previously worked as head of Department of Media Studies at Bayan College until September 2020. Prior to joining Bayan College, Samuel worked as lecturer in Public Relations and Media Management at Cavendish University in Kampala. He is a member of the Arab-European Association for Media and Communication Researchers (AREACORE).

Soheir Osman is Associate Professor of Journalism at the Department of Mass Communication at Cairo University and head of the journalism department at Ahram Canadian University in Cairo. She is an expert in journalism studies and political communication.

Carola Richter is Professor of International Communication at Freie Universität Berlin. In her research, she focuses on media systems and communication cultures in the Middle East and North Africa, foreign news coverage, media and migration as well as public diplomacy. She is the co-founder of AREACORE, the Arab-European Association of Media and

Communication Researchers, and director of the Center for Media and Information Literacy (CeMIL) at Freie Universität Berlin.

Sahar Khalifa Salim is university professor at the College of Information of al-Iraqia University in Baghdad. Her research interests include digital media education, investigative journalism and propaganda. She is the vice chairperson of al-Baseera Society for Media Research and Development and a member of the Arab-European Association for Media and Communication Researchers (AREACORE) and the Advisory Committee of Arab Research ID (ARID).

Jan Claudius Völkel is Academic Dean at IES Abroad Freiburg and associate researcher at the Arnold Bergstraesser Institute, University of Freiburg, focusing on contemporary socio-political developments in the Middle East and North Africa. He was a DAAD (German Academic Exchange Service) long-term lecturer in Euro-Mediterranean Studies at Cairo University, Faculty of Economics and Political Science (2013–17) and Marie Skłodowska-Curie Fellow at the Vrije Universiteit Brussel, Institute for European Studies with a research project on 'The Role of National Parliaments in the Arab Transformation Processes' (2017–19). In addition, he is the regional coordinator for the Middle East and North Africa at the Bertelsmann Transformation Index (BTI) and alumnus of the Arab–German Young Academy of Sciences and Humanities (AGYA). He has published widely in *Mediterranean Politics*, *Middle East Critique*, *Middle East Law and Governance*, *The Journal of North African Studies*, *European Foreign Affairs Review* and *Comparative Migration Studies*.

Fouad Yehya is a post-doctoral researcher and instructor at the Saint Joseph University of Beirut, creating learning models and strategies to implement information and computer technology (ICT) in education and strengthen educators' skills and self-awareness towards technology. Fouad's career as instructor and trainer has spanned over twenty-three years. He has published a number of articles and given workshops and conferences in Lebanon and internationally on different topics related to teaching and learning, international exams and scholarly productivity.

Joumana Stephan Yeretzian holds an MSc in Biostatistics and is currently working on a PhD in Health Management. She is a faculty member at the Higher Institute of Public Health at the Saint Joseph University of Beirut where she also serves as the coordinator of the epidemiology and biostatistics programme as well as the coordinator for research activities. Her research interests lie in designing and analysing epidemiological studies, exploring and assessing public–private partnerships and strengthening and optimising health information systems. Joumana also provides expert consultancy services for local and international non-governmental organisations.

Tobias Zumbrägel is a researcher at the Center for Applied Research in Partnership with the Orient (CARPO). He studied History, Political Science and Middle Eastern Studies in Cologne, Tubingen and Cairo and holds a PhD from the Friedrich-Alexander University Erlangen-Nuremberg. Tobias has conducted extensive field research in the Middle East and North Africa. His main research focuses on questions of legitimacy, power and state authority in the Middle East with a special interest in environmentalism and digitalisation.

Disclaimer

The Arab–German Young Academy of Sciences and Humanities (AGYA) is financing the publication *The MENA Region and COVID-19: Impact, Implications and Prospects*. The authors remain solely responsible for the content and recommendations provided in this publication, which do not reflect the positions of AGYA or any of its funding partners.

Acknowledgements

This book is the result of an open call for contributions that we launched in summer 2020 amid a still-evolving COVID-19 pandemic. After a careful selection of the incoming proposals, in October 2020 we invited all the authors to a three-day online workshop, during which the individual chapters were presented and the common themes and developments were discussed.

From the initial idea to the final publication, we were strongly supported and encouraged by the Arab–German Young Academy of Sciences and Humanities (AGYA), of which we are all members or alumni. Once more, we are very grateful for AGYA's empowerment of our interdisciplinary research and Arab–German collaboration. With funding from the Federal Ministry of Education and Research (BMBF), AGYA has facilitated this book's open-access status and its presentation at the 27th International Congress of the German Middle East Studies Association for Contemporary Research and Documentation (DAVO) in Osnabrück in September 2021. We are thankful for the support of the AGYA Berlin Office, in particular Prof. Verena Lepper, Dr Sabine Dorpmüller, Masetto Bonitz, Viktoria Fink and Jonas Reiche-Weiland.

Andrea Clausen and Tina Holze Paio have diligently and meticulously cared for the language editing, together with their colleagues from *Supertext Deutschland GmbH*, Elske Janssen has helped in assembling the index and Julia Hotopp was instrumental in conducting the initial authors' workshop. We owe them all our deepest respect and gratitude.

From Routledge, James 'Joe' Whining, Titanilla Panczel and Priyanka Mundada were highly engaged in the eventual production of the book. The collaboration with them was marked by outstandingly high levels of mutual trust and appreciation – we thank you very much indeed.

This publication is funded by the Arab–German Young Academy of Sciences and Humanities (AGYA) and is edited by AGYA members Zeina Hobaika and Lena-Maria Möller and AGYA alumnus Jan Claudius Völkel. It is an interdisciplinary research project of the AGYA working group 'Transformation'. AGYA is supported by the German Federal Ministry of Education and Research (BMBF).

SPONSORED BY THE

ARAB-GERMAN
YOUNG ACADEMY
OF SCIENCES AND
HUMANITIES

Beirut, Hamburg and Freiburg, June 2021
Zeina Hobaika, Lena-Maria Möller and Jan Claudius Völkel

Abbreviations

AI	artificial intelligence
AU	African Union
BRI	Belt-and-Road Initiative
CCP	Chinese Communist Party
CCTV	closed-circuit television
CEO	Chief Executive Officer
CERD	Centre for Educational Research and Development
COVID-19	Coronavirus disease 2019
DEBL	Digital Error Based Learning
EEBL	remote error exploitation-based learning
ESCWA	Economic and Social Commission for Western Asia
EU	European Union
FDI	foreign direct investment
G42	Group 42
GCC	Gulf Cooperation Council
GDP	gross domestic product
GoE	Government of Ethiopia
GoS	Government of Sudan
HDI	Human Development Index
HM	His Majesty
ICT	information and communications technology
ICU	intensive care unit
IDPs	internally displaced persons
iGA	Information & eGovernment Authority
IGAD	Intergovernmental Authority on Development
IHC	International Humanitarian City
IMF	International Monetary Fund
IR	International Relations
IRENA	International Renewable Energy Agency
IRGC	Iranian Revolutionary Guard Corps
IT	information technology
KSA	Kingdom of Saudi Arabia

List of abbreviations xix

LAS	League of Arab States
MEHE	Ministry of Education and Higher Education
MENA	Middle East and North Africa
MERS(-CoV)	Middle East respiratory syndrome (coronavirus)
MoPH	Ministry of Public Health
NCCHT	National Committee for Combating Human Trafficking
NGOs	non-governmental organisations
OPEC	Organisation of the Petroleum Exporting Countries
PCR	polymerase chain reaction
PHC	primary healthcare
PHCC	primary healthcare centres
PJD	Parti de la Justice et du Développement (Party of Justice and Development)
PM	Prime Minister
POGIL	Process Oriented Guided Inquiry Learning
PPE	personal protective equipment
RHUH	Rafik Hariri University Hospital
RT-PCR	reverse transcriptase polymerase chain reaction
SARS(-CoV)	severe acute respiratory syndrome (coronavirus)
SDAIA	Saudi Data and Artificial Intelligence Authority
STC	Saudi Telecom Company
STEAM	Science, Technology, Engineering, Art and Maths
TPD	Training Professional Development
UAE	United Arab Emirates
UHC	universal healthcare
UK	United Kingdom
UN	United Nations
UNDP	United Nations Development Programme
UNHCR	United Nations High Commissioner for Refugees
UNICEF	United Nations International Children Emergency Fund
USA	United States of America
USJ	Saint Joseph University
VoIP	Voice over Internet Protocol
WHO	World Health Organization
WHO-EMRO	World Health Organization's Eastern Mediterranean Regional Office

1 Introduction

The MENA region and COVID-19 – concept and content of this book

Zeina Hobaika, Lena-Maria Möller and Jan Claudius Völkel

1.1 COVID-19 in the MENA region: countering an unexpected crisis

This edited volume tackles an urgent, timely question: how has the unprecedented and far-reaching crisis caused by the COVID-19 pandemic affected social, political and individual life in countries of the region commonly referred to as the 'Middle East and North Africa' (MENA)?

Especially the MENA region's many Arab countries, which are at the centre of this book's analysis, are oftentimes perceived as a single homogeneous union due to the similarities in language and the major religion. However, they differ distinctively in many regards: while a few are (semi-)democratic, such as Lebanon and Tunisia, and some are in transformation, as is currently the case in Algeria and Sudan, others are characterised by more authoritarian forms of government, such as many Arab monarchies and Egypt. Sadly, there are also a number of war-torn countries, for example Iraq, Libya, Syria and Yemen. Similarly, while the resource-rich economies along the Persian Gulf belong to the world's most affluent countries, Yemen and the Gaza strip rank among the world's poorest regions.

Given these economic and political variances, it hardly comes as a surprise that countries in the region also differ strongly in their provisions of public policies, including health. While the rich Gulf monarchies offer world-class medical facilities and attract a large number of doctors and nursing staff from other Arab countries, less affluent countries only offer insufficient public health care systems: there are 14 doctors per 10,000 inhabitants in the 22 member states of the League of Arab States (LAS), whereas the Gulf Cooperation Council (GCC) features 25 doctors per 10,000 (Hasan, 2021: 1151). Around 20 hospital beds exist per 10,000 population in Arab countries, compared to, for example, 52 in the EU (Hasan, 2021: 1151). Tunisia was said to provide a maximum of 200 intensive care beds in public hospitals at the beginning of the pandemic, and only 550 respirators were available in Morocco (Joffé, 2020: 517). Personal protective equipment (PPE) and testing kits have remained scarce, if not completely inaccessible, for the impoverished

DOI: 10.4324/9781003240044-1

population in many parts of the Arab world. In countries with high numbers of internally displaced persons (IDPs), refugees or otherwise undocumented persons, health provisions are not extensive or specific enough to cover them all – a shortfall which becomes particularly dangerous in times of a pandemic (Wehbe et al., 2021: 3). This includes the rich Gulf monarchies, where blue-collar migrant workers – usually much more numerous than the local population – have only limited health care services at their disposal (Asi, 2020).

With 6% of gross domestic product (GDP), Arab countries spent only half as much on health than the global average in 2017 (Hasan, 2021: 1152). Unsurprisingly then, MENA countries performed only moderately to badly in the 2016 Healthcare Access and Quality Index, which measures the personal health care access and quality in 195 countries (Lozano, 2018). Overall, the MENA region scored a meagre 55.8 on a scale from 0 (worst) to 100 (best); Lebanon (in 33rd place) performed best with a score of 85.6, followed by Israel (35th/84.8), Qatar (41st/81.7), Kuwait (44th/80.7), Saudi Arabia (52nd/77.1), Oman (54th/76.2), Bahrain (65th/72.0), Iran (66th/71.8), Libya (67th/71.1), United Arab Emirate (UAE) (73rd/70.3), Jordan (74th/70.2), Tunisia (77th/69.4), Syria (88th/67.2), Algeria (99th/63.1), Egypt (111th/58.0), Morocco (112th/57.6), Palestine (114th/57.4), Iraq (125th/51.1), Sudan (136th/45.8) and Yemen (140th/43.3).

This imbalance is also reflected in the highly diverging life expectancies across the Arab world, ranging between 50 and 57.1 years in Somalia and Sudan, respectively, to 78.2 and 81.5 years in Qatar and Lebanon, respectively (Jabbour, 2013: 357). In the poorer countries, state-of-the-art health care services are usually offered in private or military clinics (for cash or only for eligible patients); meanwhile conditions in public hospitals are typically insufficient for patients and staff alike. Above all, medical research is largely underdeveloped, or, in conflict countries, completely impossible (El Achi et al., 2019). Despite some increases since the mid-2000s, the World Health Organization's Eastern Mediterranean Regional Office (WHO-EMRO) still counts Arab countries 'among the lowest producers of systematic reviews' (AlKhaldi, Al-Surimi and Meghari, 2020: 11): between December 2019 and March 2020, only 4.26% of the global research output regarding COVID-19 came from Arab countries, mostly Saudi Arabia (35.65%), Egypt (20.78%) and the UAE (11.73%) (Zyoud, 2021: 3). However, not only intra-Arab knowledge production in the field of medical research is limited: so is intra-Arab exchange of knowledge. Additionally, existing medical research is conducted in clinical laboratories without sufficient consideration of the socioeconomic aspects, as Jabbour (2013: 358) states:

> Work on social determinants, from human rights to trade policies to environmental engineering, is either in infancy or not at all part of health system mandates. The health-in-all-policies approach to health promotion has not taken root – or perhaps not even been planted across the region.

Given these grave and far-reaching shortcomings, the United Nations' Economic and Social Commission for Western Asia (ESCWA) expected the implications of the COVID-19 pandemic to rest heavily on states and societies. According to ESCWA's estimates from the initial weeks of the pandemic, approximately 1.7 million people were likely to lose their jobs in 2020, and another 8 million people, half of them children, were destined to fall into poverty. Besides the already low oil price, the pandemic threatened tourism and hospitality industries, as well as the stream of vital remittances from migrant workers in richer countries who support their families back home. A pandemic-induced economic decline would trigger devastating consequences for people's adequate nutrition and sanitation, access to clean drinking water, shelter, health care and education (Karamouzian and Madani, 2020: 886).

The region's largely insufficient health provisions are the result of grossly underperforming political systems. After decades of what political scientists perceived as 'Arab exceptionalism' in an attempt to explain why none of the 'waves of democracy' that swept the world took hold in the MENA region (Lust, 2011), a scent of 'permanent uncertainty' has become a region-wide pattern more recently. Hardly any expert on the region had predicted the breath-taking changes that affected so many Arab countries in early 2011, triggering unprecedented protests against political suppression, economic mismanagement and kleptocratic governance. Admittedly, a quiescent order appears to have been restored now in most countries and 'normality' has seemingly regained control across the region, i.e. non-democratic regimes exercising far-reaching power based on rent-generated resource distribution to their supporters, while suppressing potential opponents with uncompromised police violence and a sophisticated security apparatus. However, protesters in Algeria and Sudan have triggered a new round of regime changes in 2019, and, also surprisingly, various Arab countries started to revise their fundamental rejection of diplomatic relations with Israel in late 2020, having the potential to create completely new regional power relations.

In that particular parallelism of inertia and commotion, stagnation and dynamic, the coronavirus caught the MENA region – and the whole world – largely unprepared. While other recent epidemics had already made an impact on the MENA region – such as Middle East respiratory syndrome (MERS), which was first identified in Saudi Arabia in 2012, or Ebola, which, after being transmitted by air passengers from West Africa, threatened Dubai Airport as one of the world's leading international transport hubs two years later – these warning signs have remained largely ignored due to a 'global failure by public health systems to adequately assess and respond to such outbreaks, because of an absence of proper risk assessment and communication, transparency, and serious intent to define and control the outbreaks' (Zumla et al., 2015: 101).

The novel coronavirus SARS-CoV-2 developed a completely different dynamic. Public life around the globe changed significantly: a simple handshake could potentially bring death and suffering and face masks became an accepted part of our daily apparel. With the growing spread, clinics and hospitals in even the richest countries were pushed to the limits of their capacities, if not beyond. As of 1 July 2021, almost 3.95 million deaths in relation to the COVID-19 pandemic had been recorded by Johns Hopkins University's Coronavirus Resource Center; more than 182 million had contracted the virus (Johns Hopkins University & Medicine, 2021; on the difficulties connected with COVID-19 statistics, see Viglione, 2020). In Arab countries, more than 3.2 million infections and 55,000 deaths were reported as of December 2020, numbers that had rapidly increased since September 2020 (Wehbe et al., 2021: 1).

While in the initial months the coronavirus was said not to discriminate between rich and poor concerning its infectiousness, its consequences differ markedly: financially sound societies may be able to afford economic shutdowns, but citizens in poorer countries lack the opportunity to not go to work – if they even can afford the 'luxury' of seeing a doctor. Moreover, keeping children out of school for months can be compensated for (at least partly) through excellent learning conditions at home, but children from families with fewer resources usually lack the necessary conditions. The MENA region is believed to be especially prone to infectious diseases like COVID-19: in 'normal' times, the globally leading 'ME3 carriers' Emirates, Etihad and Qatar Airways transport millions of travellers to and from the region. This not least because the Arabian Peninsula is a prime destination for millions of labour migrants and religious pilgrims. Besides, there are the millions of refugees and IDPs who form communities that are particularly vulnerable to infectious diseases. And in general, 'Middle Eastern populations have high rates of diabetes and cardiovascular problems that have been found to be risk factors for severe COVID-19 disease' (Sawaya et al., 2020: 1).

Not only does the Arab world contain specific risk factors, but the current public health systems are often in a deplorable situation as well. While some countries had established dedicated counter-epidemic units in their public health administrative structures after their prior experiences with MERS and Ebola – as well as severe acute respiratory syndrome (SARS) in 2002–4 and the H1N1 influenza ('swine flu') in 2009, which certainly helped in formulating effective response strategies against COVID-19 in 2020 – the very limited cross-regional cooperation hindered the vital spread of knowledge about this novel coronavirus. In addition, insufficient statistics in many Arab countries regarding infection rates and COVID-19-related casualties rendered fundamental research unreliable (Sawaya et al., 2020: 2). Given the surprisingly low COVID-19 numbers that were reported from many Arab countries, especially during the infancy of the pandemic, Eberhard Kienle (2020) identified an 'Arab exceptionalism, once again', notably this time not concerning 'the deplorable large-scale absence of transitions from authoritarianism but the welcome protection of public health, perhaps even encouraged and facilitated by the former'.

Arab governments' initial COVID-19 responses partially followed the global trend: closing borders and imposing lockdowns as well as curfews to limit personal movement and contact, even by cancelling communal Friday prayers and Sunday masses and issuing guidelines for safe practices for religious occassions such as Ramadan (Karamouzian and Madani, 2020: 886), Palm Sunday and Easter. Socioeconomic support measures were launched and a number of regimes released prisoners from overcrowded jails, albeit sometimes according to questionable or problematic selection criteria, as criminals were prioritised over political prisoners in many instances (El-Sadani, 2020). Despite such measures, hospital caregivers in a number of Arab countries got desperately overwhelmed: In early 2021, videos from two Egyptian hospitals went viral, showing desperate staff and COVID-19 patients allegedly dying due to a shortage of medical oxygen – claims which the Egyptian government fervently rejected (Michaelson, 2021). Similarly, in March 2021, six COVID-19 patients in a Jordanian hospital suffocated due to a lack of medical oxygen, and the devastating blaze in a COVID-19 station of a Baghdad hospital in April 2021, killing 82 and injuring 110, showed the suffering and despair of patients, staff and families alike.

Anti-COVID-19 vaccination campaigns have picked up speed in only a few MENA countries so far. As of late June 2021, 59.7% of Israelis and 58.01% of Bahrainis were vaccinated; Qatar reported vaccination rates of 49.64%, and the UAE of 38.79%. Many other countries in the region, however, lag behind: Morocco (24.7%), Jordan (13.51%), Palestine (6.89%), Lebanon (6.24%), Tunisia (4.65%), Iran (1.95%), Kuwait (0.89%), Egypt (0.76%), Sudan (0.28%) and Syria (0.03%) all remain at a far distance. At the stage of only first doses were Saudi Arabia (51.57%), Libya (5.52%), Iraq (1.36%) and Yemen (0.79%); for Algeria, no official data were recorded.[1]

Globally, the coronavirus has drastically shown the importance of functioning governance. Countries in which the political leadership denied the seriousness of the virus at some point were hit exceptionally hard. This notably included long-standing, well-established democracies such as the United Kingdom and the United States of America. Countries where the political leadership initiated measures at an early stage, however, were able to protect their citizens astonishingly well, including countries from the middle or lower ranks of the Human Development Index (HDI) from the United Nations Development Programme (UNDP), such as Vietnam or Thailand, as a comparative analysis conducted by Bloomberg impressively showed (Hong, Chang and Varley, 2020/2021). In their updated list from 28 June 2021, some MENA countries ranked among the world's best COVID-19 responders – Israel (4th), Turkey (14th), Saudi Arabia (15th) and the UAE (18th) – even when compared with leading HDI countries such as the Netherlands (22nd), Canada (24th) or Germany (28th). Meanwhile, Egypt (33rd), Iraq (37th) and Iran (42nd) are the lowest-ranked MENA representatives out of a total of 53 analysed countries (the region's war-torn countries, Libya, Syria and Yemen, were not included).

1.2 The COVID-19 pandemic: systemic risk and societal resilience

In contrast to MERS, Ebola and a number of other endemic diseases of the past few decades, COVID-19 has quickly turned into a health challenge of global concern which meets all the criteria of a 'systemic risk': being highly complex and transboundary in nature, following random trajectories towards a catastrophic tipping point and being largely uncontained in its devastating effects (Schweizer, 2019: 4–5). Besides, systemic risks pose an imminent threat to 'a society's essential systems' (ibid.: 2), which may consist of telecommunication networks and other critical infrastructure, as well as fundamental health care arrangements, education and the provision of basic needs.

Systemic risks require systemic responses, marked by 'institutional structures and socio-political processes that guide and restrain the collective activities of a group, society, or international community' (Klinke and Renn, 2019: 2). Here, COVID-19 has brought to light major injustices on a global scale as well as at regional or even national levels. It is impossible to say whether democracies or autocracies performed better in the first year of the pandemic, but functioning governance structures seem to play an important role. Gaskell and Stoker (2020: 34–7) highlighted four qualities of governance arrangements that are relevant to successful COVID-19 responses: central capacity, decentralised capacity, mutual learning and celebrating difference. While the first two refer to institutional infrastructure, the latter two hint at a necessary minimum ability of the actors to (re)act flexibly. This includes actual decision makers and ordinary citizens.

Thus, there is a connection between the severity of the impact of the virus and a society's overall ability to withstand this major public health challenge. In abstract terms, the COVID-19 pandemic has been an external shock that has hit societies largely unprepared. As with other risks, the reaction to and eventual overcoming of this pandemic ('risk governance') result from 'complex socio-political processes, structures, and institutions that provide collectively binding agreements on the processes for identifying, framing, assessing, evaluating, managing, and communicating risks' (Klinke and Renn, 2019: 2). In that understanding, the ability of a society to cope with a threat (i.e. the resilience of this specific society) depends on two overarching independent variables: functional leadership (the *performance* of those in leadership positions) and socioeconomic potency (the *status* of a society). The behaviour of the population results from these two individual conditions as the dependent variable, in terms of both willingness and ability. The level of trust that a society has in its governance structures and political leadership works as an intervening variable.

Functional leadership depends on the structural and individual characteristics of a country's political elite. Structurally, the effectiveness and efficiency of the public administration are decisive, from the top of the state down to units at the local level. These must be met by the individual criteria of decision makers, such as factual competence, a prioritisation of rationality over ideology and communication skills to explain the decision. Since 'no single actor in our societies possesses the knowledge, capabilities, or resources to steer and manage complex risks that originate in rich ecological, social, and economic systems' (Klinke and Renn, 2019: 2), the ability to include external advice is another important element of factual leadership.

Socioeconomic potency results from the overall financial capacities a society has to counter the negative impacts of the pandemic, such as months-long closures of businesses, offices and shops, the availability of critical infrastructure such as hospitals and medical research centres for immediate responses and secondary provisions such as internet capacities for working and schooling from home or extended transportation systems to enable people to keep the necessary distance from others while riding on buses, trams or trains. Finally, the composition of a society in terms of, for example, age and health status or predominant living conditions (in individual or collective settings) also impacts the collective ability to respond to crises.

Both functional leadership and socioeconomic potency have an influence on the behaviour of citizens: individuals are more likely to comply with restrictive counter-measures if they: (1) trust the government; and (2) have the socioeconomic ability to do so; the less these conditions are fulfilled, the higher the probability that people will resist governmental orders. Trust is an important mechanism to reduce complexity in an environment that exceeds individual knowledge and thus 'enables people to maintain their capacity to act in a complex environment' (Siegrist, 2019: 2). According to Hasan (2021: 1151), '[t]rust in health systems is an important variable for effective implementation of COVID-19 health interventions'. The debate about the reliability of vaccines is a good example of how trust makes a difference in the way people react to a given uncertainty that most cannot evaluate and decipher themselves: the more people trust, the more likely they are to get the vaccine.[2]

Risk governance generally consists of three distinct phases: from the outset, the prevention of risks (i.e. for a viral epidemic, sufficient hygiene standards being in place before it can spread), the handling of risks (i.e. the management of the crisis once it becomes an epidemic) and finally the learning effects that occur during the crisis and after it has been managed (i.e. knowledge production through transparent failure analysis and knowledge application through accepted consequences for future behaviour). Obviously, despite major differences in economic ability, political leadership and social structures, almost no state was sufficiently prepared to prevent the coronavirus outbreak, even with prior warning signs from SARS, MERS and Ebola. The chapters included in this edited volume thus primarily focus on the second phase of this systemic risk governance cycle and analyse various aspects of MENA countries' reactions to the coronavirus in their handling of the crisis. The book also hints at various aspects from the third phase, policy learning from the coronavirus crisis, even though at the time of writing – mid-2021, i.e.

after several waves of the pandemic – it is still too early to draw a full, detailed picture. In summary, the findings from this collection of articles are rather worrying.

1.3 Lines of inquiry

With their broad diversity, Arab countries offer rich opportunities for comparative analyses of the COVID-19 pandemic's different trajectories and the various ways it played out in politics, socioeconomic developments and societal consequences. As illustrated by the Bloomberg ranking mentioned above, some of the MENA states weathered the challenges comparatively well, while others acted in less convincing ways. Irrespective of individual government responses, the outbreak of COVID-19 has placed 'significant stress on national economies and public services such as health and education' (KAS, 2020: 3) across the region. Unsurprisingly, the vast majority of Arab citizens polled in late 2020 saw the COVID-19 outbreak as 'very or somewhat serious', including 92% in Lebanon, 90% in Jordan, 86% in Tunisia, 84% in Algeria, 82% in Morocco and 77% in Libya (KAS, 2020: 7).

1.3.1 Geopolitical consequences

The chapters in this edited volume follow three main lines of inquiry related to the coronavirus's effects on MENA countries. The first set of articles deals with geopolitical consequences. **Thomas Demmelhuber**, **Julia Gurol** and **Tobias Zumbrägel** trace 'autocratic linkages' between the selected GCC states and China during the COVID-19 pandemic. By analysing the global IT business and international connections in digitisation and artificial intelligence, they show how the coronavirus has placed additional tools into the hands of authoritarian rulers to wield far-reaching control. For one, Arab autocrats refer to China as a role model that shows how effective containment of the virus works, i.e. through strict enforcement of governmental measures. Beyond this, and certainly more discerning, is the 'travelling of autocratic practices via technology transfer' (p. 19), the prevalence of modern mass surveillance technologies that have been promoted easily with the sudden need for 'coronavirus-tracing apps'. As the authors show, China has successfully used COVID-19 diplomacy under the label 'Health Silk Road' to further extend its influence in the MENA region. Chinese tech companies are also leading in the provision of the surveillance software that is installed on everyone's mobile phone now that coronavirus-tracing apps have become mandatory in so many countries. This is a particular concern in countries where data protection principles are not sufficiently enshrined, but not only there: Amnesty International not only levelled such claims against Bahrain and Kuwait as 'unsurprising suspects', but also criticised Norway for having 'run roughshod over people's privacy' in implementing their tracing apps (Amnesty International, 2020). This makes it clear that the scenarios of 24/7 surveillance and deep interference into any person's privacy are also of concern for citizens living in liberal democracies.

If China is an authoritarian power of global concern, Iran is a regional hegemon that tries to wield its influence through and in a number of proxy states, with fatal consequences in the case of COVID-19: in at least nine countries of Iran's immediate or broader neighbourhood – namely Afghanistan, Bahrain, Iraq, Kuwait, Lebanon, Pakistan, Oman, Qatar and the UAE – cases were identified with a history of travel through the Islamic Republic (WHO-EMRO, 2020). **Nassim AbiGhanem** analyses how the connections between Iran and Hezbollah have impaired responses to the COVID-19 pandemic in Lebanon. For one, Beirut's international airport was kept open for flights from Iran longer than might have been advisable – and longer than other important airports in the region, such as from the GCC states that had banned flights to and from Iran by 25 February 2020 (Zhuang et al., 2020: 29). Secondly, AbiGhanem argues that Hezbollah has understood that the Lebanese Ministry of Public Health (MoPH) was a veritable cash cow, furthering its aspiration to control the ministry. With the outbreak of the coronavirus, unprecedented sums of money had to be mobilised and substantial amounts have allegedly also been channelled towards Tehran. The chapter points out that because of the sanctions of Donald Trump's US administration, the MoPH represented a rare opportunity to funnel foreign money into Iran, by importing Iranian medication or as 'donations' described as humanitarian help. The COVID-19 pandemic has massively increased these questionable transactions, since in the global rush to fight the pandemic critical voices warning against such activities were hardly heard, let alone taken seriously.

1.3.2 Communication strategies

A second set of articles focusses on regimes' communicative strategies during the crisis. Citizens' awareness about the ways through which the coronavirus spreads within communities is an important precondition for successful counter-strategies and '[g]overnments play a crucial role in crisis control via adoption of different preventive and protective policies. Increasing public awareness is one of such policies to control the disease spread' (Bonyan et al., 2020: 9). However, governments use communication with the public not only to help contain the virus through higher awareness and better information (Faour-Klingbeil et al., 2021), but also to turn the crisis to their advantage. As shown by **Carola Richter, Abdulrahman al-Shami, Soheir Osman, Sahar Khalifa Salim** and **Samuel Mundua**, the strategy of 'othering' – one of the classic tools in power maintenance (Scauso et al., 2020: 86) – has also dominated COVID-19-related media coverage in Egypt, Iraq, Oman and Yemen. The authors argue that mass media have been fulfilling a particular role during the COVID-19 pandemic, since they help spread daily messages from the decision makers on the latest progress and necessary measures; at the same time, they help create the image of their own political leadership as 'saviours' against an 'external' threat. In line with Hillel Nossek (2004: 347–8), the chapter demonstrates that journalists in the four examined countries have functioned as 'local gatekeepers' during the pandemic, supposed 'to meet national ends by having a belief system such as patriotism'. The target of these 'othering' strategies can be very different, depending on the context and political need: China as the place of origin of the virus, the USA as an alleged conspiring force behind it, Saudi Arabia or Iran as hostile powers in the Yemeni civil war or simply citizens who refuse to obey the government's anti-COVID-19 requests. Much of what the authors describe will sound very familiar to readers from Europe and North America: othering creates boundaries between 'us' and 'them' that gives 'us' a feeling of safety, security and ultimately of superiority.

Giulia Cimini and **Beatriz Tomé Alonso** also identify such 'othering' strategies in their in-depth analysis of the Moroccan monarchy's behaviour, as does **Alexander Lohse** with a review of the successful handling of the pandemic by the UAE's leadership – albeit in very different directions. Cimini and Tomé Alonso describe a re-strengthening of existing authoritarian patterns in Morocco: King Mohammed VI has succeeded in taking the undisputed leadership position in the management of the crisis at the expense of the parliament and the elected government. In addition, the existing trend to 'technocratise politics' has gained further prominence by the current need for expert-based, quick decision-making; room for lengthy parliamentary debates on the pros and cons of certain measures disappears in the face of daily rising infection numbers and alarming reports about the reality in hospitals and health care centres. Thus, the authors argue how the existing hierarchy within Morocco's regime between 'primary' and 'secondary' elites has been further cemented: King Mohammed VI and his small circle of confidants, the primary elites, have been presented as 'key securitising actors', whilst the secondary elites, that is, parliament and political party leaders, and especially those who have dared to criticise the king for recent or former failures, have further lost influence. The regime indeed seems successful in this endeavour: only 9% of the Moroccans polled saw their government as the primary reason for the spread of COVID-19 in late 2020, while 41% blamed their fellow citizens as the main cause for the virus's reproduction (KAS, 2020: 10–11).

Meanwhile in the UAE, as Lohse illustrates, the regime did not implement the strategy of 'othering', at the expense of neither external nor internal rivals, but instead reacted by prolonging the country's long-term 'branding' strategy. The chapter shows that while the coronavirus-related hardships for the UAE were remarkable – the collapse of international trade and travel plus the drop in oil prices – the UAE's leadership not only handled the pandemic remarkably well, but also managed to boost its regional power ambitions through 'humanitarian diplomacy' and other status-seeking strategies. The recent normalisation of relations with Israel and the eventual moderation of the conflict with Qatar without doubt also received an important impetus through the outbreak of the pandemic.

1.3.3 Social responses

The third set of contributions considers social implications that the pandemic has had for communal life and public policies in the MENA region. **Noël van den Heuvel** and **Ulrike Freitag** investigate reasons for the distinct reactions of religious actors in Iran and Saudi Arabia to the question of whether the pandemic requires a far-reaching halt to religious ceremonies. For the first time since the establishment of the Kingdom of Saudi Arabia in 1932, the Saudi authorities banned international pilgrims from joining the *hajj* to Mecca and Medina in early summer 2020, hinting at the irresponsible risk that the mass gathering of millions of pilgrims would have meant for the further spread of the virus. Similarly, Friday prayers at mosques were cancelled as early as March 2020 (a few days after the first infection was diagnosed on 2 March 2020) and believers were encouraged to stay home. In Iran, however, there was much less willingness to stop religious ceremonies, or to even reduce the number of participants – which Younis et al. (2021: 347) see as one of the central reasons why Iran developed into the region's COVID-19 epicentre. However, while theological differences between the Shi'i interpretation prevailing in Iran and Sunni positions in Saudi Arabia can be used as one line of argumentation, van den Heuvel and Freitag also point to political reasons which equally explain the countries' diverging approaches: in Saudi Arabia, where political power is much more centralised, the clergy has always followed the directives given from the political leadership, whilst in Iran the religious authorities have acted more independently from the state. The authors' analysis shows that the often-quoted 'confrontation' between scientific rationalism and irrational belief is too short-sighted, and that the relationship between religion and science is far more complex indeed.

Manara Babiker Hassan addresses a rarely considered, yet distressing, consequence of the COVID-19 pandemic, namely how female migrants from the Horn of Africa – mostly Ethiopia – have become stranded in Khartoum after the borders were closed and international onward travel was suspended. Smugglers and traffickers use the advantageous geostrategic location of Sudan's capital as well as Sudan's relaxed travel regulations to fly women and girls to Dubai and other 'promised lands' on the Arabian Peninsula. Since the outbreak of the COVID-19 pandemic, these 'Dubai girls', as they are frequently called, are now 'at the horns of a dilemma': unable either to return or to continue their journey, they are stuck in the hands of local *samasra*, brokers who facilitate the irregular migration business. To reduce their own costs, the *samasra* often let the girls work as housemaids in wealthy Khartoum families, typically for room and board only. This is as much a traumatic situation for them as staying with the *samasra*, so unless they manage to reach the

Gulf countries in the hope of a financially more attractive and stable life, their fate remains uncertain.

A surprising paradox in the way the COVID-19 pandemic has been handled as a public health challenge in Lebanon is highlighted in the chapter by **Michèle Kosremelli Asmar** and **Joumana Stephan Yeretzian**. They describe how the private health sector, traditionally the much stronger and better-equipped part of Lebanon's health care infrastructure, has been side-lined by its public counterpart. Given the tumultuous years Lebanon has again gone through recently – with a marked lack of stability, collapsing economic and unresponsive political structures cemented in consociational stiffness – their observations truly come as a surprise, and can be read as a fervent call for public health care services. Strong and trusted public health agencies are essential to assess and manage this and potential future health threats effectively. In consequence, Kosremelli Asmar and Stephan Yeretzian's analysis is a strong reminder of the importance of a functioning and effective state with strong, empathic leaders who communicate clear, transparent messages – again an appeal that readers from other world regions will certainly find interesting as well. The fact that, as AbiGhanem describes, the MoPH in Lebanon is under the control of Hezbollah is no contradiction to Kosremelli Asmar and Stephan Yeretzian's call for a strong and effective public authority: as AbiGhanem himself argues, 'the success of the MoPH had become a priority for Hezbollah because the ministry failing would have indicated Hezbollah's inability to run the ministry' (p. 44–5); thus, the interest of having a functioning ministry is paramount to particular political ideologies.

Likewise, another global concern has been how COVID-19 has negatively affected education, after schools and universities were forced to close down and educators were suddenly obliged to instruct their pupils through alternative means. Globally, an estimated 1.58 billion learners in 200 countries are believed to have been affected – most severely in countries with low HDIs (United Nations, 2020: 6). Again, with Lebanon as a case study, **Fadi El Hage** and **Fouad Yehya** present interesting insights into the state of school education. They see a welcome opportunity in the new reality suddenly created by the COVID-19 pandemic to implement sorely needed efforts to modernise and upgrade the largely outdated and sometimes dysfunctional education system. At the same time, most educators are not qualified enough (yet) to take on this challenge and become familiar with modern e-learning platforms, for instance. Likewise, the infrastructure and affected families' ability to provide school children with sufficient learning conditions at home might differ among Arab countries (Al Lily et al., 2020). For this reason, El Hage and Yehya – as distinguished experts in education and professional development – give concrete examples of how such challenges could be successfully tackled, and their findings can be fruitfully transferred to other countries and other contexts as well, including Europe and North America, where countries also struggle with their transfer to digital education.

1.4 Concluding remarks

The COVID-19 pandemic has hit the MENA region after years, if not decades, of instability. Being 'the only region in the world where extreme poverty has been constantly increasing since 2011' (Karamouzian and Madani, 2020: 886), the economies in most countries were already struggling to fulfil citizens' basic needs, while political participation has been limited by security-focused, often kleptocratic regimes. The coronavirus, with its systemic challenges, demands systemic responses from governments and whole societies.

The contributions in this collective volume highlight the seriousness and multiplicity of the political, economic and social challenges that the pandemic has brought to the MENA region, affecting geopolitical constellations, trust-related connections between citizens and the political leadership and societal concerns. What shines through all the chapters, however, is how the unprecedented health crisis has also brought a (desperately needed) opportunity for governments, leaders and decision makers in the region 'to rebuild trust with their citizens' (KAS, 2020: 4). Indeed, it would be unrealistic to expect the coronavirus to achieve what millions of protesters and demonstrators have been unable to bring forward in almost all the MENA countries: a thorough transformation of power structures and a lasting implementation of more democratic and citizen-centred politics. Nonetheless, amidst all the human suffering the infectious disease has caused, perhaps it also brings a fresh impetus that might result in a new dynamic in the region's young and ambitious societies.

Notes

1 Data taken from 'Our World in Data', https://ourworldindata.org/covid-vaccinations (1 July 2021).
2 By reference to governmental flood preparations, Terpstra (2011) showed that a high level of trust can also lead to negative results, namely, greater unpreparedness among the population if expectations are high that the state's protective actions will suffice.

References

AlKhaldi, Mohammed / Al-Surimi, Khaled / Meghari, Hamza (2020): Health policy and systems research in the Arab world: concepts, evolution, challenges, and application necessity for COVID-19 pandemic and beyond. In: Ismail Laher (ed.): *Handbook of healthcare in the Arab world*. Cham: Springer, pp. 1–25. https://doi.org/10.1007/978-3-319-74365-3.

Al Lily, Abdulrahman Essa / Ismail, Abdelrahim Fathy / Abunasser, Fathi Mohammed / Alqahtani, Rafdan Hassan Alhajhoj (2020): Distance education as a response to pandemics: coronavirus and Arab culture. *Technology in Science*, 63: pp. 1–11. https://doi.org/10.1016/j.techsoc.2020.101317.

Amnesty International (2020): *Bahrain, Kuwait and Norway contact tracing apps among most dangerous for privacy*. 16 June, www.amnesty.org/en/latest/news/2020/06/bahrain-kuwait-norway-contact-tracing-apps-danger-for-privacy.

Asi, Yara M. (2020): *Migrant workers' health and COVID-19 in GCC countries*. Washington: Arab Center Washington D.C. www.arabcenterdc.org/policy_analyses/migrant-workers-health-and-covid-19-in-gcc-countries.

Bonyan, Ruwidah / Al-Karasneh, Aseel Fuad / El-Dahiyat, Faris / Jairoun, Ammar Abdulrahman (2020): Identification of the awareness level by the public of Arab countries toward COVID-19: cross-sectional study following an outbreak. *Journal of Pharmaceutical Policy and Practice*, 13(43): pp. 1–10. https://doi.org/10.1186/s40 545-020-00247-x.

El Achi, Nassim / Papamichail, Andreas / Rizk, Anthony / Lindsay, Helen / Menassa, Marilyne / Abdul-Khalek, Rima A. / Ekzayez, Abdulkarim / Dewachi, Omar / Patel, Preeti (2019): A conceptual framework for capacity strengthening of health research in conflict: the case of the Middle East and North Africa region. *Globalization and Health*, 15(81): pp. 1–15. https://doi.org/10.1186/s12992-019-0525-3.

El-Sadani, Mai (2020): *Detention during COVID-19: what MENA governments are, aren't, and should be doing*. Washington: Tahrir Institute for Middle East Politics. https://timep.org/commentary/analysis/detention-during-covid-19-what-mena-governments-are-arent-and-should-be-doing.

Faour-Klingbeil, Dima / Osaili, Tareq M. / Al-Nabulsi, Anas A. / Jemni, Monia / Tod, Ewen (2021): The public perception of food and non-food related risks of infection and trust in the risk communication during COVID-19 crisis: a study on selected countries from the Arab region. *Food Control*, 121: pp. 1–12. https://doi.org/10.1016/j.foodcont.2020.107617.

Gaskell, Jennifer / Stoker, Gerry (2020): Centralized or decentralized. Which governance systems are having a 'good' pandemic? *Democratic Theory*, 7(2): pp. 33–40. https://doi.org/10.3167/dt.2020.070205.

Hasan, Hasan Falah (2021): Legal and health response to COVID-19 in the Arab countries. *Risk Management and Healthcare Policy*, 14: pp. 1141–54. https://doi.org/10.2147/RMHP.S297565.

Hong, Jinshan / Chang, Rachel / Varley, Kevin (2020/2021): The Covid resilience ranking. *Bloomberg*, updated 25 May 2021. www.bloomberg.com/graphics/covid-resilience-ranking.

Jabbour, Samer (2013): Public health in the Arab world: at a crossroads. *Journal of Public Health Policy*, 34(2): pp. 356–60. https://doi.org/10.1057/jphp.2013.2.

Joffé, George (2020): COVID-19 and North Africa. *The Journal of North African Studies*, 25(4): pp. 515–22. https://doi.org/10.1080/13629387.2020.1757334.

Johns Hopkins University & Medicine (2021): *COVID-19 dashboard*. Baltimore: Coronavirus Resource Center. https://coronavirus.jhu.edu/map.html.

Karamouzian, Mohammad / Madani, Navid (2020): COVID-19 response in the Middle East and North Africa: challenges and paths forward. *The Lancet*, 8: pp. 886–7. https://doi.org/10.1016/S2214-109X(20)30233-3.

KAS (2020): *10 years after the Arab uprisings: where does public opinion in the region stand today?* Tunis: Konrad Adenauer Stiftung. www.kas.de/documents/252038/11055681/Where+does+Public+Opinion+in+the+Region+Stand+Today+-+10+Years+after+the+Arab+Uprisings.pdf/73611431-093a-3e69-8e5e-7811f1f153e9?version=1.0&t=1611755841567.

Kienle, Eberhard (2020): The corona virus in the Middle East and North Africa: 'Arab exceptionalism', once again? *Les dossiers de CERI*, 20 May. www.sciencespo.fr/ceri/en/content/corona-virus-middle-east-and-north-africa-arab-exceptionalism-again.

Klinke, Andreas / Renn, Ortwin (2019): The coming of age of risk governance. *Risk Analysis*, online first. https://doi.org/10.1111/risa.13383.

Lozano, Rafael (2018): Measuring performance on the Healthcare Access and Quality Index for 195 countries and territories and selected subnational locations: a systematic analysis from the Global Burden of Disease Study 2016. *The Lancet*, 391: pp. 2236–71. https://doi.org/10.1016/S0140-6736(18)30994-2.

Lust, Ellen (2011): Missing the third wave: Islam, institutions, and democracy in the Middle East. *Studies in Comparative International Development*, 46(2): 163–190. https://doi.org/10.1007/s12116-011-9086-z.

Michaelson, Ruth (2021): Egypt denies 'oxygen crisis' as Covid-19 ward videos allege shortage. *The Guardian*, 12 January. www.theguardian.com/global-development/2021/jan/12/egypt-denies-oxygen-crisis-as-covid-19-ward-videos-allege-shortage.

Nossek, Hillel (2004): Our news and their news. The role of national identity in the coverage of foreign news. *Journalism*, 5(3): pp. 343–68. https://doi.org/10.1177%2F1464884904044941.

Sawaya, Tania / Ballouz, Tala / Zaraket, Hassan / Rizk, Nesrine (2020): Coronavirus disease (COVID-19) in the Middle East: a call for a unified response. *Frontiers in Public Health*, 8(209): pp. 1–3. https://doi.org/10.3389/fpubh.2020.00209.

Scauso, Marcos S. / FitzGerald, Garrett / Tickner, Arlene B. / Behera, Navnita Chadha / Pan, Chengxin / Shih, Chih-yu / Shimizu, Kosuke (2020): COVID-19, democracies, and (de)colonialities. *Democratic Theory*, 7(2): pp. 83–92. https://doi.org/10.3167/dt.2020.070211.

Schweizer, Pia-Johanna (2019): Systemic risks – concepts and challenges for risk governance. *Journal of Risk Research*, online first. https://doi.org/10.1080/13669877.2019.1687574.

Siegrist, Michael (2019): Trust and risk perception: a critical review of the literature. *Risk Analysis*, online first. https://doi.org/10.1111/risa.13325.

Terpstra, Teun (2011): Emotions, trust, and perceived risk: affective and cognitive routes to flood preparedness behavior. *Risk Analysis*, 31(10): pp. 1658–75. https://doi.org/10.1111/j.1539-6924.2011.01616.x.

United Nations (2020): *Education during COVID-19 and beyond*. New York: United Nations, www.un.org/development/desa/dspd/wp-content/uploads/sites/22/2020/08/sg_policy_brief_covid-19_and_education_august_2020.pdf.

Viglione, Giuliana (2020): The true toll of the pandemic (How many people has the coronavirus killed?). *Nature*, 585: pp. 22–4. https://doi.org/10.1038/d41586-020-02497-w.

Wehbe, Sarah / Fahme, Sasha A. / Rizk, Anthony / Mumtaz, Ghina R. / DeJong, Jocelyn / Sibai, Abla M. (2021): COVID-19 in the Middle East and North Africa region: an urgent call for reliable, disaggregated and openly shared data. *BMJ Global Health*, 6: pp. 1–4. https://doi.org/10.1136/bmjgh-2021-005175.

WHO-EMRO (2020): *WHO team arrives in Tehran to support the COVID-19 response*. Press release, 2 March. Cairo: World Health Organization, Regional Office for the Eastern Mediterranean. www.emro.who.int/irn/iran-news/who-team-arrives-in-tehran-to-support-the-covid-19-response.html.

Younis, Nour K. / Rahm, Mira / Bitar, Fadi / Arabi, Mariam (2021): COVID-19 in the MENA region: facts and findings. *The Journal of Infection in Developing Countries*, 15(3): pp. 342–9. https://doi.org/10.3855/jidc.14005.

Zhuang, Zian / Zhao, Shi / Qianying, Lin / Cao, Peihua / Yijun, Lou / Yang, Lin / He, Daihai (2020): Preliminary estimation of the novel coronavirus disease

(COVID-19) cases in Iran: a modelling analysis based on overseas cases and air travel data. *International Journal of Infectious Diseases*, 94: pp. 29–31. https://doi.org/10.1016/j.ijid.2020.03.019.

Zumla, Alimuddin / Perlman, Stanley / McNabb, Scott J. N. / Shaikh, Affan / Heymann, David L. / McCloskey, Brian / Hui, David S. (2015): Middle East respiratory syndrome in the shadow of Ebola. *The Lancet*, 3(2): pp. 100–2. https://doi.org/10.1016/s2213-2600(14)70316-9.

Zyoud, Sa'ed (2021): The Arab region's contribution to global COVID-19 research: bibliometric and visualization analysis. *Globalization and Health*, 17(31): pp. 1–10. https://doi.org/10.1186/s12992-021-00690-8.

Part I
Geopolitical implications

2 The COVID-19 temptation?
Sino–Gulf relations and autocratic linkages in times of a global pandemic[1]

Thomas Demmelhuber, Julia Gurol and Tobias Zumbrägel

2.1 Introduction

In the global fight against the COVID-19 pandemic, China has emerged as an apparent role model for containing the spread of the virus and curbing the infection rate. In their urgent search for effective measures, many global leaders have sought to emulate proven models of successful containment measures. Based on the stewardship of China's digital technologies developed to control and monitor the spread of COVID-19, the Chinese state has increasingly evolved into a supplier of public health toolsets, surveillance technology and closed-circuit television (CCTV) equipment, and an artificial intelligence (AI) developer. This has resulted in a global proliferation of Chinese digital infrastructure that might provide the Chinese regime with new opportunities to promote its models of digital governance, thereby risking the undermining of democratic values (Power-Riggs, 2020).

Against this backdrop, this chapter explores whether the global pandemic and the fight against COVID-19 have fostered the travelling of autocratic practices via technology transfer, thereby supporting the emerging body of literature on the international dimension of authoritarianism. During the past decade, the increasing collaboration of autocratic countries, the regional clustering of autocracies and the parallel erosion of democracies have sparked political and public debate in democracies worldwide. The academic debate on the international dimension of authoritarianism has been thriving for the last decade (Kneuer and Demmelhuber, 2016, 2020; Tansey, 2016) and has fostered the assertion of a 'third wave of autocratisation' (Lührmann and Lindberg, 2019). After decades of normative dichotomies – as if autocratic legitimation remained an oxymoron (for a critique see Gerschewski, 2018: 652–65) or as if autocracies faced some kind of endogenous instability (Merkel, 2010: 57ff.), and the quest for legitimacy thus remained a domain of democracies – there is an emerging consensus that any regime type needs some legitimation strategies (Rothschild, 1977; Beetham, 1991). Yet it is exactly this mode of legitimation that needs to be better deconstructed in research in order to explain *how* autocrats stay in power. The scholarly debate is rich and diverse when it comes

DOI: 10.4324/9781003240044-3

to differentiating distinct modes of autocratic durability such as repression, co-optation and legitimation (Gandhi and Przeworski, 2007; Gerschewski, 2013; Kailitz, 2013), but it is also crystal clear that these 'pillars' interact and are interwoven and dependent on the subtype of the regime (Geddes, 1999).

In this chapter, we show along the lines of the COVID-19 pandemic that the sphere of digitisation is an example to demonstrate how autocrats across the globe steadily exploit cyberspace as a further means of broadening their 'digital toolkits' of autocratic regime survival (Keremoğlu and Weidmann, 2020: 1695). On the one hand, this happens through surveillance, repression, censorship and disinformation (Shahbaz, 2018; Shahbaz and Funk, 2020). On the other hand, reputational acts, image building and self-staging play crucial roles (Gunitzky, 2015).[2]

Our main argument is that the global pandemic and the fight against it in the respective domestic settings shall be understood as a window of opportunity for Middle Eastern autocrats to further fine-tune their modes of digital surveillance and repression. At the same time, we try to present circumstantial evidence to show how autocratic practices, norms and ideas of how to use digital modes of surveillance for the sake of regime survival are travelling between autocracies in an international setting. Focusing on Sino–Gulf relations, we inductively explore autocratic diffusion via technology transfer and seek to extract the modes and mechanisms of this diffusion in four case studies: the United Arab Emirates (UAE), Bahrain, the Kingdom of Saudi Arabia (KSA) and Oman.

2.2 Deepening ties: a 'China–Gulf honeymoon'?

Transregional corridors of trade, political and cultural relations between China and the Gulf monarchies have been thriving for more than a decade (Tansey, Koehler and Schmotz, 2017: 1221–54; Fulton, 2020; Sidło, 2020; Young, 2020: 236–52) and have led to a comprehensive public and academic debate about motives, content and strategies in the wider field of China's Belt-and-Road Initiative (BRI). This has resulted in stronger links, i.e. an increasing density of cross-border ties, both in terms of political relations, trade volume, arms export (plus technology) and cultural relations (e.g. the Confucius Institutes in Bahrain or the UAE).

In particular during the past few years, the density of ties has increased steadily, encompassing more and more policy fields. In this context, the Gulf region has not only become of strategic interest for China in economic terms, but it also forms part of the 'Health Silk Road'. While its health diplomacy has been secondary to the more obvious diversification of economic relations, the outbreak of the coronavirus in 2019 has resulted in the official launch of a Health Silk Road Initiative. Working on a stint of COVID-19 diplomacy, China has used the pandemic to advance its soft power, leverage and influence in the Gulf region and beyond (Zoubir, 2020). These efforts are noteworthy, not least because of the level of trust that characterises the emerging 'Chinese–Gulf honeymoon' (Lancaster, Rubin and Rapp-Hooper, 2020). Since then, China has doubled down on its efforts to recast itself as a responsible global health leader, launching a widespread public diplomacy campaign.

The Health Silk Road, albeit not an entirely novel concept,[3] has been unearthed in a way that might be advantageous to China in this moment of crisis. Not only does its health diplomacy foster the internal legitimacy of the Chinese Communist Party (CCP), but it also serves to revamp the BRI after pandemic-induced shocks (Buckley, 2020). Consequently, the digital dynamics will change in that BRI lending was already becoming more conservative before the outbreak of the pandemic, a trend that is likely to continue. Beijing will embark on taking advantage of opportunities generated by the pandemic to play a 'saviour role' and to promote digital infrastructure with the argument of ensuring global health (Greene and Triolo, 2020). This becomes particularly apparent in the Chinese rhetoric on its role in combating the COVID-19 pandemic, presenting the advantages of China's socialist system and emphasising China's role as a saviour that will help others overcome the pandemic (State Council Information Office, 2020).

China's COVID-19 diplomacy in the Gulf region could also be interpreted as an opportunity to re-brand pre-existing elements of the BRI. For instance, the health mechanism is planned to work in tandem with the Digital Silk Road for the sake of health monitoring. In this regard, the pandemic leads to increasing overlaps between two rather different policy fields and provides China with new opportunities to grow as a technological power and global provider of digital infrastructure (Blanchette and Hillman, 2020). The empirical evidence for that is abundant. Not only is China expanding 5G networks on Chinese soil, but several Gulf Cooperation Council (GCC) countries have also signed agreements with Huawei for expanding digital infrastructure (Soliman, 2020). This obvious merger of policy fields – health and digital technology – reveals once more the deepening connections and increasing density of Chinese–Gulf ties.

These observations match recent findings in the scholarly literature which have shown – in contrast to the findings of the early 2000s (Vanderhill, 2013: 6; see also Bader, 2015) – that not only has China been emerging as an economic powerhouse, but it has increasingly instrumentalised economic leverage for the sake of political influence and/or forced bandwagoning (Salman and Geeraerts, 2015; Garlick and Havlová, 2020; Kneuer and Demmelhuber, 2020: 33). It is promoting and diffusing autocratic practices, ideas and norms along the corridors of the BRI using these windows of opportunity for the promotion of autocracies and/or offering a toolbox of practices, ideas and norms for (voluntary) emulation and copying. During the global pandemic, China tried to promote a narrative of having successfully combated the pandemic, to be understood as the final evidence for the supremacy of China's own system of governance vis-à-vis the 'liberal script' of Western (democratic) systems.

2.3 Conceptual roadmap: the two-level linkage

Collaboration and exchange in fighting COVID-19 do not necessarily bring about a global resurgence of authoritarianism, but 'may lead to the unintentional strengthening of such regimes' (Yilmaz and Yıldırım, 2020: 3). Inspired by basic premises of diffusion theory, we look for circumstantial evidence that autocratic practices, norms and ideas are diffused in Sino–Gulf relations and that COVID-19 acts as a further booster. We follow Brinks in that diffusion processes are difficult to prove by causal links as 'it is hard to distinguish true diffusion from illusions of diffusion created by global trends, correlated disturbances or the regional clustering of domestic factors' (Brinks and Coppedge, 2006: 464). Having this caveat in mind, we want to feature the sequences of change and adoption. Concretely, we aim to analyse: (1) temporal sequences of adoption/change and (2) the content and (3) degree of technology transfer. By looking at some specific cases, we further intend to uncover (4) the *modus operandi*, i.e. the process of collaboration, the actors involved and the implementation or consequences of the adaptation.

In recent years, the literature on the subject has offered different conceptual mechanisms (emulation, demonstration effect, copying, etc.) concerning the travelling of autocratic practices. In this exploratory research, we do not want to test these conceptual mechanisms, but rather to extract empirical 'smoking guns' by studying different regimes' responses in the field of digital infrastructure since COVID-19 was classified as a global pandemic in March 2020 by the World Health Organization, based on a sample of four Gulf states. In doing so, we do not tackle the dimension of regional linkage – very much based on the assumption of structural similarity (O'Loughlin et al., 1998; Wejnert, 2014: 52) – that Yom called an 'epistemic community' (Yom, 2014). Instead, our focus is on studying the 'ties to the rest' – international linkages – by looking at corridors of autocratic diffusion in Sino–Gulf relations (inspired by Tansey, Koehler and Schmotz, 2017: 1222). By doing so, we contend that this exchange of ideas, practices, techniques and/or technology is more than a pragmatic, interest-driven cooperation, as scholars of authoritarian collaboration would claim (Yilmaz and Yıldırım, 2020: 2). Instead, we argue that this exchange is based on a common mindset of autocratic leadership.

2.4 Empirical spotlights

Four Gulf countries are of particular interest when examining these 'ties to the rest' in Sino–Gulf relations: Saudi Arabia, Bahrain, the UAE and Oman. All four are part of China's BRI (Fulton, 2020; Young, 2020) and have deepened their ties to China in the past decade. From a Chinese perspective, all four countries are ideally positioned to play a vital role in the implementation and expansion of the BRI. Whilst Sino–Gulf ties in the BRI context have long centred around energy – in particular crude oil and petrochemicals – their links have extended to other commodities in the context of the Digital and Health Silk Roads. Moreover, all four are considerably advanced when it comes to technology development, and therefore represent ideal cases to study the diffusion of autocratic practices via surveillance technology and tracing apps from China to the Gulf region. Instead of comparing these four cases, our aim is to provide a comprehensive overview of the different modes and mechanisms of autocratic diffusion via technology transfer in the Sino–Gulf context.

To empirically assess the mechanisms and dynamics of autocratic diffusion in Sino–Gulf ties in the context of the global pandemic, we focus on COVID-19-related tracing apps and video surveillance by looking at the networks, institutions and actors involved. Tracing apps are currently an issue of lively debate as they depict how governments worldwide thwart the issue of people's privacy 'with highly invasive surveillance tools that go far beyond what is justified in efforts to tackle COVID-19' (Amnesty International, 2020). Similarly, telecommunications technology, AI and further digital advancements have entered the debate as tools that could possibly be (mis) used for such invasive surveillance. In the following sections, we focus on empirical spotlights from the UAE, Bahrain, Saudi Arabia and Oman to study the autocratic linkages between China and the Gulf region. We thereby manage to cover four complementary cases of autocratic diffusion and to illustrate them empirically.

2.4.1 From TikTok to ToTok: the UAE as China's gateway to the Gulf

In recent years, the UAE government has heavily invested in digital surveillance techniques. The UAE-based cybersecurity company DarkMatter Group has been a crucial player therein. Founded in 2014, observers have widely considered the company to be an 'arm of the state' (Mazzetti, Perlroth and Bergman, 2019) that has recruited numerous international intelligence professionals (Bing and Schectman, 2019). Meanwhile, DarkMatter has been incorporated in the UAE-based Group 42 (G42), with the former Pegasus Chief Executive Officer (CEO), Peng Xiao, as its CEO (Pegasus was a subsidiary of DarkMatter).[4] This is an important fact because he was involved in a hacking unit (Project Raven) that had targeted UAE activists around the world in previous years. After Project Raven was exposed by media reports in 2019, DarkMatter was 'abruptly taken in hand by the authorities' (Marczak, 2020) and various units were transferred to other companies. The newly established AI and cloud computing company, G42, has become a crucial player in surveillance actions ever since. For example, it became a protagonist in programming chat apps that opened the door for mass surveillance by default based on technological know-how from China. Moreover, G42 has become a crucial hub for Sino–UAE cooperation and stands for elite networks encompassing distinct power relations with and within the ruling family in Abu Dhabi. For instance, it shares personal connections with ruling family member Sheikh Tahnoon bin Zayed Al Nahyan, who is the brother of Mohammed bin Zayed Al Nahyan, crown prince of Abu Dhabi. Nicknamed the 'spy sheikh', he has been serving as national security advisor since 2016.

Surveillance by default seems to have become the UAE standard and the role of UAE–Chinese networks therein is crucial. The rise of the tracing app ToTok serves as a vivid example of that. This popular VoIP messaging app is based on YeeCall, a VoIP app written by a Chinese company, Beijing YeeCall Interactive Network Technology. YeeCall is available from both the Apple and Google stores (the co-developer reportedly bought the code for it; Kumar and Salim, 2019). Interestingly, YeeCall's senior figures all appear to be connected to the ongoing development or promotion of ToTok (Marczak, 2020). Furthermore, YeeCall's summary on the Google Play store mentions that it provides '[f]ree unblocked video and voice calls for users who live in [the] UAE, Saudi Arabia, Oman, Qatar, Egypt, India, Pakistan, Bangladesh, Philippines, [the] U.S. and more' (Google Play, 2020a). After the New York Times coverage of the 'spy app' (Mazzetti, Perlroth and Bergman, 2019), it was removed from the Apple and Google stores. However, it is again available on company-related platforms (Samsung Galaxy Store) and the initial developer's website, 'totok.ai'. By installing the app, users agree to allow access to their microphone, pictures, geodata and more. The popularity of the app in the UAE can be linked to the highly regulated VoIP licences in the UAE, with ToTok suddenly offering services that have remained blocked for years in other apps such as WhatsApp or Skype and with the new app being merely the only one that functions via mobile data (Associated Press, 2020). Observers have mentioned the crucial advantage 'to hack people' based on their consent, 'if you can get people to willingly download this app to their phone' (Mazzetti, Perlroth and Bergman, 2019).

The COVID-19 pandemic further accelerated G42's development into a frontrunner in surveillance and data collection/storage. Reportedly, in cooperation with the Chinese global genomics leader BGI, G42 established a detection lab in Masdar City that is able to conduct thousands of PCR tests per day. The chairman of BGI was quoted as saying, 'together with our partners at G42, we can bring the world's best technology and experience in fighting global health threats to help the people of the UAE and beyond' (Group 42, 2020b). G42 further announced that it would 'set up joint lab operations, train medical and security personnel, as well as leverage its cloud infrastructure and AI platform to support data storage and provide advanced data analytics on the evolution of the epidemic' (Group 42, 2020a). This – as the statement continues – is directly related to the close relations with China that has equipped the UAE 'with the specialised knowledge to combat this virus'. This empirical spotlight shows how an evolving density of ties has eased cooperation schemes that allowed the exchange and diffusion of ideas, norms and techniques from China to the UAE. COVID-19 acts a booster for further development of AI and smart surveillance of the population for the sake of regime survival and stands for a strengthening of autocratisation for UAE citizens in daily life (also in view of the UAE context, where the crown prince, Mohammed bin Zayed, is preparing the scene for his takeover once his ailing brother passes away). Last but not least, the pandemic can be interpreted as an accelerator of the converging Digital *and* Health Silk Road initiatives.

2.4.2 Bahrain: small but smart with a little help from China

Bahrain was relatively quick to focus on investing in digital infrastructure and has promoted itself as a technology hub. Even though Bahrain lacks the financial resources from oil and gas revenues that its neighbours enjoy, it has been keen to invest in cutting-edge cybertechnology since the beginning. For instance, Bahrain was one of the frontrunners in introducing a nationwide 5G network. While Bahrain's telecom operators, Batelco and Zain, have cooperated with Ericsson to launch the first 5G service, VIVA Bahrain (a subsidiary of the Saudi telecommunication operator STC), chose the Chinese company Huawei, which sparked criticism from the USA (Calabrese, 2019). The high-speed and low-latency 5G technology is expected to provide a solid foundation for the country's future development towards AI and surveillance.

The kingdom's digital advancements, however, cannot be viewed detached from its non-democratic political setting, which has experienced a noticeable shift towards authoritarianism in the last few years. Bahrain has a historical record of restricting online speech, infiltration, censorship, internet filtering and surveillance. The control and regulation of information have dramatically increased in the wake of the Arab upheavals of 2011. In contrast to the other GCC countries, Bahrain was heavily affected by the mass protests that swept across the broader Middle East. Tactics of surveillance in particular became a key to quelling the waves of protests and preventively countering new formations of oppositional activism. There is evidence that the Bahraini government purchased intrusion software from Europe, which was then used against political dissidents, lawyers, journalists and activists during and in the aftermath of the protests (Marquis-Boire and Marczak, 2012; Currier and Marquis-Boire, 2014). As Marc Owen Jones (2020: 324) noted: 'In 2011 foreign expertise was brought in to increase the effectiveness of surveillance. CCTV cameras were installed around the country, but particularly outside Shi'i villages'.

While the majority of the Bahraini surveillance apparatus was developed with British help (Jones, 2020), China has gradually become a major source of external cybertechnological assistance and know-how. For example, Chinese AI surveillance companies such as Dahua and Plusvision (a subsidiary of the partially state-owned Chinese manufacturer and supplier of video surveillance equipment, Hikvision) have become authorised suppliers and distributors of CCTV cameras in Bahrain (Feldstein, 2019). In the early days of the global outbreak of COVID-19, CCTV footage was used for facial recognition and thermal body temperature monitoring, thereby actively contributing to tracing people's movement and tracking cross-border travel. As the pandemic spread further, monitoring and tracing techniques were further professionalised. Accordingly, China's expertise and early experience of combating COVID-19 were increasingly seen as a model to emulate.

In late March 2020, the Information & eGovernment Authority (iGA), in collaboration with the National Taskforce for Combating the Coronavirus, released the tracing application BeAware Bahrain. This COVID-19 awareness app is supposed to track the movements of people under home quarantine for two weeks and to notify its users when they are in proximity with infected people. It also provides information on public health and the status of the pandemic. In combination with the COVID-19 app, the Bahraini government launched electronic bracelets linked via Bluetooth to the users' smartphones. At the same time, the authorities declared that people confined to home quarantine were required to wear the electronic tags. Violators of the quarantine regulation were subject to a potential prison sentence of three months and a fine of several thousand Bahraini dinars under Public Health Law 34/2018. While this does not differ significantly from imposed sanctions in other – also democratic – contexts,[5] in the Bahraini context, additionally, Ministry of Health officials may randomly send photo requests to self-isolating individuals, who must respond with a photo that clearly shows their face and bracelet. An alert is also sent to the monitoring station if the wearer moves further than fifteen metres from their phone (McArthur, 2020).

The Bluetooth contact-tracing app and the digital GPS tracking devices were seen as extremely invasive and inspired by similar initiatives that had been implemented in Hong Kong and China. This included registering with one's national ID number (mandatory for quarantined individuals), uploading information to a central database and monitoring one's movement in real time. In a press release, the head of the iGA stated that the 'successful mitigation efforts, particularly the efforts of Singapore, China and Hong Kong' have been monitored and adapted to Bahraini conditions (Startup MGZN, 2020). In contrast to the digital reliance and inspirational source of tracking and monitoring, direct mechanisms of a Health Silk Road have not unfolded in Bahrain as in the UAE. However, in August 2020, Bahrain was a global frontrunner, participating in the first global clinical trials for the third phase of the Sinopharm vaccine from China. Interestingly, the testing – in which several thousand volunteers participated, including the Bahraini Crown Prince – was supervised by the above-mentioned conglomerate between G42 and BGI/Sinopharm. It is thus a good example of the diffusion of COVID-19 diplomacy within the region.

2.4.3 Saudi Arabia: China's strategic leviathan in the Gulf

Over the last few years, KSA has strategically diversified its diplomatic ties with Eastern countries. While it seems unlikely that the ruling Al Saud family will abandon the long-standing US partnership, it indicates a fundamental geopolitical shift in which the development of strategic relations to China depicts 'one of Riyadh's most important foreign policy goals in the coming years' (Al-Tamimi, 2018: 266). The strengthening of new international partnerships is closely interlinked with KSA's economic transformation, as outlined in Vision 2030 and the National Transformation Programme. The success of both development plans is a matter of regime survival (Demmelhuber, 2019). As elsewhere in the region, the expansion of digital infrastructure and the promotion of information and communications technology are considered to accompany the economic transformation. However, given its sheer size, KSA lags behind its GCC peers in terms of technological transformation. Accordingly, the kingdom has invested heavily in catching up with its neighbours over the past years, relying considerably on help from China (Soliman, 2020). This has led to closer ties to the People's Republic and has provably fostered the spread of autocratic practices.

Only a few months after the Saudi telecommunication giant STC announced a so-called joint 5G aspiration project in early 2019, Zain KSA – another leading conglomerate in the broader regional telecom space – followed suit by signing a bilateral agreement with Huawei to launch 5G services across the country (Calabrese, 2019). The initial agreement foresaw the installation of around 2,000 5G towers to deliver 5G services to more than twenty cities. While this already made KSA the largest provider of 5G services in the region (Soliman, 2020), that number has now doubled.[6] Therefore, multiple Sino–Saudi ties in the digital sphere have multiplied. The majority of these ties focus on various 'smart city' projects in the kingdom. For instance, the Chinese e-commerce giant, Alibaba Group, plans to set up a new head office in Saudi Media City,[7] whilst Huawei is engaged in several other smart city initiatives, such as Al Khobar, Dammam or Dhahran (Calabrese, 2019). Additionally, like several other Gulf states, Saudi Arabia relies mainly on Chinese companies such as Hikvision or Huawei to expand its CCTV surveillance infrastructure (Feldstein, 2019). Other sectors – transport, e-commerce, education, energy and 'industry 4.0' – are further seen as promising beneficiaries of Saudi–Sino AI cooperation. Additionally, digital health is named as a key area where China is the global leader (Taylor, 2019).

As in the UAE and Bahrain, the ongoing COVID-19 pandemic has acted as a booster to development in this area. Since the first report of a COVID-19 case, the Saudi Ministry of Health has implemented several information platforms on public health and launched multiple smartphone applications. Among these are updated versions of existing digital screening apps (i.e. Mawid and Sehhaty), as well as two newly launched contact-tracing apps (Tawakkalna and Tabaud) in July 2020. The launch of those tools and the introduction of the health e-service app, Tetamman, in June 2020 took place in collaboration with the Saudi Data and Artificial Intelligence Authority (SDAIA). The SDAIA is the leading government-led institution on AI, created by royal decree in late 2019. More recently, the SDAIA has entered a strategic partnership with Chinese digital giants Alibaba and Huawei. During the year 2020, it was reported that Huawei and the SDAIA launched the National AI Capability Development Programme in the kingdom (Huawei, 2020).

In addition to this evidently increasing Sino–Saudi cooperation in terms of AI (health) infrastructure, both countries have also collaborated closely in coordinating the fight against the COVID-19 pandemic. The evidence for that is plentiful. For instance, in March 2020, the King Salman Humanitarian Aid and Relief Centre delivered medical equipment to Wuhan. A month later, a royal decree by King Salman issued a deal with China worth $265 million to provide coronavirus tests and medical expertise. The agreement foresees the purchase of nine million test kits to fight the virus and the establishment of six laboratories, which are able to test approximately 50,000 people per day. Overseen by around 500 Chinese medical experts, the laboratories are run by Huo-yan Laboratories, which is a subsidiary of the above-mentioned Chinese genomics giant BGI (Global Times, 2020). This development went along with increasingly positive rhetoric from Saudi media outlets, praising China for its success in combating the virus. Although such media coverage may not necessarily be interpreted as the direct opinion of Saudi officials, the overtly positive media coverage on Chinese COVID-19 measures can be interpreted at least as an 'indirect reflection of official sympathies with the Chinese model of durable upgraded authoritarianism' (Leber, 2020).

In autumn 2020, KSA also started the third phase of clinical trials for a COVID-19 vaccine. Interestingly, in contrast to the UAE and Bahrain, this has not been supervised by the G42–BGI/Sinopharm joint venture, but by another Chinese company, CanSino Biologics. Around 5,000 people volunteered in this phase to receive the vaccine, which was co-developed with China's military research unit (TRT World, 2020).

2.4.4 Oman: the strategic linchpin for Chinese maritime belt politics

Oman is not a latecomer in terms of digital surveillance. Similar to Bahrain – though after more than a decade of negotiations – Huawei has become one of the companies involved in setting up 5G technology in Oman, as the three mobile network operators in Oman (Omantel, Ooredoo and – since 2020 – Vodafone) stick to a multiple-vendor model (including, for example, Omantel partnering with Ericsson and Ooredoo going for Huawei). The overall investment climate is seen as increasingly positive by China, with a senior diplomat of the Chinese mission to Oman being quoted as saying, '[w]e are looking forward to more FDI [foreign direct investment]-friendly policies. [...] The five critical non-oil sectors primed by Vision 2040 would witness a deep engagement of Chinese companies and investors' (Castelier, 2020; own omission).

China has played an important role in helping Oman tackle the COVID-19 pandemic, sharing scientific research data and pandemic prevention experience. It invited Omani experts to participate in medical webinars and actively supported Oman's pandemic prevention work (Chanda, 2020). The website of the Chinese embassy in Oman – which seems to be a collaborative hub for Chinese–Omani relations (Muscat Daily, 2020) – features the slogan of the China Daily Group: 'Fighting COVID-19 the Chinese Way'. All Chinese–Omani relations seem to be hijacked by this supremacy narrative, despite much more comprehensive bilateral cooperation schemes at play – for example, Chinese investment in the port of Duqm (Siddiqi, 2019). A former Omani official was quoted in the Chinese news agency Xinhua as saying: 'This is because China succeeded in managing the COVID-19 crisis with great intelligence' (Xinhua.net, 2020).

Meanwhile, the Omani tracing app Tarassud is strict, as are all other COVID-19 apps in the Gulf (O'Neill, Ryan-Mosley and Johnson, 2020). Though the copyright of the code remains unclear (parts of the technology come from an Indian company specialising in AI, namely Qure.ai), the mandatory combination with bracelets for people who test positive for COVID-19 within the Sultanate is a reminder of the underlying autocratic mindset of surveillance. Following an update in April 2020, Tarassud+ is an integrated platform for tracking, monitoring and clustering geodata (including access to all data on the device; Google Play, 2020b) with an interface for the mandatory bracelet for people who test positive and (since 1 October 2020) for visitors who stay more than seven days in the Sultanate. The upgrade of Tarassud+ was obviously pushed forward by the Ministry of Interior and the Ministry of Technology and Communication in cooperation with the Ministry of Health – the developer of the previous version. Tarassud+ was crucial in the resumption of international air travel on 1 October 2020, as it is mandatory for every inbound traveller to download the app, arrange a test via the app and pay 25 Omani riyals (about $65) for the test.

On the one hand, it is noteworthy that Tarassud+ is a significant upgrade in mass surveillance, as the app combines all relevant passenger details with full access to the data stored on the mobile device. On the other hand, it is interesting that again there was a partnership with the Chinese company BGI to set up testing facilities at Muscat International Airport and Salalah Airport to help passengers undergo a PCR test and boost early detection and containment of the virus (Muscat Airport, 2020). Cheng Wang – the commercial attaché at the Chinese embassy in Muscat – lauded this cooperation with a tweet on 4 October 2020: 'With the technical support from BGI, the Omani–Chinese team successfully set up a PCR testing lab at @MuscatAirport within 72 hours; such work usually takes one week according to past experience in UAE & KSA' (Wang, 2020). To sum up, though less visible and more difficult to trace, Sino–Omani relations are built on increasing links and functional elite networks that serve as fertile ground for the diffusion of autocratic norms, practices and ideas. Fighting the pandemic – as in Saudi

Arabia, the UAE and Bahrain – has served as a silver platter for the ruling dynasties.

2.5 Conclusion: COVID-19 as a window of opportunity for Gulf autocrats

The regional clustering of autocracies, the increasing collaboration of autocracies worldwide and the challenges for the 'liberal script' of Western democracies worldwide have been widely debated (see, for example, Diamond, Plattner and Walker, 2016; Tansey, 2016; Kneuer and Demmelhuber, 2020). Collaboration and exchange among autocracies in regional settings and international arenas have been on the rise for almost two decades. At the same time, autocracies have established new multilateral initiatives far away from a 'liberal script'. China's Belt-and-Road Initiative is a valid example of such parallel structures (Wientzek and Enskat, 2020). In this regard the pandemic is not a turning point, but rather a booster for what had already started. COVID-19 does not necessarily mean a global resurgence of authoritarianism, but it has led to some sort of unintentional strengthening of such regimes. Inspired by the basic premises of diffusion theory, we looked for circumstantial evidence that autocratic practices, norms and ideas are diffused in Sino–Gulf relations and that COVID-19 acts as a further booster. We focused on four Gulf countries in Sino–Gulf relations that have deepened their ties to China in the past decade: Saudi Arabia, Bahrain, the UAE and Oman. Based on the assessment that the linkages in Sino–Gulf relations have substantially increased, we tried to show that they have extended to other commodities in the context of the Digital and Health Silk Roads. By looking at tracing apps and telecommunications technology, AI and further digital advancements, we presented 'smoking guns' that show how an evolving density of ties and established political and entrepreneurial networks of collaboration facilitated cooperation schemes that allowed the exchange and diffusion of autocratic ideas, norms and digital techniques from China to the Gulf and thus stand for a further autocratisation in the respective countries.

Notes

1 This chapter is based on a research project of the authors funded by the Volkswagen Foundation (2021–2) on 'Global autocratic collaboration in times of COVID-19: game changer or business as usual in Sino–Gulf relations?' This paper focuses on the first phase of the COVID-19 pandemic, i.e. 2020 and early 2021. It thus provides a first overview how Sino-Gulf relations have generally developed since the outbreak of the pandemic. Meanwhile, we conceptualized these transregional linkages, published in 2022 in the Journal of Contemporary China (DOI: https://doi.org/10.1080/10670564.2022.2052444). Inspired by Social Network Theory we deconstruct elite networks in Sino-Emirati relations and offer conceptual thoughts for the field of transregional authoritarianism.

2 An example for this is Sheikh Mohammed Bin Rashid Al Maktoum from Dubai, who was probably one of the early frontrunners and the first 'Twitter king' in the Gulf region.
3 China already hosted a seminar titled the 'Belt and Road Forum on Health Cooperation: Toward a Health Silk Road' in Beijing in August 2017.
4 The Mohamed bin Zayed University of Artificial Intelligence, the first research-based graduate-level AI university in the world, was established in Abu Dhabi in October 2019, with Peng Xiao, the CEO of G42, on its board of trustees (Group 42, 2020a). For the role of Peng Xiao in Pegasus prior to his G42 activity, see the tweet by DarkMatter on 27 November 2016: https://twitter.com/guardedbygenius/status/802731642980691968.
5 For example, Canada has imposed fines for persons breaking their quarantine rules (14 days for all incoming travellers): up to $750,000 or up to six months' imprisonment, if not both (see https://laws-lois.justice.gc.ca/eng/acts/q-1.1/page-7.html).
6 See the official website of Zain KSA: https://sa.zain.com/en/personal/5g.
7 Saudi Media City Co. (SHAMAS) is located in Riyadh. It is designed to become a unique innovative global destination and a regional hub for the culture, media and technology sectors that play a vital role in shaping the innovation industry.

References

Al-Tamimi, Naser (2018): China's 'rise' in the Gulf: a Saudi perspective. In: al-Rasheed, Madawi (ed.): *Salman's legacy. The dilemmas of a new era in Saudi Arabia*. London: Hurst, pp. 251–72.

Amnesty International (2020): *Bahrain, Kuwait and Norway contact tracing apps among most dangerous for privacy*. Press release, 16 June. www.amnesty.org/en/latest/news/2020/06/bahrain-kuwait-norway-contact-tracing-apps-danger-for-privacy.

Associated Press (2020): Co-creator defends suspected UAE spying app called ToTok. *Voice of America*, 2 January. www.voanews.com/middle-east/co-creator-defends-suspected-uae-spying-app-called-totok.

Bader, Julia (2015): China, autocratic patron? An empirical investigation of China as a factor in autocratic survival. *International Studies Quarterly*, 59(1): pp. 23–33. https://doi.org/10.1111/isqu.12148.

Beetham, David (1991): *The legitimation of power*. Basingstoke: Macmillan. https://doi.org/10.1007/978-1-349-21599-7.

Bing, Christopher / Schectman, Joel (2019): Inside the UAE's secret hacking team of American mercenaries. *Reuters Investigates*, 30 January. www.reuters.com/investigates/special-report/usa-spying-raven.

Blanchette, Jude / Hillman, Jonathan (2020): *China's digital Silk Road after the coronavirus*. Washington: Center for Strategic and International Studies. www.csis.org/analysis/chinas-digital-silk-road-after-coronavirus.

Brinks, Daniel / Coppedge Michael (2006): Diffusion is no illusion: neighbor emulation in the third wave of democracy. *Comparative Political Studies*, 39(4): pp. 463–89. https://doi.org/10.1177%2F0010414005276666.

Buckley, Peter J. (2020): China's Belt and Road initiative and the COVID-19 crisis. *Journal of International Business Policy*, 3(3): pp. 311–14. https://doi.org/10.1057/s42214-020-00063-9.

Calabrese, John (2019): *The Huawei wars and the 5G revolution in the Gulf*. Washington: Middle East Institute. www.mei.edu/publications/huawei-wars-and-5g-revolution-gulf.

Castelier, Sebastian (2020): Oman kicks off ambitious reform project. *Al-Monitor*, 21 August. www.al-monitor.com/pulse/originals/2020/08/oman-ministerial-reshuffle-sultan-haithan-economy-employment.html.

Chanda, Amit (2020): China-Oman ties to scale greater heights: Chinese envoy. *China Global Television Network*, 28 September. https://news.cgtn.com/news/2020-09-28/China-Oman-ties-to-scale-greater-heights-Chinese-envoy-U9MYTJPMxG/index.html.

Currier, Cora / Marquis-Boire, Morgan (2014): Leaked files: German spy company helped Bahrain hack Arab Spring protestors. *The Intercept*, 7 August. https://theintercept.com/2014/08/07/leaked-files-german-spy-company-helped-bahrain-track-arab-spring-protesters.

Demmelhuber, Thomas (2019): Playing the diversity card: Saudi-Arabia's foreign policy under the Salmans. *The International Spectator*, 54(4): pp. 109–24. https://doi.org/10.1080/03932729.2019.1678862.

Diamond, Larry Jay / Plattner, Marc F. / Walker, Christopher (eds.) (2016): *Authoritarianism goes global: the challenge to democracy*. Baltimore: Johns Hopkins University Press.

Feldstein, Steven (2019): *The global expansion of AI surveillance*. Washington: Carnegie Endowment for International Peace. https://carnegieendowment.org/files/WP-Feldstein-AISurveillance_final1.pdf.

Fulton, Jonathan (2020): China–UAE relations in the Belt and Road era. *Journal of Arabian Studies*, 9(2): pp. 253–68. https://doi.org/10.1080/21534764.2019.1756135.

Gandhi, Jennifer / Przeworski, Adam (2007): Authoritarian institutions and the survival of autocrats. *Comparative Political Studies*, 40(1): pp. 1279–301. https://doi.org/10.1177%2F0010414007305817.

Garlick, Jeremy / Havlová, Radka (2020): China's 'Belt and Road' economic diplomacy in the Persian Gulf: strategic hedging amidst Saudi–Iranian regional rivalry. *Journal of Current Chinese Affairs*, 49(1): pp. 82–105. https://doi.org/10.1177%2F1868102619898706.

Geddes, Barbara (1999): What do we know about democratization after twenty years? *Annual Review of Political Science*, 2(1): pp. 115–44. https://doi.org/10.1146/annurev.polisci.2.1.115.

Gerschewski, Johannes (2013): The three pillars of stability: legitimation, repression, and co-optation in autocratic regimes. *Democratization*, 20(1): pp. 13–38. https://doi.org/10.1080/13510347.2013.738860.

Gerschewski, Johannes (2018): Legitimacy in autocracies. Oxymoron or essential feature? *Perspectives on Politics*, 13(3): pp. 652–65. https://doi.org/10.1017/S1537592717002183.

Global Times (2020): Chinese firm cooperates with Saudi Arabia to build six COVID-19 testing labs. *Global Times*, 27 April. www.globaltimes.cn/content/1186853.shtml.

Google Play (2020a): YeeCall – HD video calls for friends & family. https://play.google.com/store/apps/details?id=com.yeecall.app&hl=en_IN&gl=US.

Google Play (2020b): Tarassud+. https://play.google.com/store/apps/details?id=om.gov.moh.tarassudapplication&hl=gsw&gl=US.

Greene, Robert / Triolo, Paolo (2020): *Will China control the global internet via its digital Silk Road?* Washington: Carnegie Endowment for International Peace. https://carnegieendowment.org/2020/05/08/will-china-control-global-internet-via-its-digital-silk-road-pub-81857.

Group 42 (2020a): *Group 42 helps China combat coronavirus outbreak*. Press release, 29 January. https://g42.ai/news/healthcare/group-42-helps-china-combat-coronavirus-outbreak.
Group 42 (2020b): *G42 and BGI announce COVID-19 detection lab*. Press release, 31 March. https://g42.ai/news/g42/g42-and-bgi-announce-covid-19-detection-lab.
Gunitzky, Seva (2015): Corrupting the cyber-commons: social media as a tool of autocratic stability. *Perspectives on Politics*, 13(1): pp. 42–54. https://doi.org/doi:10.1017/S1537592714003120.
Huawei (2020): *SDAIA partner with Huawei to launch National AU Capability Development Program*. Press release, 22 October. www.huawei.com/en/news/2020/10/huawei-sdaia-national-ai-capability-development-program.
Jones, Marc O. (2020): *Political repression in Bahrain*. Cambridge: Cambridge University Press. https://doi.org/10.1017/9781108558822.
Kailitz, Steffen (2013): Classifying political regimes revisited: legitimation and durability. *Democratization*, 20(1): pp. 38–59. https://doi.org/10.1080/13510347.2013.738861.
Keremoğlu, Eda / Weidmann, Nils (2020): How dictators control the internet: a review essay. *Comparative Political Studies*, 53(10/11): pp. 1690–703. https://doi.org/10.1177%2F0010414020912278.
Kneuer, Marianne / Demmelhuber, Thomas (2016): Gravity centres of authoritarian rule: a conceptual approach. *Democratization*, 23(5): pp: 775–96. https://doi.org/10.1080/13510347.2015.1018898.
Kneuer, Marianne / Demmelhuber, Thomas (eds.) (2020): *Authoritarian gravity centers: a cross-regional study of authoritarian promotion and diffusion*. London: Routledge.
Kumar, Ashwani / Salim, Sahim (2019): ToTok founder explains why app was allowed in UAE. *Khaleej Times*, 29 December. www.khaleejtimes.com/business/local/ToTok-founder-explains-why-app-was-allowed-in-UAE.
Lancaster, Kirk / Rubin, Michael / Rapp-Hooper, Mira (2020): *Mapping China's Health Silk Road*. New York: Council on Foreign Relations. www.cfr.org/blog/mapping-chinas-health-silk-road.
Leber, Andrew (2020): China and COVID-19 in Saudi media. *War on the Rocks*, 23 April. https://warontherocks.com/2020/04/china-and-covid-19-in-saudi-media.
Lührmann, Anna / Lindberg, Staffan I. (2019): A third wave of autocratization is here: what is new about it? *Democratization*, 26(7): pp. 1095–113. https://doi.org/10.1080/13510347.2019.1582029.
Marczak, Bill (2020): A breej too far: how Abu Dhabi's spy sheikh hid his chat app in plein sight. *Medium*, 2 January. https://medium.com/@billmarczak/how-tahnoon-bin-zayed-hid-totok-in-plain-sight-group-42-breej-4e6c06c93ba6.
Marquis-Boire, Morgan / Marczak, Bill (2012): From Bahrain with love. FinFisher's spy kit exposed? *Citizen Lab*, 25 July. https://citizenlab.ca/2012/07/from-bahrain-with-love-finfishers-spy-kit-exposed.
Mazzetti, Mark / Perlroth, Nicole / Bergman, Ronen (2019): It seemed like a popular chat app. It's secretly a spy tool. *The New York Times*, 22 December. www.nytimes.com/2019/12/22/us/politics/totok-app-uae.html.
McArthur, Rachel (2020): Bahrain launches electronic bracelets to keep track of active COVID-19 cases. *Mobile Health News*, 8 April. www.mobihealthnews.com/news/emea/bahrain-launches-electronic-bracelets-keep-track-active-covid-19-cases.

Merkel, Wolfgang (2010): *Systemtransformation: Eine Einführung in die Theorie und Empirie der Transformationsforschung*. Wiesbaden: VS.

Muscat Airport (2020): *Drive-through coronavirus PCR test facilities now available for citizens and residents*. Press release, 26 September. www.muscatairport.co.om/news/drive-through-coronavirus-pcr-test-facilities-now-available-for-citizens-and-residents-oman-airports-announces-coronavirus-pcr-testing-requirements-for-all-travelers-muscat-oman-oman-airports-in-partnership-with-supply-international-in-collaboration-with-.

Muscat Daily (2020): Chinese envoy lauds effective measures by Omani government. *Muscat Daily*, 4 May. https://muscatdaily.com/Oman/386564/Chinese-envoy-lauds-effective-measures-by-Omani-government.

O'Loughlin, John / Ward, Michael D. / Lofdahl, Corey L. / Cohen, Jordin, S. / Brown, David S. / Reilly, David et al. (1998): The diffusion of democracy, 1946–1994. *Annals of the Association of American Geographers*, 88(4): pp. 545–74. https://doi.org/10.1111/0004-5608.00112.

O'Neill, Patrick Howell / Ryan-Mosley, Tate / Johnson, Bobbie (2020): A flood of coronavirus apps are tracking us. Now it's time to keep track of them. *MIT Technology Review*, 7 May. www.technologyreview.com/2020/05/07/1000961/launching-mittr-covid-tracing-tracker.

Power-Riggs, Aidan (2020): *Covid-19 is proving a boon for digital authoritarianism*. Washington: Center for Strategic and International Studies. www.csis.org/blogs/new-perspectives-asia/covid-19-proving-boon-digital-authoritarianism.

Rothschild, Joseph (1977): Observations on political legitimacy in contemporary Europe. *Political Science Quarterly*, 2(3): pp. 487–501.

Salman, Mohammad / Geeraerts, Gustaaf (2015): Strategic hedging and China's economic policy in the Middle East. *China Report*, 51(2): pp. 102–20. https://doi.org/10.1177%2F0009445515570440.

Shahbaz, Adrian (2018): *Freedom on the net 2018: the rise of digital authoritarianism*. New York: Freedom House. https://freedomhouse.org/report/freedom-net/2018/rise-digital-authoritarianism.

Shahbaz, Adrian / Funk, Allie (2020): *Freedom on the net 2020: the pandemic's digital shadow*. New York: Freedom House. https://freedomhouse.org/report/freedom-net/2020/pandemics-digital-shadow.

Siddiqi, Sabena (2019): After billions in Chinese investment Oman's Duqm port could help bypass Hormuz. *Albawaba*, 16 June. www.albawaba.com/opinion/after-billions-chinese-investment-omans-duqm-port-could-help-bypass-hormuz-1291468.

Sidło, Katarzyna W. (2020): The Chinese Belt and Road project in the Middle East and North Africa, in: IEMed (ed.): *Mediterranean Yearbook 2020*. Barcelona: European Institute of the Mediterranean, pp. 272–5.

Soliman, Mohammed (2020): *COVID-19 and the digital landscape in the Gulf*. Washington: Middle East Institute. www.mei.edu/publications/covid-19-and-digital-landscape-gulf.

Startup MGZN (2020): *BeAware app officially launched by iGA*. Press Release, 31 March. www.startupmgzn.com/english/news/beaware-bahrain-app-officially-launched-by-iga.

State Council Information Office (2020): 国务院新闻办就中国关于抗击疫情的国际合作情况举行发布会 *[The State Council Information Office held a press conference on China's international cooperation in the fight against the epidemic]*. www.gov.cn/xinwen/2020-03/26/content_5495712.htm#1.

Tansey, Oisín (2016): *The international politics of authoritarian rule*. Oxford: Oxford University Press.
Tansey, Oisín / Koehler, Kevin / Schmotz, Alexander (2017): Ties to the rest: autocratic linkages and regime survival. *Comparative Political Studies*, 50(9): pp. 1221–54. https://doi.org/10.1177%2F0010414016666859.
Taylor, Nick Paul (2019): China leads world in digital health adoption, Philips survey finds. *MedTech Dive*, 12 June. www.medtechdive.com/news/china-leads-world-in-digital-health-adoption-philips-survey-finds/556699.
TRT World (2020): Saudi Arabia to begin human trials with Chinese Covid-19 vaccine. *TRT World*, 10 August. www.trtworld.com/middle-east/saudi-arabia-to-begin-human-trials-with-chinese-covid-19-vaccine-38779.
Vanderhill, Rachel (2013): *Promoting authoritarianism abroad*. Boulder, CO: Lynne Rienner.
Wang, Cheng (2020): With the technical support from BGI, the Omani–Chinese team successfully set up PCR testing lab at @MuscatAirport within 72 hours… *Twitter*, @SadiqChengWang, 3 October. https://twitter.com/SadiqChengWang/status/1312 600794848530432.
Wejnert, Barbara (2014): *Diffusion of democracy. The past and future of global democracy*. Cambridge: Cambridge University Press. https://doi.org/10.1017/S153759271 500047X.
Wientzek, Olaf / Enskat, Sebastian (2020): The Trojan horse of multilateralism: why authoritarian regimes favour international cooperation while simultaneously undermining it. *International Reports*, 3: pp. 89–99. www.kas.de/documents/259121/10240919/The+Trojan+Horse+of+Multilateralism.pdf/a42971c0-e7cf-8dba-83fc-da0ab0bd1631?version=1.0&t=1601545214595.
Xinhua.net (2020): News analysis: Oman-China ties to prosper under BRI after COVID-19, say experts. *Xinhua*, 9 June. www.xinhuanet.com/english/2020-06/09/c_139125323.htm.
Yilmaz, Gözde / Yıldırım, Nilgün Eliküçük (2020): Authoritarian diffusion or cooperation? Turkey's emerging engagement with China. *Democratization*, 27(7): pp. 1202–20. https://doi.org/10.1080/13510347.2020.1777984.
Yom, Sean L. (2014): Authoritarian monarchies as an epistemic community: diffusion, repression, and survival during the Arab Spring. *Taiwan Journal of Democracy*, 10(1): pp. 43–62.
Young, Karen E. (2020): The Gulf's eastward turn: the logic of Gulf–China economic ties. *Journal of Arabian Studies*, 9(2): pp. 236–52. https://doi.org/10.1080/21534 764.2019.1768655.
Zoubir, Yahia H. (2020): *China's 'Health Silk Road' diplomacy in the MENA*. Konrad Adenauer Stiftung, Med Dialogue Series 27. www.kas.de/documents/282499/282548/MDS_China+Health+Silk+Road+Diplomacy.pdf/3b0af715-8671-cb10-5022-5e4a94eec086?t=1595341252822.

3 The reverse impact of politics on the COVID-19 response

How Hezbollah determined the choices of the Lebanese government

Nassim AbiGhanem

3.1 Introduction

Lebanon's sovereignty has been continuously questioned since Hezbollah monopolised the decision of war and peace for the Lebanese state. The COVID-19 pandemic has been no different, and has demonstrated the obvious political insovereignties in Lebanon when combating this pandemic. In this chapter, I explore how the influence of Iran over the Lebanese government was a main driver for the cabinet's decisions on dealing with the spread of COVID-19.

Albeit a single case study, this chapter allows us to reflect not only on what the realities are for many countries in the Arab world, exemplified by Lebanon, but also the extent to which protracted conflicts and regional influences intermingle. The literature on COVID-19 in politics, specifically, has so far focused on answering questions regarding governments' responses to the crisis and the policies being formulated and implemented. Little has however been written on how the relational ties between countries have impacted the responses and shaped the policies. Various opinion and analytical pieces have tapped into such questions, but they lack theoretical grounding.

I therefore argue that political research on COVID-19 needs to take into consideration political variables other than regime type (democratic or authoritarian) that factor into a government's policies in times of crisis. In other words, there are country-specific variables that matter to some countries and not to others – for example, how different geopolitical alliances play out and what effects economic sanctions have on the sanctioned states. In cases where the governments are geopolitically embedded in wider regional coalitions, the responses from the governments have not strictly addressed the interests of the people based on the health sector's capabilities but, in instances, were driven by the interests of geopolitical alliances.

Lebanon is a case in point – a country entrenched in protracted political and sectarian divisions, coupled with an economic crisis that emerged towards the end of 2019. The COVID-19 crisis came at a time that exposed how unprepared the government was to address a health crisis and how political

DOI: 10.4324/9781003240044-4

affiliations to regional powers are prioritised over the health of the Lebanese citizens. The government failed to develop a long-term strategy to combat COVID-19, which begs the question: how has the regional embeddedness of Lebanon and, in particular, the allegiance to Iran of the strongest Lebanese political party – Hezbollah – influenced the Lebanese government's response to the COVID-19 pandemic since February 2020?

This chapter demonstrates Hezbollah's systematic plan since early 2018 to consolidate the Lebanese health sector under its control. Hezbollah's influence on the government manifested in January 2020, allowing them to delay closing the borders and halting flights from Iran – the regional epicentre of COVID-19 – in order to ensure that Lebanese people and Iranians could return from Iran for medical help and that Hezbollah could deliver medical resources to Tehran. This, in turn, opened the door for the virus to spread further and suggests that regional hegemons can utilise their proxies to receive tributary support during a global or regional crisis, putting the incubator state in which the proxy operates at risk.

More broadly, this chapter showcases that going forward, research on the politics of health and the impacts of health crises in countries with strong proxy connections requires an unpacking of the political dynamics and the impacts of the health crisis on the state of the proxy actor, the proxy actor itself and the patron state. The case of Lebanon can set the stage for trying to understand how smaller countries overwhelmed with regional and international political divisions, including the presence of proxies, react to a pandemic. The chapter lays out one possible academic approach to help understand state interference through proxies and the subtleties that prevail in such situations. Methodologically, I utilise primary and secondary sources to ground my argument with sufficient evidence. Primary sources included five interviews with Lebanese health experts, activists, journalists and analysts.[1] Secondary sources were a culmination of reported news, press releases and announcements from the government as well as Hezbollah. This allowed me to validate each event more than once from all available sources.

The initial phases of the research included analysing secondary data and tracing the processes and patterns of the decisions taken at every juncture as the pandemic unfolded, starting with the date of the first case of COVID-19 recorded in Lebanon (21 February 2020) and followed by the chain of announcements made and decisions taken. Through the secondary sources, I followed the trends in the increase or decrease in the number of cases. Based on my findings, I created interview protocols, with questions focused on filling in the gaps that were left by the secondary sources, which either remained ambiguous or were never made public. Because of the sensitivity of its operations, Hezbollah is well practised in implementing plans that remain undisclosed to the public.

My argument proceeds as follows: section 3.2 provides a brief background on the political divisions in Lebanon to date and highlights the regional alliances and allegiances of some Lebanese sects and political parties.

Section 3.3 conceptualises proxy theory as one way to understand the actions of actors and regional states' inter-reference, either in the decisions of the governments that suffer from internal divides or in countries that have always been influenced by international politics in their internal and external policies. Section 3.4 establishes Hezbollah as an Iranian proxy and describes the influence of Iran on the health sector in Lebanon before and during the outbreak of COVID-19. The last section concludes with insights on future prospects and proposes further cases where this approach may be applicable.

3.2 The political divisions in Lebanon

Lebanon's contemporary history is a story of yet another political cleavage between political actors who swore allegiance to a pro-Syrian, pro-Iranian alliance and those who called for alignment with the anti-Syrian and anti-Iranian policies in the region. A few marginalised political parties remained opposing the external influences on statehood in Lebanon, with little influence on unifying the nation. This division took place back in 2005, after the assassination of the late Prime Minister Rafik al-Hariri. The Syrian President, Bashar al-Assad, in August 2004 was determined to force Lebanese politicians to vote for an extended presidential term for the then president of Lebanon, Émile Lahoud, despite such an extension requiring constitutional amendments. The Syrian president assumed that the Lebanese people would accept this interference because Syria had got its way in Lebanon throughout the fifteen years of command since the Lebanese civil war ended (Harris, 2009). This would also allow Assad to control Iranian interests in Lebanon.

Al-Hariri refused to extend Lahoud's presidential term and turned against the Syrian hegemony of Lebanon. In the aftershock of his assassination on 14 February 2005, outrage against Syrian influence – internationally and locally – meant that ethnic sects, who were oppressed by the Syrian regime, mobilised their groups to take part in significant demonstrations against the regime. This was marked by a large protest that took place after the first monthly memorial of Hariri's death and culminated in a new coalition, which was subsequently called '14 March' movement. At the opposite end of the spectrum, Hezbollah and other allies of Syria in Lebanon who had been benefiting from the Syrian hegemony and Iranian support in the post-war years also took to the streets to show appreciation on 8 March 2005 in a show of allegiance to Syria. The group later came to be known as 'March 8th'. The result is a political split along the lines of allegiance (or not) to Syria and by extension Iran.

After the 2011 Syrian uprising turned into a civil war, the intertwined political cleavage in Lebanon – coupled with the influx of refugees – meant that the naturally pro-Syrian and pro-Iranian regime (in support of Alawites and Shi'ites) and the anti-Syrian, anti-Iranian proponents in Lebanon would be fighting a proxy war (Darwich and Fakhoury, 2016). The logical outcome of the Lebanese political situation should place Lebanon inside the regional conflict that has been surging, since it is another country that is nested within the US–Iranian, Sunni–Shi'ite conflict from the Gulf, Iraq and Syria (see Jenne, 2015). As Kramer (2017: 118) puts it:

> The civil war in neighbouring Syria is no longer a Syrian domestic affair, but includes religious extremists declaring the aim of establishing an Islamic caliphate that includes the entire Levant. Arms and supplies are purchased by the emirates in the Arabian Gulf and channelled through Lebanon to factions opposing President Assad in Syria, which has led to Syrian incursions and divided much of Lebanon into supporters and opponents of Assad.

Ten years after the start of the Syrian civil war, it became clear to Hezbollah that consolidating power in Lebanon is necessary in order to maintain the interests of the Iranian and Assad's regimes. Hezbollah saw a political and security vacuum that can be filled after the withdrawal of the Syrian troops from Lebanon (Alagha, 2005). This is not a new objective for Hezbollah; since the party's establishment, it has intended to give the Shi'ite Muslims in Lebanon a leg up in the government and to slowly hegemonise Lebanon's foreign policy (Azani, 2012). Hezbollah gradually began to utilise the excess of power at their disposal by intimidating other political actors. For example, in 2008, Hezbollah responded violently to a governmental decision to dismantle its communication network by attacking areas in Beirut and Chouf. In 2014, Hezbollah's members of parliament blocked the vote for a new president by not attending the parliamentary session and preventing the necessary quorum for a constitutional vote. Hezbollah simultaneously pressurised its allies to do the same. Ultimately, this allowed Hezbollah to place its own Christian ally, veteran politician Michel Aoun (then head of the Free Patriotic Movement), in the Lebanese presidency. The first government formed after Aoun's election in 2016 also gave in to pressure for a new electoral law which gerrymandered the districts to ensure that Hezbollah would achieve a relative majority in the parliament and an absolute majority together with its loyal allies. These conditions were presented in an ultimatum that meant there would be no moving forward on the presidential or parliamentary elections unless Hezbollah's demands were met, hindering any institutional progress and risking major positions remaining vacant.

3.3 Hezbollah as an Iranian proxy in Lebanon

Proxy alliances are understood as partnerships formed between dyadic, asymmetrically capable states or between states and non-state groups (Byman, 2007: 92). This is often the case between a state, referred to as a patron or sponsor state, and a non-state group, referred to as the proxy actor. As such, the state provides the non-state group with financial resources, arms, training and political support in exchange for the latter agreeing to fight on its behalf or act in favour of the foreign policy objectives of the patron state (Salehyan, 2010). Some proxy alliances, particularly ideological ones, last beyond wars and violent conflicts and extend to a strong, long-term governance alliance. If the proxy comes out as a winner in the war, the patron state invests in an alliance that constitutes governing know-how (Khan and Zhaoying, 2020). As such, the proxy actor maintains a strong representation in the apparatuses of the government and operates in its own interest and in that of the sponsor state simultaneously (Moghadam and Wyss, 2020).

The tenets of proxy relationships are: (1) shared political interests and a basis for military partnerships and objectives; (2) a partnership between a principal (patron state) and an agent (proxy); and (3) a partnership that can shift between or combine transactional or exploitative associations (Borghard, 2014: 50). The principal–agent dynamic is essentially the determinant relationship in proxy environments (Eisenhardt, 1989). The principal (sponsor state) is usually the first mover; that is, it has a goal that it wants to achieve and delegates to the proxy the tasks which need to be carried out. The relationship is based on serving the needs of the principal (Hovil and Werker, 2005).

Hezbollah has been a core component in a proxy alliance with Iran for four decades now and is successful in implementing Iran's interests. Iran has been providing millions of dollars, military training, technical assistance and weapons to Hezbollah. In return, Hezbollah has strongly supported Iran's foreign policy goals in Lebanon and the region at large (Norton, 2007: 106). Hezbollah's operations allowed Iran to achieve its strategic objectives in the Middle East without direct military intervention. The Iran–Hezbollah symbiotic relationship of state–proxy cooperation has been consistently progressing, reaching the pinnacle when Hezbollah began controlling Lebanon's foreign policy and bilateral relationships with European and North American states (Byman and Kreps, 2010: 10).

Hezbollah became a well-trained and highly effective organisation that is now indispensable to Iran (Byman, 2007; Levitt, 2014). Hezbollah offers Iran a form of 'power projection, enabling Iran to indirectly attack its adversaries and influence events far from its shores, even attacking Iran's enemies in Europe' (Byman and Kreps, 2010: 4). Iran established Hezbollah as a challenge to the more secular Shi'ite group, Amal Movement, which was as old as the Lebanese state and had worked to integrate Shi'ite Muslims into the diverse Lebanese social fabric (Kramer, 1994: 21). By weakening Amal, Iran was sowing the seeds for a proxy that would have a strong ideological pact with the revolutionary movement it aimed to spread to the region. Countries where Shi'ite communities can form a sectarian majority are targets. The former Amal hardliners formed the basis of Hezbollah, and a number of Iranian Revolutionary Guard Corps (IRGC) and Iranian intelligence personnel helped establish Hezbollah in Lebanon back in 1982. Hezbollah's founders agreed on two principles in return: the belief in 'velāyat-e faqīh' [guardianship of the Islamic jurist] and in the armed struggle against Israel

(Malakoutikhah, 2020: 921). Hezbollah became a successful model that Iran tried to replicate elsewhere in the region, i.e. Iraq and Yemen (Shapira, 1987; Ranstorp, 1997; Hajjar, 2002; Hamzeh, 2004; Byman, 2007).

Iran contributes approximately $700 million annually to Hezbollah (Mandelker, quoted in Karam, 2018). Some of the funding is spent on the welfare of its own fighters, their families and the families of the martyrs, while a major chunk is spent on recruit training and salaries for party leaders and members of parliament (Malakoutikhah, 2020: 922). The new manifesto of Hezbollah, published in 2009, emphasises cooperation with other Islamic states and Iran's importance as a 'central state in the Muslim world' (El Husseini, 2010: 809). Furthermore, military training in Iran has been key for Hezbollah's fighters. Ahmad Nizar Hamzeh (2004: 71) even argues that

> [r]eportedly, [Hezbollah's] military operational headquarters include top-ranking officers of Iran's Islamic Revolutionary Guards. Although the guards withdrew in the early 1990s, Secretary General Nasrallah has referred to their continued stay in some parts of Lebanon. Without disclosing [… their number], the party's military apparatus seems to rely extensively on the logistics and military training of the guards.
> (own omission and clarification)

Hezbollah publicly declared on several occasions their position as a party within a structure spearheaded by the IRGC. In a speech by Hezbollah's Secretary General Hassan Nasrallah on 16 March 2016, he emphasised that 'we are open about the fact that Hezbollah's budget, its income, its expenses, everything it eats and drinks, its weapons and rockets, come from the Islamic Republic of Iran' (Nasrallah, quoted in Rafizadeh, 2016). Hezbollah has developed a strong political influence in the Lebanese government. Since the withdrawal of the Syrian troops from Lebanon in 2005, Hezbollah has been consistently represented in every Lebanese cabinet. In addition, Hezbollah manages a vast network of social services that includes infrastructure, schools and even healthcare facilities. Previously, the healthcare facilities focused on assisting long-term injured combatants from the war with Israel. They then expanded to include the injuries from Syria. Hence, healthcare facilities operating in times of war would later on be mobilised to operate in aiding the COVID-19-infected individuals close to Hezbollah's network.

There are many instances in which Tehran directly gave orders to Hezbollah. Hezbollah is a Shi'ite Muslim political party and a militant group; its longstanding alliances with Iran embroiled the group in the civil war in Syria, where Hezbollah is an effective military force assisting the Assad regime. Hezbollah publicly confirmed its involvement in the Syrian civil war in 2013, joining Iran and Russia in supporting the Syrian regime against the rebel groups (Levitt, 2014). More than 7,000 Hezbollah militants are estimated to have fought for Assad (Robinson, 2020). In 2015, Hezbollah participated in the battle of Aleppo, whilst prior to the battle they had justified their participation in the

Syrian war to the Lebanese public as serving to protect Shi'ite villages and the Shi'ite shrines in Damascus. However, the city of Aleppo has no Shi'ite shrines nor a Shi'ite population and certainly does not border Lebanon. The real reason for participating was the direct order from Iran to mobilise Hezbollah in support of the Assad regime so that Assad could regain control of Aleppo (Ghaddar, 2019). Ghaddar claimed that a number of Hezbollah fighters and officials confirmed to her that the IRGC al-Quds Brigades commanded by Qassem Soleimani had forced Mustafa Badreddine, Hezbollah's Elite Commander in Syria, to participate in the Aleppo war against his will and ultimately had him killed in 2016 in Syria (Ghaddar, 2019).

The weak reasoning provided by Hezbollah for fighting in Syria left ambiguities that the war in Yemen cleared up. Any doubt that Hezbollah's direct orders were delivered top-down from Iran disappeared when Hezbollah got involved in the war in Yemen in support of the Iranian-backed Houthi rebels. Secretary General Nasrallah eventually admitted, in another speech on 15 February 2019, that they had a presence in Yemen, saying,

> we tell you in all honesty we will not hide [the truth about martyrs in Yemen], we are not ashamed and we are proud of these martyrs [...] We are only ashamed when we do not support the people of Yemen.
> (Nasrallah, 2019; own omission and clarification)

This was another clear indicator of Hezbollah's actions and involvements not serving Lebanon's security or foreign relations, but serving the interests of Iran.

3.4 Hezbollah's control of the Lebanese Ministry of Public Health

Since 2018, Hezbollah has continuously asserted a claim on the Ministry of Public Health (MoPH) because of the interesting portfolio the ministry presents. The motivation to take control of the ministry is mostly driven by the local and regional challenges Hezbollah faces. As the US sanctions on Iran increased, Hezbollah's financial network was hit hard, forcing the party to seek additional resources – through the ministry they can do so. After the Defence, Education and Interior Ministries, the MoPH commands Lebanon's fourth largest budget annually (Government of Lebanon, 2020). The funds at the MoPH are also mostly distributed to the public rather than to salaries and other expenses within the ministry (Ghaddar, 2018). As Iran began to struggle under the US sanctions, it turned its focus to continuing military spending for Hezbollah. Fearing the loss of cash flow from Iran for its social services, Hezbollah needed new sources of financial support. The US sanctions do not apply to health services, so Hezbollah shifted its focus to controlling the MoPH. According to historian Makram Rabah,

> health institutions are exempted from the sanctions and the plan to hand the MoPH to Hezbollah was something the U.S. government warned

the Lebanese Prime Minister [about] in 2018, but [Prime Minister Saad] Hariri ignored the warnings and went ahead with appointing Jamal Jabak as Minister of Health.

(personal interview, online, 28 October 2020)

The opportunity for Hezbollah to flex their muscles and force the prime minister to designate the MoPH to them became a priority that was achieved in two consecutive government formations.

As previously mentioned, Hezbollah's infrastructure includes thousands of fighters who have been battling in Syria and who require essential and advanced medical care. In other words, Hezbollah needs the health sector and hospital services in order to treat the injured. The five hospitals and hundreds of medical centres and infirmaries that Hezbollah owns are barely able to meet the needs of the wounded (Ghaddar, 2018). Additionally, to circumvent the sanctions on Iran, medications imported or produced in Lebanon can be delivered to Tehran through unofficial channels. Thus, the MoPH has become a great opportunity for Hezbollah to 'funnel the much-needed funds and possibly to conceal them within the framework of the [ministry]' (Rabah, 2019; own addition). Another plan for funnelling financial resources is for the MoPH to register Iranian medicines that have not yet met international standards and are not yet approved by the US Food and Drug Administration or the World Health Organization. The importation of these drugs to the Lebanese market enables cash to flow back into Iran. In this way, the revenue generated from their sale is sufficient to cover the financial needs of Hezbollah and enough to be transferred to Iran. Hadi Mourad, a Lebanese medical doctor, activist and whistle-blower against the MoPH policies on registering uncertified and unapproved drugs from Iran, estimated that '$900,000million to $1 billion of profits are generated from selling Iranian medications on the Lebanese market' (personal interview, online, 10 November 2020). Therefore, Hezbollah taking control of the MoPH eases their financial burden and enables them to capture the resources of the Lebanese healthcare system to help them respond to the injured militants, ultimately allowing them to maintain their military presence in Syria.

Consequently, the 2019 and 2020 cabinets headed by Prime Ministers Saad al-Hariri and Hassan Diab, respectively, assigned the MoPH to Hezbollah. In 2019, the minister was Jamal Jabak, former personal physician for the party's Secretary General Hassan Nasrallah. Swiftly after the appointment, Jabak signed a memorandum of understanding with Iran for a five-year plan that includes cooperation between the Lebanese and Iranian ministries of health. The memo stipulated that Lebanon would import medicine from Iran and initiate an exchange programme for medical students (*Tehran Times*, 2019). Accordingly, the former Minister of Health in Iran announced in a press conference with Jabak that

we place great focus on transferring our technical knowledge to Lebanon. However, at first, we need to export some medicine to Lebanon to meet the immediate medical needs of people. Then, the private sector of both countries can cooperate on exchanging their technical knowledge.

(*Tehran Times*, 2019)

This signalled that the export of medicine is a condition for any further cooperation. Nevertheless, as previously mentioned, the Iranian medicines have not yet received worldwide international certification, thus the scheme is 'risking the health of millions in Lebanon for the benefit of the Iranian state' (Hadi Mourad, personal interview, online, 10 November 2020). The only countries that import medicine from Iran are Russia, Iraq, Syria, Afghanistan, Ukraine and Azerbaijan. The political affiliations of these states speak volumes on the direction Iran's allies and proxies took in order to support Iran in its fight against sanctions.

Additionally, Jabak announced that he sees no limitations in cooperation with Iran, in that, alluding to the decision to ignore the US sanctions on Iran, even at the risk of discontinuing work with wider international healthcare providers. Jabak added that

> I think many countries in the region have the same opinion about sanctions against Iran. In our visits from Iranian pharmaceuticals, we are amazed at the high quality of medicine produced in Iran and we want to use Iran's technical knowledge and expertise in Lebanon.
>
> (*Tehran Times*, 2019)

It was clear that the Lebanese minister, and behind him Hezbollah, saw the sanctions on Iran as unjust and the abuse of power at Lebanese state institutions as one way to fight against them.

3.5 Hezbollah during COVID-19: influencing Lebanon's government for Iran's benefit

Since the start of the pandemic, Hezbollah has run an assertive public health policy campaign showing off its fleet of ambulances and its control over various hospitals and health centres (Fiore, 2020). The close links with Iran and the slow response to COVID-19 from the Lebanese government have left Hezbollah at a disadvantage, as Iran became the Middle East epicentre of the pandemic: nearly 200,000 cases and 9,272 deaths had been recorded by mid-June 2020, when the virus was spreading throughout the region (Reuters Staff, 2020). However, it was clear to many opponents of Hezbollah that the party insisted on delaying any response that would involve shutting down the airport in order not to stop flights from Iran. In this way, the support to Iran as it battled with COVID-19 could come from Lebanon (Clarke, 2020).

At first, Hezbollah did not announce that it would mobilise its resources to be at the disposal of the government, but claims of support were made by Nasrallah in his speech on 16 March 2020. At that point, the success of the MoPH had become a priority for Hezbollah because the ministry failing would have indicated Hezbollah's inability to run the ministry – and they very much wished to hold on to it. However, while Hezbollah was pushing not to stop flights from Iran for strategic reasons, the party went on to formulate an independent programme to fight COVID-19 in the hope that controlling the spread of the virus in the community would lift some of the burden off the MoPH and the government could avoid the decision to shut down the airport. Therefore, the narrative of a successful MoPH operation went hand in hand with a strong operation led by Hezbollah. As the Executive Council Chairman Sayyid Hashem Safi al-Din put it:

> Our job is to work in harmony with the government mechanisms, and in no way to act instead of them. Does anyone have any doubt today that the relevant government ministries engaged in containment are in need of assistance?
>
> (Al-Manar, 2020)

The programme was officially presented in detail by Hezbollah's executive council chairman on Al-Manar TV, the network owned solely by Hezbollah. Hezbollah's programme focused primarily on their areas of influence in South Beirut, South Lebanon and the Beqaa Valley, reflecting the sectarian nature of their social services. However, images of Hezbollah's ambulance fleet indicated that the plan was initiated as early as 18 February 2020. The programme utilised the decades of support the party had received from Iran. In the plan 1,500 doctors, 3,000 medics and nurses, 5,000 medical teams working in hospitals and clinics and 15,000 individuals were divided into teams in cities and towns to manage contact tracing. To control all that, Hezbollah set up an operations room to manage the complex operation, which itself was divided into different committees dealing with different aspects of handling the spread of the virus (Perry and Bassam, 2020).

The Lebanese government continued the scheduled flights from the regional epicentre and delayed any airport shutdowns, despite the first case in Lebanon being recorded on 21 February, from a passenger arriving from the city of Qom in Iran. The outcry of the Lebanese public and political opposition calling for a halt to flights from Iran was largely ignored for almost a month. Even after later agreeing to close the airport (more details in the following paragraph), the Lebanese government insisted on repatriation flights and – given the nature of the relationship between Hezbollah and Iran – many of the flights still came from different cities around Iran. To respond to the accusations that Hezbollah was pushing for the flights from Iran to continue, Sayyid Hashem Safi al-Din in the same interview with Al-Manar on 25 March 2020 specified the steps taken by Hezbollah's team when flights from Iran landed, indicating that Hezbollah was completely replacing the state in governing the precautionary measures needed upon the arrival of at least those flights arriving from Iran, if not all flights. Safi al-Din insisted that

Hezbollah were responding swiftly by forming teams that got in touch with passengers arriving from Iran and made sure that they were tested and that they followed self-isolation instructions (Al-Manar, 2020). If this indicates anything, it provides clear evidence that Hezbollah preferred to mobilise its own resources to enforce the necessary precautionary measures for the passengers rather than to stop all flights completely. Moreover, other incidents demonstrated that Hezbollah was not entirely competent in dealing with the matter. A Lebanese reporter for the newspaper *An-Nahar*, Asrar Shbaro, was interviewing passengers from an Iranian flight from Tehran, who were indicating that there was no testing or registration, when Shbaro was assaulted in full view of the public by a member of Hezbollah who grabbed her phone and erased what she had recorded. Airport security agents watched the incident unfold and acted a bit too late, aware that Hezbollah had already tightened its grip on security over the airport through infiltrating governmental security apparatuses masterminded by Hezbollah Security Chief Wafiq Safa (Asrar Shbaro, personal interview, online, 28 November 2020).

To be able to support patients coming from Iran, Hezbollah freed all 86 beds at St George's Hospital, owned by the Martyrs Foundation of Hezbollah, and the hospital was transformed into a medical centre designated for the treatment of COVID-19 patients. Reports suggest that Hezbollah was quarantining and treating infected Iranian personnel at its own private hospitals as well (Badran, 2020). As Makram Rabah, with reservation, stated: 'A number of Hezbollah hospitals were rumoured to have hosted high-ranking regime members and elites transferred from Iran due to the healthcare system's struggles' (Makram Rabah, personal interview, online, 28 October 2020). However, Hadi Mourad insisted that 'many Iranians who were infected have been treated at these hospitals and the health ministry intended to help and they mostly attended the hospitals that are in the South of Beirut' (Hadi Mourad, personal interview, online, 10 November 2020). It is important to note that the government had officially designated the Hariri Public Hospital to be the one responsible for treating COVID-19 patients, signifying that the St George's Hospital was strictly used for the needs of Hezbollah's soldiers and/or Iranian elite commanders. Furthermore, Hezbollah began working on seventeen sites to be used for isolating patients in case of a larger outbreak and twenty-three diagnostic centres for testing. All the diagnostic centres were set up in southern Lebanon, a Hezbollah stronghold (Janoubia website, quoted in ITIC, 2020).

Hezbollah gave up its stance against closing the airport three weeks after reporting that the first case of COVID-19 had been detected in a passenger arriving from Iran. Hezbollah's position shifted as public pressure mounted on the government and the party itself. Through its strong influence on the government, Hezbollah wanted to protect its patron's image and to address the party's logistical needs for transferring money and sophisticated Iranian precision-guided weapons (Fiore, 2020). The obscured motivations for maintaining the flights from Iran with packed passengers also suggested the transfer of more than weapons: 'there was further hostile scrutiny [...] with allegations in the Arab media that Hezbollah was secretly treating Iranian military leaders in hospitals it controlled' (Fiore, 2020; own omission). Until that point, Hezbollah had fully imposed its own agenda on the government, forcing the continuation of the flights from Iran to Beirut with no plan for dealing with pilgrims arriving from Qom, even though the first case of coronavirus infection in Lebanon was a person who had visited Qom (Nassar, 2020). Only after three weeks and strong demands from the populace through traditional and social media did Hezbollah find itself cornered for not doing more to combat the spread of the virus; needing to show a commitment to fighting the pandemic, Hezbollah were finally pushed not to veto a governmental decree to close the airport. The Lebanese minister of health in 2020, Hassan Hamad, who is supported by Hezbollah and who served as mayor of the city of Baalbek (a Hezbollah stronghold in the Beqaa Valley), personally declared that stopping flights is a political decision and not one based on health policy. Essentially, the delay in closing the airport allowed Hezbollah to initiate a Plan B for smuggling in Iranian elite commanders for treatment as well as money and weapons which no longer was limited to land borders.

To further emphasise the extent of the control that Hezbollah has exerted on the Lebanese government for the benefit of Iran, the blatant example of the incident at Beirut International Airport with the reporter demonstrates the lengths Hezbollah are willing to go to defend the interests of Iran. Such oppression and insistence on covering up the passengers' situation on the flights are further indication and evidence of the ambiguous motivations behind the continuation of flights coming from Iran.

3.6 Prospects and conclusion

This chapter looked at how the regional interference and non-state proxies have shaped the governmental responses to the COVID-19 crisis. In Lebanon, by prioritising the needs of Iran, the sponsor state, Hezbollah – as a proxy actor – institutionally navigated processes to maintain flights from Tehran to Beirut that included religious tourism and high-ranking officials who needed to receive medical treatment in Lebanon. After a few years attempting to control the MoPH to circumvent the economic sanctions imposed on Iran and Hezbollah, Hezbollah envisioned the MoPH as a concealed source of income for itself and Iran. In doing so, it jeopardised the preparedness of the Lebanese government to combat the pandemic. A simultaneous crisis with Iran, which in turn is struggling to contain the spread of the virus, allowed Hezbollah to mobilise Lebanon's resources to the benefit of Iran.

The chapter established Hezbollah as an Iranian proxy and discussed in detail the slow encroachment of Hezbollah over the MoPH. Hezbollah saw an opportunity to manipulate the sanctions imposed on the party and Iran by controlling the Lebanese MoPH. Despite international warnings, the Lebanese opposition parties, including Prime Minister Saad al-Hariri, could not break through the political deadlock Hezbollah had created when forming cabinets without succumbing to Hezbollah's demands. The pandemic coincided with Hezbollah's two-term tenure over the reins of the Lebanese MoPH in two consecutive cabinets. On the one hand, Hezbollah wanted the ministry as an opportunity to demonstrate to the Lebanese public that the party can govern well without corruption when it is granted control over ministries, and while doing so can maintain its image as a political party that gets things done. On the other hand, it needed to ensure that the patron state and ally, Iran, got the support it needed. Ultimately, this meant that borders needed to remain open longer in order to serve the Iranian leaders and Hezbollah travellers between Lebanon and Iran at the expense of the Lebanese people. After Hezbollah set a contingency plan for the transfer of personnel and material, Hezbollah agreed to the airport's closure, after which Hezbollah's resources were mobilised to address the needs of its own supporters rather than the population, leaving the Lebanese healthcare system struggling to control the pandemic.

Apart from the proxy relationships having detrimental effects on Lebanese citizens, the Lebanese government also underperformed in providing a clear communication strategy, collaborating with local authorities and providing education, awareness and a wider social safety net (Abi-Rached et al., 2020). Diwan and Abi-Rached (2020: 3) referred to Lebanon's initial low number of cases as a 'lucky start'. The low number was also a reflection of the fact that only 1% of the population was tested for the virus. Without transparency in the figures on mortality, infection and testing, the foundational lack of trust between the population and the government will continue to cause dissent among people asked to abide by the precautionary rules set to stop the virus spreading. Moreover, Lebanon has set out no plan for the crowded settlements of refugees, and while there might have been cases in the camps that went unregistered, the lack of any plan for refugee camps and settlements leaves these spaces prone to various forms of contamination in the future (Diwan and Abi-Rached, 2020). More recently, there is a wide suspicion that the numbers are lower than they are due to the relatively high PCR test costs on the strained economic situation for the households.

Going forward, political research and analysis on state responses to crises need to take into consideration the wider geo political variables that have a significant impact on policy choices. Context matters, and not all governments have the same political sovereignty to respond as a unified actor towards a crisis. In certain instances we need to look at patron states that influence national governmental responses more than the government itself. Conceptually, principal–agent theory in proxies can provide one approach to understanding why certain non-state actors are more adamant to push for one decision over another. Certainly, the political and military strength of the proxy are prerequisites for their ability to strongly influence national government decisions.

For the case of Lebanon, this chapter showed not only how Hezbollah as an Iranian proxy has affected government responses to the COVID-19 health pandemic so far, but also teased out questions on how governments incubating a strong proxy can shape their policies based on the dynamics between a proxy and a regional state sponsor. What can one expect for future crises of similar extent, may they be health pandemics, climate change-induced crises or any other devastating disasters? Further research is merited to provide more in-depth evidence on external intervention in state institutions, and comparative cases can be drawn from Iraq and Yemen, Libya and Nigeria as well as Paraguay to explore mechanisms of the impact of strong proxies in times of crisis.

Note

1 Expert interviews were possible through my connections in Lebanon. The interviews were conducted online by videoconference so that they could be recorded if permitted by the participant. The interviews were then transcribed, and insightful information was extracted that either confirmed or disconfirmed the data collected from the secondary sources.

References

Abi-Rached, Joelle / Issa, Nahla / Khalife, Jade / Salameh, Pascale / Karra-Aly, Ayah / Kosremelli Asmar, Michèle (2020): *Towards a zero-COVID Lebanon: a call for action*. Paris: Arab Reform Initiative. www.arab-reform.net/publication/towards-a-zero-covid-lebanon-a-call-for-action.

Alagha, Joseph (2005): Hizballah after the Syrian withdrawal. *Middle East Report*, 237: pp. 34–9. https://doi.org/10.2307/30042473.

Al-Manar (2020): Hashem Safi al-Din announces Hezbollah's plan to combat coronavirus [in Arabic]. *Al-Manar*, 25 March. https://almanar.com.lb/6444187.

Azani, Eitan (2012): Hezbollah's strategy of 'walking on the edge': between political game and political violence. *Studies on Conflict and Terrorism*, 35(11): 741–59. https://doi.org/10.1080/1057610X.2012.720238.

Badran, Tony (2020): *Lebanon, Hezbollah and COVID-19*. Washington: Foundation for Defense of Democracies, 23 April. www.fdd.org/analysis/2020/04/23/lebanon-hezbollah-and-covid-19.

Borghard, Erica D. (2014): *Friends with benefits? Power and influence in proxy warfare* (doctoral thesis). New York: Columbia University. https://doi.org/10.7916/D8Q81B7Z.

Byman, Daniel (2007): Israel and the Lebanese Hizballah. In: Art, Robert J. / Richardson, Louise (eds.): *Democracy and counterterrorism: lessons from the past*. Washington: United States Institute of Peace, pp. 305–42.

Byman, Daniel / Kreps, Sarah E. (2010): Agents of destruction? Applying principal–agent analysis to state-sponsored terrorism. *International Studies Perspectives*, 11(1): pp. 1–18.

Clarke, Colin P. (2020): Yesterday's terrorists are today's public health providers. *Foreign Policy*, 8 April. https://foreignpolicy.com/2020/04/08/terrorists-nonstate-ungoverned-health-providers-coronavirus-pandemic.

Darwich, May / Fakhoury, Tamirace (2016): Casting the other as an existential threat: the securitization of sectarianism in the international relations of the Syria crisis. *Global Discourse*, 6(4): 712–32. https://doi.org/10.1080/23269995.2016.1259231.

Diwan, Ishac / Abi-Rached, Joelle (2020): *Lebanon: managing COVID-19 in the time of revolution*. Paris: Arab Reform Initiative. www.arab-reform.net/wp-content/uploads/pdf/Arab_Reform_Initiative_en_lebanon-managing-covid-19-in-the-time-of-revolution_10411.pdf?ver=a8eaf5bc86a17a87e8005dde74b0cbac.

Eisenhardt, Kathleen M. (1989): Agency theory: an assessment and review. *Academy of Management Review*, 14(1): pp. 57–74. https://doi.org/10.2307/258191.

El Husseini, Rola (2010): Hezbollah and the axis of refusal: Hamas, Iran and Syria. *Third World Quarterly*, 31(5): pp. 803–15. https://doi.org/10.1080/01436597.2010.502695.

Fiore, Massimiliano (2020): Lebanon's economic crisis: an opportunity to contain Hezbollah? *E-International Relations*, 25 June. www.e-ir.info/2020/06/25/opinion-lebanons-economic-crisis-an-opportunity-to-contain-hezbollah.

Ghaddar, Hanin (2018): *Why does Hezbollah want Lebanon's health ministry?* Washington: The Washington Institute for Near East Policy. www.washingtoninstitute.org/policy-analysis/why-does-hezbollah-want-lebanons-health-ministry.

Ghaddar, Hanin (2019): *Hezbollah–Iran dynamics: a proxy, not a partner*. Washington: The Washington Institute for Near East Policy. www.washingtoninstitute.org/policy-analysis/view/hezbollah-iran-dynamics-a-proxy-not-a-partner.

Government of Lebanon (2020): *Budget law 2020* [in Arabic]. Beirut: Ministry of Finance. www.finance.gov.lb/en-us/Finance/BI/ABDP/Annual%20Budget%20Documents%20and%20Process/Budget%20%20Law%202020.pdf.

Hajjar, Sami G. (2002): *Hizballah: terrorism, national liberation, or menace*. Pennsylvania: Strategic Studies Institute, U.S. Army War College.

Hamzeh, Ahmed Nizar (2004): *In the path of Hizbullah*. Syracuse: University of Syracuse Press.

Harris, William (2009): Lebanon's roller coaster ride. In: Rubin, Barry (ed.): *Lebanon: liberation, conflict, and crisis*. New York: Palgrave Macmillan, pp. 63–82. https://doi.org/10.1057/9780230622432.

Hovil, Lucy / Werker, Eric (2005): Portrait of a failed rebellion: an account of rational, sub-optimal violence in western Uganda. *Rationality and Society*, 17(1): pp. 5–34. https://doi.org/10.1177%2F1043463105051775.

ITIC (2020): *Hezbollah's coping with Covid-19: a test case of the conduct of the ministate established by Hezbollah in Lebanon*. Ramat Hasharon: Meir Amit Intelligence and Terrorism Information Center. www.terrorism-info.org.il/app/uploads/2020/04/E_076_20.pdf.

Jenne, Erin K. (2015): *Nested security lessons in conflict management from the League of Nations and the European Union*. Cornell: Cornell University Press.

Karam, Joyce (2018): Iran pays Hezbollah $700 million a year, US official says. *The National News*, 5 June. www.thenationalnews.com/world/the-americas/iran-pays-hezbollah-700-million-a-year-us-official-says-1.737347.

Khan, Akbar / Zhaoying, Han (2020): Iran-Hezbollah alliance reconsidered: what contributes to the survival of state–proxy alliance? *Journal of Asian Security and International Affairs*, 7(1): pp. 101–23. https://doi.org/10.1177%2F2347797020906654.
Kramer, Martin (1994): Hizbullah: the calculus of jihad. In: Marty, Martin E. / Appleby, R. Scott (eds.): *Fundamentalisms and the state: remaking polities, economies, and militants*. Chicago: University of Chicago Press, pp. 539–56.
Kramer, Christian R. (2017): *Network theory and violent conflicts: studies in Afghanistan and Lebanon*. Basingstoke: Palgrave Macmillan.
Levitt, Matthew (2014): Hezbollah's Syrian quagmire. *PRISM*, 5(1): pp. 100–15.
Malakoutikhah, Zeynab (2020): Iran: sponsoring or combating terrorism? *Studies in Conflict and Terrorism*, 43(10): pp. 913–39. https://doi.org/10.1080/1057610X.2018.1506560.
Moghadam, Assaf / Wyss, Michel (2020): The political power of proxies: why nonstate actors use local surrogates. *International Security*, 44(4): pp. 119–57. https://doi.org/10.1162/isec_a_00377.
Nasrallah, Hassan (2019): Speech. *Al-Manar TV*, 15 February. www.youtube.com/watch?v=Ey4LVXnTcEw&ab_channel=NewsUpdateLive.
Nassar, Adid (2020): Iran before the health of the Lebanese. *The Arab Weekly*, 1 March. https://thearabweekly.com/iran-health-lebanese.
Norton, Augustus Richard (2007): *Hezbollah: a short history*. Princeton: Princeton University Press.
Perry, Tom / Bassam, Laila (2020): Hezbollah deploys medics, hospitals against coronavirus in Lebanon. *Reuters*, 26 March. www.reuters.com/article/us-health-coronavirus-hezbollah/hezbollah-deploys-medics-hospitals-against-coronavirus-in-lebanon-idUSKBN21C3R7.
Rabah, Makram (2019): Hezbollah's control of Lebanon's health ministry poses a grave danger. *Al Arabiya*, 11 February. https://english.alarabiya.net/en/views/news/middle-east/2019/02/11/Hezbollah-s-control-of-Lebanon-s-health-ministry-poses-a-grave-danger.
Rafizadeh, Majid (2016): In first, Hezbollah confirms all financial support comes from Iran. *Alarabiya*, 25 June. https://english.alarabiya.net/en/features/2016/06/25/In-first-Hezbollah-s-Nasrallah-confirms-all-financial-support-comes-from-Iran.
Ranstorp, Magnus (1997): *Hizb'Allah in Lebanon: the politics of the Western hostage crisis*. New York: St. Martin's Press.
Reuters Staff (2020): Iran's death toll from coronavirus outbreak approaches 10,000. *Reuters*, 19 June. www.reuters.com/article/us-health-coronavirus-iran-idUSKBN23P3BM.
Robinson, Kali (2020): *What is Hezbollah?* Washington: Council on Foreign Relations. www.cfr.org/backgrounder/what-hezbollah.
Salehyan, Idean (2010): The delegation of war to rebel organizations. *Journal of Conflict Resolution*, 54(3): pp. 493–515. https://doi.org/10.1177%2F0022002709357890.
Shapira, Shimon (1987): The Imam Musa al-Sadr: father of the Shiite resurgence in Lebanon. *Jerusalem Quarterly*, 44: pp. 121–44.
Tehran Times (2019): Iran, Lebanon to prepare five-year plan for health cooperation. *Tehran Times*, 7 August. www.tehrantimes.com/news/439032/Iran-Lebanon-to-prepare-five-year-plan-for-health-cooperation.

Part II
Communication strategies

4 'American Corona' vs. 'The Chinese virus'
Blaming and othering in Arab media

Carola Richter, Abdulrahman al-Shami, Soheir Osman, Sahar Khalifa Salim and Samuel Mundua[1]

4.1 Introduction

A pandemic is by nature a transnational phenomenon. It does not stop at land borders drawn by humans. It affects humanity as a whole, not only a particular group. It could thus stimulate global solidarity and empathy. However, with regard to the COVID-19 pandemic, we can observe completely opposite reactions: a discursive and real re-bordering in an attempt to protect a nationally defined group and an attribution of guilt toward certain groups or countries. On an individual level, the aim to protect oneself can be explained with what psychologists call the 'behavioral immune system', which is 'an unconscious psychological process that constantly scans environments for harmful pathogens' (Reny and Barreto, 2020: 5). On a societal level, however, applying a discursive nationalism and blaming specific groups can stimulate xenophobia, racism and social fragmentation (Ahmed, 2004). For example, in the USA, former President Donald Trump's rhetoric on the 'Chinese virus' or the seemingly funny pun 'Kung Flu' has created an atmosphere in which anti-Chinese or anti-Asian attitudes have grown in US society (Reny and Barreto, 2020). In Hungary, Prime Minister Viktor Orbán linked the spread of the virus to migrants and refugees in order to reinforce the fear of immigration among the Hungarian populace (Inotai, 2020). In general, worldwide travel restrictions and the closing of borders were accompanied by a nationalist rhetoric characterised by the fear of and protection from the foreign 'other' (Bieber, 2020).

Mass media play an important role in constructing the 'other' and in reinforcing discourses of othering. There are two main reasons for this in the context of the coronavirus crisis. Firstly, because of the media's typical focus on political elites, they help circulate problematic political statements. Secondly, particularly in times of crisis and alleged threats to the nation, according to Nossek (2004: 347–8), journalists function as 'local gatekeepers' and are supposed to 'handle any tensions between their journalistic values and the need to meet national ends by having a belief system such as patriotism'.

DOI: 10.4324/9781003240044-6

56   *Richter et al.*

Thus, a nationalist focus and discursive othering can be the result. However, Nossek also argued that the media or journalists' 'behavior is actually context dependent' (2004: 348). Turning our focus away from Europe and the USA to Arab countries in the Middle East and North Africa (MENA), we have to indeed acknowledge different political and media system contexts through which othering may take specific shapes.

COVID-19 has provided many regimes in the MENA region with a justification to restrict critical media and investigative reporting against the pretext of saving the public from false information spread by the media (Farmanfarmaian, 2020: 855; for the case of Morocco, see also the contribution of Cimini and Tomé Alonso in this volume). At the same time, most media in the MENA region have never been as independent from regime influences as would be wished from a libertarian point of view. In fact, the media have often been actively instrumentalised to reinforce the regimes' official discourses. Even media that are not in the hands of the incumbents are often considered loyalist, the term used by William Rugh (2004), hinting at the fact that media licences are often given to businessmen close to the regime, who do not then bite the hand that fed them. Thus, looking at the media discourse not only helps us to understand how journalists have dealt with the pandemic, but it also allows us on a broader scale to learn more about political and societal discourse as it is reflected in the media. Since the focus on media discourse concerning the COVID-19 pandemic has been mainly on the Global North so far, we aim to fill the gap by looking at different MENA countries. Thus, this article comparatively investigates processes of 'othering' in the media with regard to COVID-19 in four MENA countries – Egypt, Iraq, Oman and Yemen.

Below, we will first provide a theoretical framework by looking at what othering is and how it is constructed through the media. Second, we will provide some contextual information about the political and media systems in the four countries under investigation. Third, we will explain our methodology for doing qualitative content analysis and fourth, we will present the results country by country.

4.2   Theoretical framework: othering in the media

While the concept of othering is said to go back to the master–slave dialectic of the German philosopher Hegel, it has taken a post-colonial turn through the writings of Gayatri Spivak (1985) and in Edward Said's book *Orientalism* (1978/1995). By analysing the Western perception of the 'East' or the 'Orient', they determined that a discursive construction of the other as inferior dominates both fictional and non-fictional writing, reinforcing a societal discourse of superiority in the Western hemisphere. Said also spoke of an 'imagined geography' of Western scholars and writers that constructs a certain territory in a distancing and reductionist way (Said, 1978/1995). While Spivak, Said and other post-colonial scholars particularly focused on the ways colonial power relations are upheld through discourse, the concept of othering is not bound to a certain part of the world. It ultimately refers to the fact that power relations can be discursively constructed and reinforced. Jensen (2011: 65) argued that othering describes 'discursive processes by which powerful groups, which may or may not make up a numerical majority, define subordinate groups into existence in a reductionist way which ascribe problematic and/or inferior characteristics to these subordinate groups'. She also referred to Lister (2004: 101), who provided a more general definition of othering as a 'process of differentiation and demarcation, by which the line is drawn between "us" and "them" [...] and through which social distance is established and maintained' (own omission).

The media are part and parcel of this process of differentiation and demarcation. Typically, the media use stereotypes to reduce the complexity of the world in their coverage (Kleinsteuber, 1991). Stereotypes usually have an exclusionary tendency, because they are used to attribute certain characteristics to groups or people, ultimately creating an ingroup and an outgroup. The consequence of stereotyping is often the devaluation of the outgroup along with an overestimation of the ingroup. According to Lippmann (1922/2012), stereotypes are thus used to maintain a specific view of the world and to form the basis of a specific moral system. Especially in the case of reporting on distant countries, regions and societies, stereotypical representations in the media may have a strong impact on public opinion and may increase social stratification because personal experiences with the other are missing (Hafez, 2002). The media's impact on othering may also be stronger during times of perceived crises, in which the media become an important source of information. One of the rare studies on public trust during the early phase (the spring of 2020) of the pandemic in the MENA region – a study done by Open Think Tank in Iraqi Kurdistan – revealed that people's trust in mass media, particularly in television, is higher than their trust in news spread through social media and even information from friends and family (Beaujouan, Rasheed and Taha, 2020: 10). While this finding may not be representative of the region as a whole, we can conclude that it is important to look at the media discourse to get an impression of what shapes public opinion regarding processes of othering.

Processes of othering in the media are often shaped by stereotypical dichotomic attributions such as own/alien, good/bad or morally superior/ inferior that ultimately create an 'us vs. them' logic. A vocabulary of dehumanisation and homogenisation of the respective other is characteristic in this context (Said, 1978/1995). The bond of belonging that is discursively created in such a manner may refer to a variety of ingroups, such as a certain political group or a religious current or a class, race or ethnicity. However, Bieber (2020: 3) detected over the past few years a global rise of 'exclusionary nationalism'. He has defined nationalism as a 'narrow ideology that values membership in a nation more than belonging to other groups' (Bieber, 2020: 2). Othering is an essential part of nationalism, because the formation of a national identity requires the demarcation of others through the self-attribution of certain values and a drawing of borders. During the pandemic, Bieber (2020: 8) noticed that the 'importance of citizenship' has been reemphasised as well as the 'primacy of the state'. Thus, the discursive line that is drawn between the self and the other in the context of nationalism may not only result in a homogenised view of one's own and the other nation, but may also draw a line between citizens and foreigners, privileging the former against the latter.

Othering can easily be instrumentalised to blame specific groups for phenomena that threaten the status of the self. The other is seen as if they were jeopardising a particular order of which the self is part. Castro Varela and Mecheril (2016) have spoken of the 'demonisation of the imagined other' as a typical consequence of this construction and indicated racial, religious or nationalistic discrimination in the media, politics and society as a possible result. Given the rise of nationalism, the blaming and shaming of national outgroups have become common. Anti-Chinese and nationalist rhetoric has shaped not only the US discourse, but also public opinion in the MENA region. A study on the level of public awareness conducted by scientists from Al-Ain University in the United Arab Emirates (UAE) among respondents of six Arab countries in February and March 2020 revealed that the closing of borders was strongly supported. A huge majority (95.5%) of the respondents agreed with the survey item 'Travel bans to/from areas of the disease should be implemented by the government to prevent COVID-19 spreading'. At that time, China was seen as the dangerous other: in the same study, 95.1% considered travelling to China a risk and 47.2% even considered Chinese goods to be a source of exposure to the virus (Bonyan et al., 2020: 6). Blaming a national other became mainstream, and has continued as such, underpinning Bieber's (2020: 3) observation that 'exclusionary nationalists shift the agenda and change acceptable public discourse'.

In our own study, it has thus been important to look at the manifestations of othering in the media and to see which ingroups and outgroups are being constructed and if and how the latter are being blamed for spreading the virus.

4.3 Cases of investigation: Egypt, Iraq, Oman and Yemen

We examined four different country cases in the MENA region, aiming to include a variety of different forms of government, media control and affectedness by the pandemic. Even though all countries can be considered to have an authoritarian political system, they are not homogeneous. In order to understand the specific results for each country, it was important to learn more about: (1) the general political approach of the country, which we assumed would shape decision-making processes and discourses during the pandemic; (2) the degrees of freedom and (governmental) control in the media system; and (3) the respective situation regarding COVID-19 cases and measures discussed and taken during the spring of 2020. Below, we will review these three elements briefly for each case.

Since 2013, *Egypt* has been ruled by a military regime under formally elected president Abdel Fattah El-Sisi. Egypt has returned to hard authoritarian rule after an interrupted transition (Roll, 2016). The regime is known for its heavy grip on the media and limitation of oppositional and independent media to a minimum. Only in the press is there a bit of a variety of ownership models and opinions to be detected, while the broadcasting media are in the hands of loyalist businessmen or the secret service (Badr, 2021).

The first coronavirus case was reported on 14 February 2020, at Cairo airport and involving a tourist from Asia. During March and early April, according to Joffé (2020: 518), the regime downplayed the crisis and even sent two planeloads of medical supplies to Italy, which had been strongly affected. Even after many countries reported that tourists who had travelled to Egypt had been testing positive for the coronavirus, Egyptian officials continued to downplay the pandemic in Egypt, and referred only to foreign nationals and tourists as being infected. Only after two army generals died of COVID-19 did the government start to act, and schools, universities and mosques were closed in April. In early April, no more than 2,000 cases in a country of 100 million inhabitants were officially reported – the peak would not be reached until June 2020, with more than 40,000 cases (Johns Hopkins University & Medicine, 2020).

Since 2003, *Iraq* has been a federal republic in which elections play a significant role in the distribution of power. The country is characterised by strong confessional and ethnicity-based parties, with different Shiite, Sunni and Kurdish parties struggling for power (Wimmen, 2014). The beginning of the coronavirus epidemic in Iraq coincided with a period of political instability after the resignation of the former government. The various parties were busy choosing candidates for prime minister, and the media was busy covering this political struggle. The media system itself is characterised by strong political parallelism with most of the media aligned with one political party or another (Khalifa Salim, 2021). However, a small number of media outlets are still in the hands of the government. Several are also in the hands of private entrepreneurs, thus making the Iraqi media system comparatively diverse.

In Iraq, COVID-19 was first detected on 24 February 2020, in Najaf, in the case of an Iranian student. The number of confirmed cases remained rather low, but neighbouring Iran at that time was in the spotlight for having the highest number of coronavirus-related deaths outside of China. The Iraqi government officially closed its borders to Iran by 8 March. The central government imposed several measures, including partial or local lockdowns, after mid-March. This also affected the work of the media – many newspapers have been appearing only irregularly since then. Nevertheless, the number of cases kept rising significantly. According to Johns Hopkins University & Medicine (2020) Coronavirus Research Center, the peak of coronavirus infections only hit Iraq in September 2020, with more than 120,000 new cases per month in a country of 40 million people.

Oman is a unitary absolute monarchy ruled by Sultan Haitham bin Tariq, who in January 2020 succeeded his cousin Qaboos, who had ruled Oman for almost fifty years. Through its petroleum and gas reserves, the country has created considerable wealth. Due to late modernisation and a limited indigenous workforce, like many other Gulf countries it relies heavily on guest workers from abroad. Around 42% of the population are expatriates, mainly coming from India, Pakistan, Bangladesh and the Philippines (Oman News Agency, 2020).

The media are considered part of the modernisation plan of the country and are supposed to support the ruling elites and follow a conflict-avoiding political line. The government considers it extremely important not to offend any of its international partners, mainly for economic reasons (Al-Kindi, 2021).

Oman had its first reported COVID-19 cases on 24 February 2020, when two of its citizens returned from Iran. By March, cruise ships were not allowed to dock in Oman, and schools and universities had switched to online teaching. Starting in mid-April, the government imposed a number of local lockdowns. However, the number of infections kept rising steadily until reaching a peak in July 2020, with around 40,000 newly infected in a country of roughly 5 million inhabitants. It was reported that, in the early stages of the pandemic, the expat community was disproportionately affected by the virus, while the ratio changed later (*Times of Oman*, 2020).

Yemen has been embroiled in a devastating war since 2015. It started with violent conflicts between the Houthi movement that conquered the northern part of Yemen, including the capital, Sana'a (Transfeld, 2015). The internationally recognised government under President Abdrabboh Mansour Hadi finally fled to exile in Saudi Arabia. A Saudi-led coalition, including the UAE, has since launched airstrikes and sent troops to reconquer northern Yemen. Meanwhile, another anti-Houthi transitional council was installed in the southern city of Aden. Due to the war, in the spring of 2020, 24 million – out of a population of 30 million – required humanitarian assistance (International Crisis Group, 2020: 4). Confirmed COVID-19 cases, however, amounted to no more than 3,000 by the end of 2020, which is most likely related to a very low testing rate. On 10 April 2020, the first infection was reported in the south. In the Houthi-controlled north, no casualties were reported, and this was described by the Houthi-owned media as a 'divine miracle' (*Al-Thawrah*, Sana'a version, 2020a), a blessing from God, who 'singled out Yemen for many of its worshipper around the globe for not spreading the Corona epidemic inside it' (*Al-Thawrah*, Sana'a version, 2020b), until 3 May 2020 when a Somali migrant was found dead in one of the hotels in Sana'a.

The Yemeni media system has also suffered from the war, and the fragmentation of the country into different interest groups has led to extremely high political parallelism in the media. The two main conflict actors – the Houthis and the exiled government in Saudi Arabia – operate their own media, whilst other conflict actors such as the Muslim Brotherhood or the Southern Transitional Council in Aden also use the media as instruments to disseminate their respective propaganda (al-Shami, 2021).

These four cases will allow us to gain insights into how, in the MENA region, different political preconditions and differing political–media relations result in a variety of forms of othering mirrored in the media discourse.

4.4 Methodology

In our study, we were interested in answering the following questions:

1. Are 'others' held responsible for the coronavirus crisis in the countries under study? Who are those 'others'?
2. Which forms and manifestations of 'othering' can be detected in media discourse?
3. What language and terminologies are being used that stimulate xenophobic and nationalistic feelings?

To answer these questions, we conducted a qualitative content analysis of major newspapers (in print or their respective online versions) in the four different Arab countries described above. While (online) newspapers cannot compete with TV in terms of audience reach in the MENA region, they are relevant for this research because they reflect the mainstream political discourse due to their closeness to the regimes and/or major political actors in the respective countries. With regard to qualitative content analysis, we refer to Kuckartz (2016), who suggested as a first step an in-depth reading of the material and an initial coding of relevant phrases that pertain to the research questions, which can be seen as abstract deductive categories. In the second step, these initial codes are reviewed, systematised and summarised so as to find distinct patterns of argumentation that can be related to three categories: (1) who is held responsible; (2) forms of othering; and (3) the language used. At the same time, this method is not meant to employ rigid categories, but leaves room for the identification of specific arguments and statements that help to underpin the general findings.

The time period investigated covers the first two months during which COVID-19 first hit the respective countries and during which the virus could still be seen as an external threat. Thus, in three cases we opted for March and April 2020, while in the case of Yemen, we chose April and May 2020. In all media outlets we searched for articles with the search terms 'Corona' and 'COVID-19'. This added up to several hundred articles in each country case. From this initial sample, all articles were selected that were suitable for a qualitative content analysis with our focus, meaning that in particular longer news stories, opinion and analytical pieces were included.

For *Egypt*, 194 articles from three different types of newspapers were qualitatively analysed: the state-owned *Al-Ahram*, *Al-Wafd* – the only remaining daily partisan newspaper, but which no longer has an oppositional political profile – and *Al-Shorouk*, a privately owned newspaper that can be considered the most autonomous from regime control in the Egyptian sample.

For *Iraq*, we examined *Al-Sabah*, which is the only state-owned newspaper in Iraq, *Al-Bayna Al-Jadeeda* – a party newspaper – and the privately owned *Al-Mustaqbal Al-Iraqi* newspaper. In the two months of investigation, in particular the two latter newspapers have not been published regularly because of the lockdown, leading to fewer articles being published on the topic. The number of articles used in the qualitative analysis came to 120.

For *Oman*, the online editions of the three English-language daily newspapers, *Times of Oman*, *Muscat Daily* and *Oman Daily Observer*, were selected. Stories that only reproduced articles from international news agencies were excluded. After examining a total of 183 daily editions only thirty articles qualified for a qualitative content analysis. The *Oman Daily Observer* is government-owned, while the *Muscat Daily* and the *Times of Oman* are privately owned. In the Omani case, however, all newspapers can be considered loyal to the ruling incumbents, despite some diversity in ownership.

For *Yemen*, we included 161 articles in the qualitative analysis. The sample was selected from the online platforms of three strongly partisan newspapers representing the major oppositional players in Yemen. *Al-Thawra* (Sana'a version) is under the control of the Houthis, while *Al-Thawra* (Riyadh version) represents the internationally recognised but exiled government operating from Saudi Arabia. *Al-Sahwa*, published by the Muslim Brotherhood-affiliated Al-Islah party, operates from Riyadh in Saudi Arabia, and is considered anti-Houthi.

In the next section, we present the main findings and observations separately for each country. This includes (translated) statements from the analysed material and an implicit answering of the research questions. In the conclusion, we will answer the research questions in a comparative manner.

4.5 Results: othering in different shapes

4.5.1 Egypt: denying one's own responsibility and blaming the other

In the Egyptian case, the notion that 'the disease came over us from others' dominated the media discourse throughout March 2020. *Al-Ahram* began its coverage of the coronavirus pandemic by simply denying a relation between Egypt and the discovery of any new infections. 'There is no single case of Corona in the land of Egypt' (*Al-Ahram*, 1 March) was one of the early headlines published. In its attempt to attribute responsibility to foreigners and tourists, it was seconded by the party newspaper, *Al-Wafd*, and the more independent *Al-Shorouk*. A Taiwanese tourist was accused of having spread the virus in Egypt through contact with a number of tourists and crew members on a Nile cruise to Luxor (*Al-Wafd*, 7 March).

Consequently, the focus of the media discourse was on border control and travel restrictions to save Egypt from external threats. *Al-Wafd* dealt with the preparations in Egyptian ports, focusing on foreigners and goods coming from China in particular (*Al-Wafd*, 2 March). *Al-Ahram* took the same approach of blaming the open borders and the continuation of air traffic as the main reasons for the spread of the coronavirus. It did so by referring to the positively evaluated decision of then US President Donald Trump to suspend travel to Europe and the decision of the Iraqi authorities to close the border crossings with Iran after the outbreak of the epidemic there (*Al-Ahram*, 13 March). Interestingly, the Egyptian media discourse thereby mirrored a political foe–friend discourse of seconding its perceived ally, the USA, and blaming political enemies such as Iran and Qatar. After Qatar had closed its borders to anyone flying in from Egypt, Egypt prohibited entry for Qataris – and the media followed both decisions with a great deal of interest (*Al-Ahram*, 5 March; *Al-Wafd*, 5 March). Moreover, Europe came into the focus of the media discourse. One of the analytical articles in *Al-Ahram* blamed some European countries for delaying taking full precautionary measures to prevent the spread of the epidemic, describing Europe as the 'epicentre' of the outbreak of the epidemic (*Al-Ahram*, 16 March). A columnist in *Al-Wafd* called on the Egyptian government to stop flights to Europe (*Al-Wafd*, 13 March). The less government-influenced *Al-Shorouk* also published a story on the Egyptian president's orders to tighten control over any entry points to Egypt to stop the virus spreading (*Al-Shorouk*, 2 March). At the same time, it criticised how the control mechanisms were arbitrary and obviously only applied to specific nationalities: 'Quarantine at Cairo Airport: There are no instructions to examine travellers to Kuwait' (*Al-Shorouk*, 2 March).

In addition to a strong focus on securing the national borders from infiltration, in parts of the coverage a xenophobic discourse toward specific groups could be detected, reflecting anti-Asian and anti-refugees stereotypes. *Al-Shorouk* published a news report about migrants being considered a 'time bomb about to explode' in Italy, as a result of the first case of the virus being discovered in a reception centre for migrants in Italy (*Al-Shorouk*, 19 March). Most of the other xenophobic coverage, however, dealt with Asians in general and China in particular. One *Al-Ahram* writer used the term 'the great Chinese virus' (*Al-Ahram*, 10 March), while another writer argued to 'seek knowledge away from China', which is a distortion of a prophetic Hadith that says, 'seek knowledge even in China' (*Al-Ahram*, 12 March). In another column entitled 'World War III', a journalist mentioned that China could be seen as the greatest enemy in this alleged war that the world was now witnessing, describing the virus as the 'Chinese dragon' that must be eliminated (*Al-Ahram*, 25 March). Interestingly, one article strongly criticised the policies of some countries against China as well as the xenophobic pictures used in German and Danish magazines to discredit China, pointing to the Europeans as the problem creators (*Al-Ahram*, 26 March). But this reverted othering remained a rare exception. In an *Al-Wafd* article, the writer exclaimed, 'May God protect the brothers in the Gulf because of the presence of many Asian communities working and living there' (*Al-Wafd*, 1 March), suggesting that anything Asian could be a source of the coronavirus epidemic. Another writer repeated this sentiment by referring to a book critical of China which argued that China should be 'fought' and 'eliminated' because it was the main cause of the epidemic that now affected the whole world (*Al-Wafd*, 28 March). *Al-Shorouk*'s coverage also used some of these xenophobic stereotypes (e.g. *Al-Shorouk*, 3 March), but it also contained a critique of the media in which it reflected on possible reasons for attacks on Chinese people in Egypt. It referred to a case in which a taxi driver bullied a potential customer because he considered him to be Chinese and concluded that anti-Asian racism was a product of the Egyptian media discourse (*Al-Shorouk*, 2 March). In addition, *Al-Shorouk* (17 March) in particular contained several pieces on China's successful dealing with the crisis, thus positing an ambivalent evaluation of 'the Chinese other' between blaming and praising.

4.5.2 Iraq: being caught in the midst of a US–China battle

The Iraqi media coverage in the spring of 2020 took a different course than the Egyptian one. Since the epidemic had already spread tremendously in neighbouring Iran, the Iraqi government started to take measures early on. Most coverage therefore dealt with internal measures to confront the virus, such as curfews for many Iraqi governorates and preparing places for quarantine. However, not all newspapers were able to publish during the curfew restrictions of March and April. The government-owned *Al-Sabah* newspaper was able to do so and was therefore found to have published the most articles that dealt with the epidemic.

In general, the pandemic was described as a global threat, but the responsibility was not solely attributed to China. In fact, there was even a substantial number of articles in all three newspapers that highlighted Chinese cooperation and medical aid to Iraq. *Al-Bayna Al-Jadeeda* (16 March), for example, reported that the Chinese Red Cross 'brings Iraqi citizens the materials to prevent and control the virus and the Chinese experience in fighting the epidemic in order to help the Iraqi government'.

The Iraqi newspapers, whether government-, party- or privately owned, located the reasons for the pandemic in a broader political conflict in which the USA was seen as the opponent of China (and also of neighbouring Iran). Indeed, many articles mentioned that the virus was actually the result of a conflict between China and the USA, who were defined as the most powerful actors – both capable of launching biological warfare – and the rest of the world seemed to be left to their mercy. The government-owned *Al-Sabah* published an edition in which two contradictory versions of the origin of the virus in the context of this biological warfare frame were explained: 'Those who believe in the conspiracy theory say that it is a biological weapon and was manufactured in U.S. laboratories to strike China and Iran' (*Al-Sabah*, 13 April), while in another article it argued that 'an American senator and others have also spread a theory claiming that the virus had originally emerged from a biological weapons laboratory in Wuhan' (*Al-Sabah*, 13 April).

In general, many contradictory and unproven claims were circulated, and it was undecided who could be held more responsible – the USA or China. The privately owned *Al-Mustaqbal Al-Iraqi*, for example, argued that Trump was behind the virus (*Al-Mustaqbal Al-Iraqi*, 12 March). *Al-Bayna Al-Jadeeda* even carried a piece on 11 March that took up Iran's accusation of the USA being responsible for biological 'terrorism'. It quoted an Iranian official as saying that

> [w]hat we understood is that there are two types of coronavirus spread in the country, one of which is the Chinese Wuhan virus and the other is an unknown virus. The different virus did not have mercy on a 25-year-old nurse and killed her immediately. This virus is likely to be a kind of American bioterrorism that Washington has spread in the country.

Moreover, it was also mentioned that the sanctions on Iran or, respectively, the isolation of China by the USA are instrumentalised to spread the virus, emphasising again the notion of biological warfare: 'America's goal is to isolate Iran and China from the world so that America remains in the forefront' (*Al-Bayna Al-Jadeeda*, 2 March).

On the other hand, in several articles, China was identified as the source of the pandemic. Indeed, *Al-Sabah* (4 April) argued that

> it is known that the source is the Chinese city of Wuhan, from which it spread with lightning speed to all parts of the planet, leaving an unprecedented state of panic among the poor and backward peoples who have no power to face any danger.

In some of its articles, *Al-Sabah* adopted the term 'Chinese virus', and in one case also referred to 'Corona being a socialist disease' (*Al-Sabah*, 15 March). However, this was even presented positively because the author argued that 'Corona embodied [China's] socialism in making the world stand together to confront it', while in previous catastrophes, such as 'famines that have killed millions of people in many places, especially in Africa, South Asia [and] Latin America', the (capitalist) world stands by watching. Clear anti-Asian language could not be detected; on the contrary, some articles were even concerned with racist anti-Asian feelings in the USA due to the virus (e.g. *Al-Mustaqbal Al-Iraqi*, 11 March).

4.5.3 Oman: emphasising national cohesion

In Oman, all the selected newspapers sourced their news from the government and its agencies, such as the Supreme Committee mandated to oversee the control of the spread of the pandemic and the Ministry of Health, thus reflecting the official state discourse. There were no investigative stories on COVID-19 conducted by the journalists of the newspapers under review.

Unlike other international or Arab media, the newspapers in Oman did not publish any article in which the authorities directly blamed any country, nationality or race for the spread of the coronavirus. The Omani media thus reflected the careful management of the country's international relations (IR) and its main goal of not offending anyone.

Still, as in the Egyptian case, the closing of borders was a main issue reported in the media. One article reported that Saudi Arabia had banned its citizens from travelling to Oman, and Oman felt obliged to take its own measures, by suspending flights to Europe in mid-March (*Oman Daily Observer*, 9 March). An article in the *Oman Daily Observer* (16 March) reported that a decision of the Supreme Committee was made to ban entry of non-Omanis into the Sultanate via land, air or sea borders, with the exception of citizens of Gulf Cooperation Council (GCC) countries. In this context of border control, othering was obvious in the constant distinction of Omani vs. non-Omani citizens in the official and media discourse. People coming from other countries were specifically identified by their nationalities and countries of origin. What is even more important in Oman is that the population was also separated into two different groups. In terms of wording, Omanis were mainly referred to as 'citizens', whilst non-Omanis were called 'residents' and 'expatriates', indicating a clear distinction – though stopping short of directly apportioning blame. Also, daily graphical updates in the newspapers on the development of cases in Oman clearly distinguished between Omanis and non-Omanis. The same sentiment of separating the to-be-protected 'us' from the potentially threatening 'them' was reflected in the *Times of Oman* (4 March) in an article entitled 'Expats from COVID-19 nations can't return'. The article reported that expatriates of Chinese, Italian, Iranian and South Korean nationalities who live in Oman would not be allowed to return to the Sultanate should they travel overseas, even if their visas were valid.

What was even more telling were the efforts to highlight national cohesion, in which – first and foremost – Omani citizens mattered more than others. The Omani government took special measures for the repatriation of Omanis who were stranded abroad (*Muscat Daily*, 14 April). This was accompanied by intensive coverage employing a patriotic tone in the three newspapers. Interviews with repatriated individuals were given large and prominent space in the media, highlighting the caretaking of the government for its citizens (e.g. *Oman Daily Observer*, 24 and 25 March). To also emphasise patriotism in the context of the pandemic, Omani doctors working in the UK, France and Australia were interviewed on whether they would be ready to return.

One of them was quoted as saying, 'I am one of the frontline fighters against COVID-19. The situation in my country is currently under control. However, once my mother country needs me back to my duty, I will fly back immediately [...] without thinking twice' (*Muscat Daily*, 19 April; own omission).

4.5.4 Yemen: constructing conspiracies of the enemy other

In Yemen, the coronavirus pandemic has been clearly politicised by all parties – and so it was reflected in the media, being the mouthpieces of the parties which owned them. Each party used the pandemic to attack the other, claiming that the measures it took in the areas under its control were for the sake of the Yemeni people, while the respective other was attacked. In doing so, alleged and actual supporters of the other faction were included in the argumentation, creating a dichotomy of 'us' vs the cruel 'enemy other'.

When the country was still considered to be free of COVID-19 in April 2020, but threatened by the first cases, the Houthi-affiliated media in Sana'a repeatedly described the pandemic as 'biological warfare' waged by a 'coalition of aggression', meaning the USA, its intelligence agency and the Saudi regime, to deliver the pandemic to Yemen in order to achieve what they had not been able to achieve during the war (e.g. *Al-Thawra*, Sana'a version, 5 April). Many articles in Houthi-affiliated media considered the USA the main responsible actor, arguing that the coronavirus was the product of 'American industry' (*Al-Thawra*, Sana'a version, 10 April). It was also claimed that 'American Corona' (*Al-Thawra*, Sana'a version, 22 April) is a virus that was created and developed by America to subjugate the world. It was also speculated that 'there is an American tendency to spread the Corona epidemic and to exploit it even if it harms the American society itself' (*Al-Thawra*, Sana'a version, 4 April). COVID-19 was seen as being similar to what they did to 'the American Indians when they introduced them to the smallpox virus through blankets, deceived them with so-called humanitarian aid and killed and exterminated hundreds of thousands of them' (*Al-Thawra*, Sana'a version, 2 April). It was thus concluded in the Houthi media that the USA is the 'enemy of the people' (*Al-Thawra*, Sana'a version, 3 May) and it is 'the one that causes humanity all this pain'.

A review of the Houthi-media discourse indicates that the coronavirus pandemic has provided an opportunity to vent the state of anger against the West, especially the USA, and to generally attack what is considered to be the double standard of Western values. In this context, there was also talk about the 'suspicious roles' of the United Nations and other international organisations operating in Yemen (*Al-Thawra*, Sana'a version, 2 May). These actors were accused of utilising the suffering of Yemenis to receive more funding, whilst only distributing the crumbs of that funding to the Yemenis.

Once the first casualty, a Somali migrant, was found in the Houthi-controlled area in Sana'a, the discourse changed from constructing an abstract

American or Western conspiracy to more concrete accusations toward the direct conflict actors. Using war-infused language, the Houthi-affiliated media accused Saudi Arabia and the UAE – as the 'countries of aggression' – of purposefully and systematically planting the virus in Yemen through continuous flights that allegedly transported mercenaries infected with the virus (*Al-Thawra*, Sana'a version, 19 May). It was further claimed that, in the southern ports of Yemen, thousands of illegal immigrants from the Horn of Africa, or even from Chad and Nigeria, were being let in without any medical inspections and that the Saudi regime had established camps for Africans on the Yemeni border to traffic them to Yemeni cities and governorates with the help of networks of smugglers who work with Saudi intelligence (*Al-Thawra*, Sana'a version, 11 April).

The media outlets of the internationally recognised government in Saudi exile, as well as *Al-Sahwa*, which is close to the Al-Islah party, took an anti-Houthi stance, but used the same kind of accusations, just turning them round. Since the Houthis are said to cooperate with Iran, their measures were discredited as mimicking the ineffective Iranian measures against the virus. According to *Al-Thawra*, the Riyadh version, the 'Iranian mercenaries' (meaning the Houthis) had falsified the facts, disavowing responsibility and concealing the true numbers and statistics of the spread of the pandemic in their areas of control. Thus, according to *Al-Sahwa*, they duplicated the Iranian regime's way of managing the coronavirus crisis through political utilisation of the global pandemic (*Al-Sahwa*, 26 May). At the same time, this article argued that Houthi senior leaders were themselves infected with the virus, which they had brought back from their visits to Iran.

The references to Iran were clearly meant to emphasise what was being seen as a disastrous influence of a political actor that strongly opposes Saudi politics in the MENA region, which is the protecting power of the internationally recognised Yemeni government. Using this as a pretext, the alleged practices of the Houthis were illustrated in gruesome pictures. In a report it was speculated that the Houthis were killing patients under quarantine in hospital, burying them and strictly instructing their families to conceal their deaths (*Al-Thawra*, Riyadh version, 17 May). Furthermore, it was said that the Houthis were 'intentionally bringing people infected with the coronavirus to prisons' (*Al-Thawra*, Riyadh version, 27 May) or sending security services to arrest those suspected of being infected with the coronavirus instead of sending medical teams (*Al-Thawra*, Riyadh version, 17 May). Likewise, using the same tone, *Al-Sahwa* repeated several accusations toward the Houthis. In one of the articles, it was said that the Houthis were dealing with the coronavirus with a police mentality, as if it were a global conspiracy against Islam. The article argued that this was the same kind of denial that the Iranians were using (*Al-Sahwa*, 2 May). *Al-Sahwa* also disgustedly described how, in a northern neighbourhood, a local Houthi leader claimed that the coronavirus pandemic was 'contrived and faked by Western countries' and 'merely an international conspiracy aimed at preventing Muslims from congregational prayers and family kinship' (*Al-Sahwa*, 7 May), while another article talked about rumours that, in hospitals, 'Houthis will use lethal injections for people with the coronavirus to get rid of them directly' (*Al-Sahwa*, 19 May).

4.6 Conclusion

By focusing on four different MENA countries with political and media systems that clearly differ from each other, we aimed to learn more about how this is reflected through discursive othering in the media. We asked who is being blamed for the coronavirus crisis and what manifestations of othering in relation to exclusionary tendencies and nationalistic rhetoric can be detected. In all four countries, the discursive line of the political elites defined the media coverage. In Egypt and Oman, the official line of the government was followed, resulting in Egypt in an aggressive, alarmist tone against China in particular and foreigners in general, whilst in Oman the tone remained harmonious but with a subtle othering of non-Omani citizens. In war-struck Yemen, a clear political instrumentalisation could be observed with blame attributed to the respective opponent. In particular, in the Yemeni case, but also in Egypt and Iraq, the blaming and shaming included those seen as opponents in international politics, while blame was not (or to a lesser degree) attributed to presumed allies. In Yemen, the Houthis held the USA, Saudi Arabia and the UAE responsible for the virus, while the exiled government pointed to Iran. Also, in Iraq, a China/Iran–USA battle could be detected, albeit from a more distanced perspective. In Egypt, Oman and Yemen, a strong focus was on border control, emphasising that the threat came from abroad and employing nationalist and exclusionary rhetoric.

In all four cases, the media played a questionable role by not taking a stand against political othering. On the contrary, the media emphasised discursive othering by attributing blame to others, avoiding expressions of empathy and abrogating responsibility.

Note

1 This is an expanded version of the article 'The virus of the "others"? Corona and discursive othering in Arab media', published in April 2021 in Journal of Arab & Muslim Media Research, 14(1): pp. 3–24. https://doi.org/10.1386/jammr_00022_1.

References

Ahmed, Sara (2004): Collective feelings or, the impressions left by others. *Theory, Culture & Society*, 21(2): pp. 25–42. https://doi.org/10.1177%2F0263276404042133.

Al-Kindi, Abdullah (2021): Oman: time for fundamental changes. In: Richter, Carola / Kozman, Claudia (eds.): *Arab media systems*. Cambridge: Open Book Publishers, pp. 181–95. https://doi.org/10.11647/OBP.0238.11.

Al-Shami, Abdulrahman (2021): Yemen. Unsettled media for an unsettled country. In: Richter, Carola / Kozman, Claudis (eds.): *Arab media systems*. Cambridge: Open Book Publishers, pp. 197–214. https://doi.org/10.11647/OBP.0238.12.

Al-Thawrah, Sana'a version (2020a): Danger threatening the lives of millions of Yemenis: Yemen in the 'time of corona' ... a faith strengthened. *Al-Thawra News*, 5 April. http://althawrah.ye/archives/619390.

Al-Thawrah, Sana'a version (2020b): In the time of Corona... 'Hold it down and trust'. *Al-Thawra News*, 18 May. http://althawrah.ye/archives/624585.

Badr, Hanan (2021): Egypt. A divided and restricted media landscape after the interrupted transformation. In: Richter, Carola / Claudia Kozman (eds.): *Arab media systems*. Cambridge: Open Book Publishers, pp. 215–32. https://doi.org/10.11647/OBP.0238.13.

Beaujouan, Juline / Rasheed, Amjed / Taha, Mohammedali Yaseen (2020): *Political trust and social cohesion at a time of crisis. The impact of Covid-19 on Kurdistan Region-Iraq*. Dohuk: Open Think Tank. www.politicalsettlements.org/wp-content/uploads/2020/07/Covid-19-KRI.pdf.

Bieber, Florian (2020): Global nationalism in times of the Covid-19 pandemic. *Nationalities Papers*, online first. https://doi.org/10.1017/nps.2020.35.

Bonyan, Ruwidah / Al-Karasneh, Aseel Fuad / El-Dahiyat, Faris / Jairoun, Ammar Abdulrahman (2020): Identification of the awareness level by the public of Arab countries toward Covid-19: cross-sectional study following an outbreak. *Journal of Pharmaceutical Policy and Practice*, 13(43): pp. 1–10. https://doi.org/10.1186/s40545-020-00247-x.

Castro Varela, Maria do Mar / Mecheril, Paul (2016): Die Dämonisierung des Anderen. Einleitende Bemerkungen [The demonisation of the other: introductory remarks]. In: Castro Varela, Maria do Mar / Mecheril, Paul (eds.): *Die Dämonisierung der Anderen. Rassismuskritik der Gegenwart* [The demonisation of the other. Contemporary criticque of racism]. Bielefeld: transcript, pp. 7–20. https://doi.org/10.14361/9783839436387.

Farmanfarmaian, Roxane (2020): The pandemic and the media in North Africa. *The Journal of North African Studies*, 25(6): pp. 855–61. https://doi.org/10.1080/13629387.2020.1831337.

Hafez, Kai (2002): *Die politische Dimension der Auslandsberichterstattung* [The political dimension of foreign reporting]. Vol. 1: Theoretische Grundlagen. Baden-Baden: Nomos. https://doi.org/10.1007/s11616-003-0017-5.

Inotai, Edit (2020): How Hungary's Orban blamed migrants for coronavirus. *EU Observer*, 20 March. https://euobserver.com/coronavirus/147813.

International Crisis Group (2020): *Covid-19 and conflict: seven trends to watch*. New York: International Crisis Group. www.crisisgroup.org/global/sb4-covid-19-and-conflict-seven-trends-watch.

Jensen, Sune Qvotrup (2011): Othering, identity formation and agency. *Qualitative Studies*, 2(2): pp. 63–78. https://doi.org/10.7146/qs.v2i2.5510.

Joffé, George (2020): COVID-19 and North Africa. *The Journal of North African Studies*, 25(4): pp. 515–22. https://doi.org/10.1080/13629387.2020.1757334.

Johns Hopkins University & Medicine (2020): *COVID-19 dashboard*. Baltimore: Coronavirus Resource Center. https://coronavirus.jhu.edu/map.html.

Khalifa Salim, Sahar (2021): Iraq: media between democratic freedom and security pressures. In: Richter, Carola / Kozman, Claudia (eds.): *Arab media systems*.

Cambridge: Open Book Publishers, pp. 73–90. https://doi.org/10.11647/OBP.0238.05.

Kleinsteuber, Hans J. (1991): Stereotype, Images und Vorurteile – Die Bilder in den Köpfen der Menschen [Stereotypes, images and prejudices – the pictures in the heads of the people]. In: Trautmann, Gunter (ed.): *Die häßlichen Deutschen? Deutschland im Spiegel der westlichen und östlichen Nachbarn* [The ugly Germans? Germany in the mirror of its western and eastern neighbours]. Darmstadt: Wissenschaftliche Buchgesellschaft, pp. 60–8.

Kuckartz, Udo (2016): *Qualitative Inhaltsanalyse: Methoden, Praxis, Computerunterstützung* [Qualitative content analysis: methods, practice, computer support]. Weinheim: Beltz.

Lippmann, Walter (1922/2012): *Public opinion*. Eastford: Martino Fine Books.

Lister, Ruth (2004): *Poverty*. Cambridge: Polity Press.

Nossek, Hillel (2004): Our news and their news. The role of national identity in the coverage of foreign news. *Journalism*, 5(3): pp. 343–68. https://doi.org/10.1177%2F1464884904044941.

Oman News Agency (2020): Expatriates make up 41.7 percent of total population of the Sultanate. *Oman News Agency*, 2 May. https://omannews.gov.om/NewsDescription/ArtMID/392/ArticleID/12456/Expatriates-Make-up-417-percent-of-Total-Population-of-the-Sultanate.

Reny, Tyler T. / Barreto, Matt A. (2020): Xenophobia in the time of pandemic: othering, anti-Asian attitudes, and Covid-19. *Politics, Groups, and Identities*, online first. https://doi.org/10.1080/21565503.2020.1769693.

Roll, Stephan (2016): Managing change: how Egypt's military leadership shaped the transformation. *Mediterranean Politics*, 21(1): pp. 23–43. https://doi.org/10.1080/13629395.2015.1081452.

Rugh, William A. (2004): *Arab mass media: newspapers, radio, and television in Arab politics*. Westport: Praeger.

Said, Edward W. (1978/1995): *Orientalism*. London: Penguin Books.

Spivak, Gayatri Chakravorty (1985): The Rani of Simur. An essay in reading the archives. *History and Theory*, 24(3): pp. 247–72. https://doi.org/10.2307/2505169.

Times of Oman (2020): Covid-19: 79 per cent of cases in Muscat are among expats. *Times of Oman*, 20 May. https://timesofoman.com/article/3015149/oman/health/covid-19-79-of-cases-in-muscat-are-among-expats.

Transfeld, Mareike (2015): *The failure of the transitional process in Yemen. The Houthi's violent rise to power and the fragmentation of the state*. Berlin: Stiftung Wissenschaft & Politik, www.swp-berlin.org/en/publication/yemen-transitional-process-failed.

Wimmen, Heiko (2014): *Divisive rule. Sectarianism and power maintenance in the Arab Spring: Bahrain, Iraq, Lebanon and Syria*. Berlin: Stiftung Wissenschaft & Politik. www.swp-berlin.org/en/publication/arab-spring-sectarianism-and-power-maintenance.

5 Securitisation dynamics and COVID-19 politics in Morocco
Old wine in new bottles?

Giulia Cimini and Beatriz Tomé Alonso[1]

5.1 Introduction

Moroccan authorities detected the first cases of COVID-19 at the beginning of March 2020. Soon afterwards, they issued a series of early and restrictive measures to avoid the spread of the pandemic. At first, all events with foreign participants were cancelled, as were public gatherings. Later on, the maritime and land borders were sealed and restrictions on domestic travel were imposed. Mosques, hammams, cafés, schools and universities were ordered to close. On 20 March, a national health state of emergency was declared. After more than three months of strict lockdown, authorities opted for more targeted measures and selective confinements. Partial closures were thus newly imposed, but mainly on major cities such as Tangier and Casablanca over the summer.

While Morocco successfully avoided a major outbreak during the first wave, it nonetheless saw a significant increase in the number of infections after the summer. Although those numbers were not as high as in neighbouring Europe, Morocco emerged as the one of the African countries to have the highest number of confirmed cases of COVID-19 (Xinhua, 2020). At the beginning of December 2020, it had recorded 372,620 cases and just over 6,100 deaths since the pandemic started (Hekking, 2020a).

Against this backdrop, this chapter centres around the following question: how did the emergence of an unexpected and non-traditional security threat such as the COVID-19 pandemic impact Morocco's national politics?

Virtually, crises can also be an opportunity for change. With respect to this, this chapter explores to what extent political dynamics have changed in response to the health crisis or simulated a change. Put it differently, whether Moroccans were served 'old wine in new bottles'. Our main argument is that the management of the crisis can be framed as a 'securitisation process' capitalised on by the Palace and providing no exception to the traditional logics of governance in the country. In other words, the monarchy took the lion's share to the detriment of the parliament and government that followed its roadmap and blessed its decisions. In addition, the tendency of Morocco's

DOI: 10.4324/9781003240044-7

politics toward technocratisation was equally confirmed, while securitising the pandemic also allowed for attempts to crack down on rights like freedom of expression, possibly contrasting with mainstream narratives dictated by authorities.

The chapter is organised as follows: first, it will illustrate the theoretical underpinnings of our reflection borrowing from the Copenhagen School of Security Studies. Next, it will analyse the discursive framing of COVID-19 as a 'security threat' to both citizens and the nation by looking at two key traditional royal speeches. It will then illustrate the extent to which the monarchy led in practice in crisis management. Finally, it will highlight how the 'securitisation' of the COVID-19 crisis connects with two previous tendencies already present in the Moroccan context, namely, the technocratisation of politics and the limitation of the freedom of speech.

5.2 Securitisation and the COVID-19 pandemic: health, human and national security

By the outset of the twenty-first century, health issues were back on the international agenda as a matter of high politics. Whereas infectious diseases such as HIV/AIDS, tuberculosis and malaria remained endemic – and largely 'confined' in terms of their most harmful effects – for many countries in the Global South, a number of potentially lethal viruses responsible for Ebola, severe acute respiratory syndrome (SARS) or Middle East respiratory syndrome (MERS) gave way to a 'renewed sense of microbial unease' (Elbe, 2019: 380). As Elbe recalls, health issues have been 'increasingly articulated in the language of security' (ibid.) – hence the rising diffusion of the concept of health security – and in connection to the developing 'human security' approach revolving around 'people-centric' accounts of threats. Health security – defined in relation to diseases and inadequate health care affecting the needs and welfare of ordinary individuals – was thus outlined as a 'sub-dimension' or component of human security in the pioneering *Human Development Report* by the United Nations Development Programme (UNDP) (UNDP, 1994). In addition, health security has been increasingly linked to national security, whose potential effects on populations, economies and social stability are amplified by globalisation and international travel.

The COVID-19 outbreak ruthlessly exposed how fragile countries can be in the face of a virus that knows no borders, and it pointed to the multidimensional impact of infectious diseases, which by their very nature lend themselves particularly well to securitisation dynamics.

In the words of the leading scholars of the Copenhagen School, which first laid out the securitisation theory, an issue becomes 'securitised' – hence a security issue – inasmuch it 'is presented as an existential threat, requiring emergency measures and justifying actions outside the normal bounds of political procedure' (Buzan, Wæver and de Wilde, 1998: 25–6). Central to this process is the importance of the 'speech act', understood as the discursive representation of certain issues – migration, illicit trafficking and drug abuse being the most glaring examples – as existential threats to the survival of given referent objects. These can be individuals, groups or issues (e.g. national sovereignty or the economy). In doing so, the 'securitising' actors are provided the right and legitimacy to use exceptional measures. This process, however, is far from being automatic. In other words, 'only once an actor has convinced an audience of its legitimate need to go beyond otherwise binding rules and regulations (emergency mode) can we identify a case of securitization' (Taureck, 2006: 55). Remarkably, these moves do not occur in a vacuum. The securitisation processes are influenced and modulated by power relations in a given context. In turn, they 'have an impact on power relations among securitizing actors and the relevant audiences to whom they address their securitizing moves' (Balzacq, Léonard and Ruzicka, 2016: 501). The social context is also relevant since it is the 'field of power struggles' where securitising actors attempt to swing the audience's support toward a specific policy or course of action (Balzacq, 2005: 173).

In our particular case, we suggest that the COVID-19 pandemic has been securitised by Moroccan state authorities, and by the Palace in particular, and framed as a threat to both citizens and the nation. To a certain extent, the securitisation of the pandemic is even more evident exactly because Morocco was not struck with the same virulence as many other European, Asian or American countries. By no means does this underestimate the detrimental effects on the Maghrebi kingdom – particularly concerning the economy – but we contend that securitising the pandemic has been instrumental in consolidating traditional power dynamics in the short term, and the related tendency toward technocratisation. It was therefore a missed opportunity for other institutional actors to recover their legitimacy and claim a greater role in the domestic political arena.

5.3 The securitisation of the pandemic: the Palace's central role through discourse and political practice

Since the very beginning of the pandemic, the Palace has been distinguished for being the most proactive stakeholder – unsurprisingly, to certain extents. The 2011 constitution meaningfully, albeit only partly, reassessed the balance of power among state offices and institutions. One of the most significant changes, for example, concerned the extended functions and powers of the head of the government (Abouzzohour and Tomé Alonso, 2019: 451). According to Article 47, in fact, he must be named from within the party receiving the most votes in the election, and no longer at the king's will. This remarkable shift should have been accompanied by a *de facto* new legitimacy and relevance for the prime minister (PM), that is not always the case. In fact, amongst persisting constitutional and unwritten constraints, personalities more than institutional prerogatives seem to be able to make the difference, as evidenced by the more charismatic leadership of former PM Abdelilah

Benkirane in comparison to his successor, Saadeddine El-Othmani, both issued from the Islamist Party of Justice and Development (Parti de la Justice et du Développement, PJD). The constitution still recognises the very broad powers and responsibilities of the king, which is the reason why Morocco is often referred to as an 'executive' monarchy (Szmolka, 2021). Suffice it to say that the king, even before being labelled the 'head of state', is the 'commander of the faithful', the most powerful religious authority of the country. By virtue of this title, he rules by royal decrees (*dahirs*) without being subject to the principle of accountability or responsibility. The king's role in national politics is of primary relevance. This is particularly evident if one considers that his annual speeches before parliament dictate the political agenda, along with the fact that he presides over the council of ministers, which is responsible for state orientations, among other things. Last but not least, the monarchy's influence on the executive branch is always assured by the presence of technocratic figures within the cabinet and by the choice of the 'ministries of sovereignty'.

Beyond constitutional prerogatives, the centrality of the monarchy is more entrenched with a 'traditional' understanding of power in a Weberian sense, that is a power legitimised by long-standing customs and practices. In this, the monarchy's authority is deeply rooted in the Moroccan way of governance and defines a kind of informal 'hierarchy' in the decision-making process. A distinction between 'primary' and 'secondary' elites can thus be traced: among the former are King Mohammed VI and his small circle of confidants, whilst the latter include political parties and parliamentary leaders (Feliu and Parejo Fernández, 2009: 108–12). With regard to this, the pandemic has further highlighted the imbalance of power and resources in favour of primary elites.

As mentioned above, the 'securitisation' approach is inextricably linked to 'speech acts', the vehicles through which a previously non-politicised issue comes to the forefront of public debate as an existential threat that needs to be dealt with using exceptional measures. Crisis management thus goes through the discursive construction of the threat and the responses to it. The ways in which both are framed and addressed deserve further attention.

Traditionally, the king addresses a speech to the nation on two main occasions: the Throne Commemoration on 29 July and the Anniversary of the Revolution of the King and the People on 20 August. Less than a month apart, these two speeches were substantially different in 2020, the former being imbued with optimism and pride, and the latter with sombre tones and pessimism. This shifting approach may be in part due to the upsurge of cases over the summer with the most restrictive measures being relaxed. In both cases, three core clusters emerge – what we may define as a tripartite structure – in which two are recurrent themes. The triad 'claiming – giving thanks – calling for' in the discourse of the first speech stands in contrast to the triad 'claiming – blaming – calling for' in the discourse of the second.

In July 2020, the king claimed the need for strict measures serving a dual priority: protecting the citizens and the highest interest of the nation (Kingdom of Morocco, 2020a). He praised their effectiveness whilst also acknowledging the harsh impact they had on weaker sections of the population. After that, he proudly acknowledged the 'awareness, discipline and positive responsiveness' of Moroccans and the nation coming hand in hand with solidarity and patriotism. Lastly, he called for national unity to realise social justice all across the country, and to develop a more inclusive model of development – also in light of the criticalities highlighted by the pandemic, such as the dependence of certain sectors on external hazards, the size of the informal sector and the weakness of social protection networks.

The speech in August was in a completely different vein. As elsewhere, war-related terminology has been the mainstream discursive framework of the pandemic. In this royal speech, references to past hardships and sacrifices were combined with mentions of the current 'fight' and the 'unfinished battle' that characterises these 'difficult, unprecedented times for everyone' (Kingdom of Morocco, 2020b). The king's heavy and pessimistic tone – a novelty in itself – further highlighted the gravity of the circumstances. The king claimed the genuineness of the measures taken and praised their effectiveness, as evidenced by the low number of deaths and infection in comparison to many other countries. However, he quickly transferred the responsibility for the increased number of cases after the lockdown was lifted on to those who deny the existence of the pandemic or believe it has passed, those who do not respect the prescriptions of public authorities or who do not take appropriate hygiene measures. This unspecified 'significant fringe of the population' was blamed head-on for its 'inadmissible relaxation'. Lastly, he called to patriotism, equating it with individual responsibility to take care of the well-being and safety of the collective. Against the backdrop of a nation portrayed as cohesive, patriotic and in solidarity, where the monarchy and the people act in concert, the rule-breakers are consequently depicted as running against the core values of the nation.

By defining the extent of the emergency and framing it, the king acted as the key securitising player. In so doing, he not only defined the boundaries of discourse and the trajectories of action, but also emerged as an actor capable of assuming the leadership in difficult times. He did this without resorting to a typical paternalistic tone.

Two interesting aspects emerge from these royal discourses: firstly, the transfer of responsibility away from the authorities to the citizenry, or at least part of it, according to a rhetoric approach that is by no means exclusive to Morocco. Indeed, regime type does not seem to be the crucial variable in this sense, as this has been a practice largely observed internationally. In this chapter we are arguing that the crisis triggered by the pandemic has confirmed the centrality of the Palace: remarkably, this statement holds true except for its liability for any deficiencies or failures. This is not new, either. Notably, political parties are the main traditional scapegoats of the country's missed development objectives, and they are perceived as such by the citizenry at large. On this occasion, irresponsible citizens were blamed and held accountable for a possible recrudescence of the pandemic. It is worth noting that, by virtue of these discourses, the king reiterated a 'direct' communication with his 'dear people', thus bypassing any intermediaries, and highlighted the relevance of the unity between the crown and the people, which is a unity of purpose as well.

Secondly, in sync with the securitisation process, this rhetoric leaves no room for questioning either the current choices or those in the past that have led to the present crisis (Laaroussi, 2020). For example, almost no debate was held on the neoliberal economic model that led to the systematic dismantlement of the public health care system, which is highly penalised in comparison to the private sector and accessible only to a small segment of the population, thereby reinforcing existing inequalities (Cimini and Mansouri, 2020).

In this sense, the Moroccan government has completely endorsed the king's 'securitisation' speech and has also itself become a 'securitising' actor. In the parliament, current PM Saadeddine El-Othmani referred to the COVID-19 pandemic as a crisis 'without precedents' which

> requires from the government and from all national forces – parliament, trade unions and professional organisations, the media and intellectuals, civil society and citizens – a high level of patriotism and commitment, solidarity and mutual aid, as well as innovation, to overcome this virus and face its repercussions.
>
> (Moroccan Parliament, 2020)[2]

Not only discursively, but also in practice, the Palace took the lead. Our next section will explore this dimension.

5.4 Leading the crisis: measures and domains of intervention

To better appreciate who securitised the COVID-19 and how, it is useful to recall here what impact the virus had in the country. According to the International Monetary Fund (IMF), Morocco's gross domestic product (GDP) is expected to shrink by 7% by the end of the year (IMF, 2020). The National Tourist Confederation estimates that tourism-related revenues decreased by 92% in the first three quarters of 2020 (CNT, 2020). In particular, the informal economy, precarious workers, women and migrants suffered the most during the lockdown measures and saw their social and economic rights reduced (Zaireg, 2020).

This deterioration in the economic situation and the increasing uncertainties regarding the future come at a difficult time for Morocco. In 2019, King Mohammed VI indirectly acknowledged the failure of the development model which has been the centrepiece of the strategy to fight poverty since the 2005 launch of the National Human Development Initiative (Desrues,

2007; Tomé-Alonso and García de Paredes, 2020). Indeed, a 2019 Oxfam report ranks Morocco as the most unequal country in North Africa (Oxfam, 2019). As Desrues and García de Paredes (2019) point out, these inequalities affect rural areas and young people most of all. A recent UNDP *Human Development Report* also highlights the fact that 'inequality stagnated in Morocco' (UNDP, 2019: 118), whilst its progress in the Human Development Index went from an average annual growth of 1.53% to 1.14%.

The COVID-19 crisis has also exposed 'educational inequalities' and 'enduring fragilities', such as the digital divide, the school system's inability to quickly switch to online platforms and the difficulty of poor families in densely populated households (Chalfaouat and Cimini, 2020; see also Chapter 10 by El Hage and Yehya in this volume).

Even more remarkably, it was immediately evident that the fragility of public health care and its incapacity to absorb the shock led to a much greater outbreak of cases. After all, since 2019 public sector doctors and medical students have been denouncing substandard infrastructure, unfair 'competition' with the private sector and the uneven distribution of facilities and personnel across regions and between urban and rural areas, among other problems (Cimini and Chalfaouat, 2020).

It is therefore plausible to think that Morocco focused on a prevention strategy through early restrictive measures being well aware of the poor capacity of its public health sector. At the same time, remarkable financial resources were injected into the system to the extent that some describe these efforts as the 'Moroccan Marshall Plan' (Laaroussi, 2020).

Along with restrictive corrective measures such as the lockdown, the mandatory closure of establishments or travel bans, Moroccan authorities have indeed been proactive in taking health- and economic-related measures quickly. When tracing back the decisions taken along their chain of command, it becomes evident that the Palace is at the heart of the decision-making process. Most of the initiatives were spearheaded by it, and the leading figures or forces all gravitated around it. As early as March 2020, the king designed the roadmap to face the crisis. He launched a special fund 'to cover the costs of upgrading the medical system, support the national economy to cope with the shocks induced by this pandemic' (MAP, 2020c). Under the king's input, many corporations and businessmen contributed to this fund with donations, also encouraged by the promise of tax relief (Morocco World News, 2020). In his speeches, the king proudly claimed his role in mobilising the aid needed for the population. Informal workers also receive 80–1,200 Moroccan dirhams (€7–110) per month based on the size of their household (OECD, 2020: 3). In the first weeks of the pandemic, Morocco doubled the available intensive care beds from 1,640 to 3,000 units (Hatim, 2020). Moreover, upon the instructions of Mohammed VI – the Commander in Chief of the Armed Forces – the Royal Armed Forces (Forces Armées Royales) quickly took action and deployed, for example, a military hospital in Benslimane in the Casablanca-Settat region, which was one of the most affected ones (MAP,

2020a). In fact, the king ordered the mobilisation of military medical infrastructure and personnel as further support in facing COVID-19 (Hekking, 2020b). The armed forces, then, played a key role in the management of the pandemic, not only in relation to health care facilities but also to ensure that the measures imposed by the authorities were complied with.

Not only does the deployment of the army emphasise the royal leadership, but it also has a positive impact on an already much-trusted institution. As a 'rule', Moroccan institutions hardly win their citizens' trust, with few exceptions. With the necessary caution that every survey brings with it, the Moroccan 'Trust in Institutions' Index points out very high levels of confidence for both the army and the police: 83.3% and 78%, respectively. By contrast, representative and elective institutions score much lower: only 22.6% trust political parties and 32.7% trust the parliament (MIPA, 2019).

With great media visibility, additional initiatives included the royal-sponsored campaign of testing in the private sector, as well as the royal amnesty granted to more than 5,000 prisoners for humanitarian reasons, but with no benefit for the most troubled and politicised cases, such as the prisoners from the Rif social movement. With a strong emotional impact, Mohammed VI also ordered the repatriation of thousands of Moroccan citizens who had been stranded abroad since the earlier border closures after months of waiting and uncertainty. Finally, and in line with his pivot to Africa and commitment to cooperation among countries in the Global South or South–South cooperation, the king boosted the country's role internationally by allocating aid to African countries.

Indeed, the centrality of the monarchy is not only produced in the domestic space, but also in the international arena, traditionally considered the 'reserved domain' of Mohammed VI (Hernando de Larramendi and Fernández Molina, 2014). In the context of the pandemic, Mohammed VI reaffirmed his 'African vocation' – which began after Morocco's return to the African Union (AU) in 2017 (Hernando de Larramendi and Tomé Alonso, 2017) – by ordering the shipment of medical supplies to African countries (MAP, 2020b). One relevant aspect of this cooperation is that the materials which have been sent are completely manufactured in Morocco, 'which is interpreted as a message to all the countries of the continent: we must count on our own forces; Africa must mobilize its own resources against the pandemic and its dire consequences' (Canales, 2020). Thus, Morocco wants to emerge as a leading actor in cooperation as well as in trade exchanges, deploying its soft power and becoming a resource hub in the African continent. The king's proposal to create a Joint African Operation structure can also be understood in this sense (Medias24, 2020b).

Moreover, Morocco has confirmed its increasing interest in establishing new partnerships with non-traditional allies like China (Abouzzohour and Tomé Alonso, 2019). In this sense, the expected vaccination campaign is also an opportunity to develop closer links with China. As stated by the Ministry of Foreign Affairs, 'the two cooperation agreements related to anti-COVID-19 vaccine clinical trials', which were signed between Rabat and Beijing, 'come to consolidate and flesh out the dynamic of cooperation between Morocco and China, with a new and promising dimension of cooperation' (MAEC, 2020).

In sum, and despite the challenges faced during the COVID-19 crisis and the foreseeable economic and social consequences, Morocco has sought to strengthen its image at international level. In this sense, some European political figures and media outlets have praised the management of the pandemic, specifically the drastic response from the regime and its ability to quickly adapt production to face the new needs to the extent that it can be considered as a model to follow. For example, French leftist member of parliament Jean-Luc Mélenchon stated that 'Morocco has performed well in its plan to combat COVID-19 by commandeering its textile industry to make protective masks. France should be inspired by it' (Laaroussi, 2020).

5.5 Old wine: the impetus of technocratisation and a legalist, punitive approach

The aforementioned securitisation process takes place in a broader, particular context of power relations and dynamics. Two trends in particular seem to be confirmed in 2020 during the pandemic: on the one hand, the technocratisation of politics, already boosted since the arrival of Mohammed VI to the throne, and the parallel 'retreat' of the more purely political actors.

On the other hand, freedom of expression and freedom of the press have never ceased to be questioned, even long before the pandemic.

Hence, citizens have been called to adhere to top-down orders and to close their ranks around 'those who know'. During the first and second waves of the pandemic, 'technical knowledge' remained unquestioned. Beyond widespread calls for the security of society, a broader debate on the political actors charged with providing security has largely been absent, as has a deeper reflection on the meanings and referent objects of security (Laaroussi, 2020). Without disregarding the relevance of specific expertise, it is nonetheless worth observing that 'technocracy' and 'technocratic figures' are traditionally double-edged swords in Morocco.

More specifically, they have been the instruments used by the monarchy for interference and control over national politics and public affairs. The idea of authority in the country thus combines the rise of technocratic elites and an executive monarchy that 'governs and controls the limit of what is politically permissible' (Ojeda García and Suárez Collado, 2015: 51). Public management is then depoliticised and de-democratised (Brown, 2015: 18) and the figure of the monarch appears reinforced compared to that of other actors in the Moroccan political space. It is no coincidence that, starting from the coordination meeting held in Casablanca in March 2020 under the king's auspices which produced the roadmap for action against the pandemic, those appearing in the front line next to Mohammed VI were not only his 'royal' ministers (for example, the Minister of the Interior) but also technocrats. Notably, Mohamed El Youbi, the director of epidemiology at the Ministry of Health, completely overshadowed the minister himself, Khalid Aït Taleb.

By moving away from the other Moroccan institutions and reinforcing the logic of the executive monarchy, technocratisation runs in the direction of consolidating citizens' distrust in elected institutions. The parliament and the political parties have once again relegated themselves to a marginal position, renouncing their role as 'the link between society and political decision-makers' (Maghraoui, 2019: 18). Like the parliament, they have simply echoed the king's words and blessed the decisions taken. In a follow-up to the measures undertaken against the pandemic, and in line with the overall securitisation framework, PM Saadeddine El-Othmani stated:

> For its part, the government is mobilised, under the enlightened leadership of HM King Mohammed VI, may God preserve him, to assume its full responsibility, as a united team, and to undertake whatever the situation requires in terms of actions and decisions, in an energetic and orderly manner. [...] These measures, which were able to distinguish our country and allow it to be at the level of the requirements of this conjuncture, were taken in accordance with the Directives of HM King Mohammed VI [...] and under his direct supervision [...]. His Majesty had thus given his High instructions in order to take all the necessary measures to bring our country to safety, including the organisation of the operation for the return of Moroccans from the Chinese city of Wuhan.
> (Moroccan Parliament, 2020; own omissions)

In doing so, from the very beginning, Othmani validated the leadership role of the monarchy while exposing the government's role of implementing royal decisions. At least implicitly, he corroborates the current balance of power and the marginalisation of elected institutions in the decision-making process. By calling for 'national unity', it is difficult for political parties – even within the government coalition – to propose debates or alternative policies. Indeed, a division between leadership and management responsibility is established.

As for the second trend mentioned before, it is important to observe that securitisation dynamics also play out when the identified threat becomes an all-encompassing category in the name of which a number of rights are restricted. Freedom of expression is a case in point.

In 2019, Reporters Without Borders warned about the judicial harassment suffered by journalists in Morocco (Reporters Without Borders, 2019) when it was obvious that social networks were being used for political criticism (Tomé Alonso and García de Paredes, 2020). Social networks were thus the targets of the controversial draft law number 22.20, which attempted to criminalise false information on the internet ('fake news'; see also Chapter 4 by Richter et al. in this volume). Presented to the government council by the Ministry of Justice in late March 2020, the draft law provided a basis for prison sentences and high fines (Medias24, 2020a). Indeed, some people had already been arrested for 'false rumours' (BBC, 2020). International human rights institutions and civil society organisations have been particularly critical of the draft law and expressed their concern about the vagueness of notions such as 'threatening public order, security and the Monarchy's constants'. These charges have been considered as pretexts 'to censor relevant information uncomfortable for the government or use the COVID-19 crisis as a pretext to silence the voices of dissent' (Kacha, 2020).

In addition to the socio-economic measures listed before, Moroccan authorities have taken some punitive measures. Remarkably, during the first month after the state of medical emergency was declared, 2,593 people were prosecuted for disrespecting the health-related restrictions (Medias24, 2020c). Among the arrests, one of the most notorious and debated was that of the Salafist Abou Naim, who was sentenced to one year in prison and a pecuniary sanction after uploading a video criticising the decision of the High Council of Ulemas to close Moroccan mosques to fight the spread of COVID-19 (Sefrioui, 2020). Likewise, the pandemic did not stop arbitrary arrests of outspoken journalists and activists on charges that seem backed by scant evidence but which are punctually linked to sexual or espionage offences (Cimini and Mansouri, 2020).

5.6 Conclusion

The COVID-19 crisis in Morocco has undergone a clear securitisation process. The king Mohammed VI has not only confirmed himself to be the key securitising actor, but has also strengthened his authority. By centralising all the major initiatives to curb the pandemic and address its socio-economic consequences without losing direct contact with 'his dear people' (not only through his speeches, but also through official media) and by boosting diplomatic international activities traditionally in his domain, the monarch has emerged as the key actor and the only one capable of leading the country through this delicate and uncertain period.

Under the 'instructions of the king' (following the formula used by media outlets), restrictive measures as well as health- and economic-related ones have been taken. These measures have not aroused remarkable resistance from any political parties, organisations or social movements, nor have they called into question the structural, dysfunctional allocation of resources to the public health sector and domestic power balance.

For its part, both the government and the 'opposition' have been marginalised in the decision-making process. At the same time, they have not claimed a major role, self-limiting themselves to follow the decisions of the Palace. Interestingly, the centrality of the latter – even in these exceptional circumstances – holds true except for its liability for any shortcomings or failures to manage the pandemic that, in this context, fall on irresponsible citizens.

Lastly, the process of securitisation has not only confirmed an enduring trend of technocratisation but has also favoured a clampdown on the restrictions of freedom of expression as the thwarted attempt of draft law against fake news and arbitrary arrests shows.

In conclusion, rather than old wine in new bottles, we could say that the 'bottles' – understood here as dynamics and actors at stake – are also the same. In this, the exceptionality of the pandemic was not taken as an input or trigger to alter the status quo, but rather as a tool to further consolidate it.

Notes

1 Dr Cimini acknowledges the financial support of the Germany-based Gerda Henkel Foundation in the context of the project 'Security for whom? Reshaping notions of state legitimacy for a new social contract'. Dr Tomé Alonso also acknowledges the financial support of the Research Project, 'Crisis and Regional Change Processes in North Africa: The Implications for Spain' (CSO2017-84949-C3-3-P), financed by the Spanish Ministry of the Economy, Industry and Competitiveness (MINECO), the State Research Agency (AEI) and the European Regional Development Fund (ERDF).
2 Here, as in the case of other non-English biographical references, the translation is by the authors.

References

Abouzzohour, Yasmina / Tomé Alonso, Beatriz (2019): Moroccan foreign policy after the Arab Spring: a turn for Islamists or persistence of royal leadership? *The Journal of North African Studies*, 24(3): pp. 444–67. https://doi.org/10.1080/13629 387.2018.1454652.
Balzacq, Thierry (2005): The three faces of securitization: political agency, audience and context. *European Journal of International Relations*, 11(2): pp. 171–201. https://doi.org/10.1177%2F1354066105052960.
Balzacq, Thierry / Léonard, Sarah / Ruzicka, Jan (2016): Securitization revisited: theory and cases. *International Relations*, 30(4): pp. 494–531. https://doi.org/10.1177%2F0 047117815596590.
BBC (2020): Arrestation d'auteurs de fake news au Maroc [Fake news authors arrested in Morocco]. *BBC Afrique*, 20 March. www.bbc.com/afrique/region-51969309.
Brown, Wendy (2015): *Undoing the demos: neoliberalism's stealth revolution*. Cambridge: MIT Press, Zone Books.
Buzan, Berry / Wæver, Ole / de Wilde, Jaap (1998): *Security: a new framework for analysis*. Boulder: Lynne Rienner.
Canales, Pedro (2020): COVID-19: Morocco encourages Africa to mobilize its resources. *Atalayar*, 17 June. https://atalayar.com/en/blog/COVID-19-morocco-enc ourages-africa-mobilize-its-resources.
Chalfaouat Abderrahim / Cimini, Giulia (2020): Despite drastic measures, COVID-19 exposes educational inequalities in Morocco. *Middle East Monitor*, 15 April.

www.middleeastmonitor.com/20200415-despite-drastic-measures-COVID-19-exposes-educational-inequalities-in-morocco.

Cimini, Giulia / Chalfaouat, Abderrahim (2020): *Coronavirus in Morocco opens possibilities for new social contracts.* 23 April. Washington: Carnegie Endowment for International Peace. https://carnegieendowment.org/sada/81631.

Cimini, Giulia / Mansouri, Hicham (2020): Securing essential rights in times of pandemic: health care access in Morocco during the Covid-19 crisis. *Rowaq Arabi*, 25(4): pp. 127–41. https://rowaq.cihrs.org/securing-essential-rights-in-times-of-pandemic-healthcare-access-in-morocco-during-the-covid-19-crisis/?lang=en.

CNT (2020): *Le Maroc va investir plus de 49 millions EUR dans le tourisme et le transport aérien en 2021* [Morocco will invest more than 49 million euros in tourism and air transport in 2021]. Rabat: Confédération Nationale du Tourisme. www.cnt.ma/le-maroc-va-investir-plus-de-49-millions-eur-dans-le-tourisme-et-le-transport-aerien-en-2021.

Desrues, Thierry (2007): Entre État de droit et droit de l'état, la difficile émergence de l'espace public au Maroc [Between the rule of law and the right of the state, the difficult emergence of the public space in Morocco]. *L'Année du Maghreb*, 2: pp. 263–92. https://doi.org/10.4000/anneemaghreb.123.

Desrues, Thierry / García de Paredes, Marta (2019): Political and civic participation of young people in North Africa: behaviours, discourses and opinions. *Revista de Estudios Internacionales Mediterráneos*, 26: pp. 1–22. https://doi.org/10.15366/reim2019.26.001.

Elbe, Stefan (2019): Health and security. In: Collins, Alan (ed.): *Contemporary security studies*. New York: Oxford University Press, pp. 379–92.

Feliu, Laura / Parejo Fernández, María Angustias (2009): Marruecos: la reinvención de un sistema autoritario [Morocco: the reinvention of an authoritarian system], in: Izquierdo Brichs, Ferran (ed.): *Poder y regímenes en el mundo árabe contemporáneo* [Power and regimes in the contemporary Arab world]. Barcelona: Fundació CIDOB, pp. 105–43.

Hatim, Yahia (2020): Morocco to boost intensive care capacity to 3,000 beds. *Morocco World News*, 28 March. www.moroccoworldnews.com/2020/03/297832/morocco-to-boost-intensive-care-capacity-to-3000-beds.

Hekking, Morgan (2020a): Morocco confirms 4,966 new COVID-19 cases, 82 deaths in 24 hours. *Morocco World News*, 15 November. www.moroccoworldnews.com/2020/11/326070/morocco-confirms-4966-new-COVID-19-cases-82-deaths-in-24-hours.

Hekking, Morgan (2020b): King Mohammed VI deploys military medicine in fight against COVID-19. *Morocco World News*, 22 March. www.moroccoworldnews.com/2020/03/297206/king-mohammed-vi-deploys-military-medicine-in-fight-against-COVID-19.

Hernando de Larramendi, Miguel / Fernández-Molina, Irene (2014): Relaciones internacionales y políticas exteriores de los estados norteafricanos tras el despertar Árabe [International relations and foreign policies of North African states in the wake of the Arab awakening]. In: González del Miño, Paloma (ed.): *Tres años de revoluciones árabes* [Three years of Arab revolutions]. Madrid: Los libros de la Catarata, pp. 239–63.

Hernando de Larramendi, Miguel / Tomé Alonso, Beatriz (2017): The return of Morocco to the African Union. In: IEMed (ed.): *IEMED Mediterranean yearbook 2017*. Barcelona: Institut Europeu de la Mediterrània. www.iemed.org/publicacions/historic-de-publicacions/anuari-de-la-mediterrania/sumaris/iemed-mediterranean-yearbook-2017.

IMF (2020): *IMF staff completes 2020 Article IV mission with Morocco*. Washington: International Monetary Fund. www.imf.org/en/News/Articles/2020/11/02/pr20329-morocco-imf-staff-completes-2020-article-iv-mission.
Kacha, Yasmine (2020): In a post-COVID-19 world, 'fake news' laws, a new blow to freedom of expression in Algeria and Morocco/Western Sahara? *Amnesty International*, 29 May. www.amnesty.org/en/latest/news/2020/05/in-a-post-COVID19-world-fake-news-laws-a-new-blow-to-freedom-of-expression-in-algeria-and-morocco-western-sahara.
Kingdom of Morocco (2020a): *HM the King delivers a speech to the nation on occasion of Throne Day*. 29 July. www.maroc.ma/en/royal-activities/hm-king-delivers-speech-nation-occasion-throne-day.
Kingdom of Morocco (2020b): *Royal speech on the occasion of the 67th anniversary of the King's and People's revolution*. 20 August. www.maroc.ma/en/royal-speeches/full-text-royal-speech-67th-anniversary-revolution-king-and-people.
Laaroussi, Mohammed Issam (2020): How Arab states take on coronavirus: Morocco as a case study. *Al Jazeera*, 20 May. https://studies.aljazeera.net/en/reports/how-arab-states-take-coronavirus-morocco-case-study.
MAEC (2020): *M. Nasser Bourita: Les accords de coopération entre Rabat et Pékin relatifs aux essais cliniques du vaccin anti-COVID-19 'consolident et étoffent' la dynamique de coopération entre les deux pays* [Mr. Nasser Bourita: Cooperation agreements between Rabat and Beijing on clinical trials of the COVID-19 vaccine 'consolidate and expand' the dynamics of cooperation between the two countries]. Rabat: Moroccan Ministry of Foreign Affairs and Cooperation. www.diplomatie.ma/fr/m-nasser-bourita-les-accords-de-coop%C3%A9ration-entre-rabat-et-p%C3%A9kin-relatifs-aux-essais-cliniques-du-vaccin-anti-COVID-19-%E2%80%9Cconsolident-et-%C3%A9toffent%E2%80%9D-la-dynamique-de-coop%C3%A9ration-entre-les-deux-pays.
Maghraoui, Driss (2019): On the relevance or irrelevance of political parties in Morocco. *The Journal of North African Studies*, 25(6): pp. 939–59. https://doi.org/10.1080/13629387.2019.1644920.
MAP (2020a): COVID-19: Benslimane field hospital ready to provide health care. *Moroccan Agency of Press*, 2 April. www.mapnews.ma/en/actualites/regional/COVID-19-benslimane-field-hospital-ready-provide-health-care.
MAP (2020b): COVID-19: very high royal instructions for sending medical aid to several African countries. *Moroccan Agency of Press*, 14 June. www.mapnews.ma/en/actualites/world/COVID-19-very-high-royal-instructions-sending-medical-aid-several-african-countries.
MAP (2020c): Covid-19: special fund collects MAD 33.3 billion in first half of 2020. *Moroccan Agency of Press*, 17 July. www.mapnews.ma/en/actualites/social/covid-19-special-fund-collects-mad-333-billion-first-half-2020.
Medias24 (2020a): Fake news: Enfin une loi marocaine pour encadrer l'usage des réseaux sociaux [Fake news: finally a Moroccan law to regulate the use of social networks]. *Medias24*, 19 March. www.medias24.com/fake-news-enfin-une-loi-marocaine-pour-encadrer-l-usage-des-reseaux-sociaux-8566.html.
Medias24 (2020b): Covid-19: Le Roi Mohammed VI propose une initiative commune pour l'Afrique [COVID-19: King Mohammed VI proposes a joint initiative for Africa]. *Medias24*, 13 April. www.medias24.com/covid-19-le-roi-mohammed-vi-propose-une-initiative-commune-pour-l-afrique-9434.html.
Medias24 (2020c): 25.857 personnes poursuivies en justice, dont 1.566 en état d'arrestation [25,857 people prosecuted, including 1,566 under arrest]. *Medias24*,

18 April. www.medias24.com/bilan-des-poursuites-et-arrestations-liees-a-l-etat-d-urgence-sanitaire-9569.html.

MIPA (2019): *Trust in institutions index: preliminary findings*. Rabat: Moroccan Institute for Policy Analysis. https://mipa.institute/7141.

Moroccan Parliament (2020): *Les mesures prises par le Royaume du Maroc pour faire face au COVID-19, à travers les réponses du Monsieur Chef du Gouvernement au Parlement* [The measures taken by the Kingdom of Morocco to deal with COVID-19, through the responses of the Head of Government to Parliament]. Rabat: Moroccan Parliament. www.cg.gov.ma/ar/%D8%A7%D9%84%D8%AA%D9%86%D8%B2%D9%8A%D9%84%D8%A7%D8%AA/les-mesures-prises-par-le-royaume-du-maroc-pour-faire-face-au-COVID-19-a-travers-les.

Morocco World News (2020): King Mohammed VI orders creation of $1 billion fund to face COVID-19. *Morocco World News*, 15 March. www.moroccoworldnews.com/2020/03/296311/king-mohammed-vi-orders-govt-to-create-over-1-billion-to-address-coronavirus.

OECD (2020): *The COVID-19 crisis in Morocco*. Paris: Organisation for Economic Cooperation and Development. www.oecd.org/mena/competitiveness/The-Covid-19-Crisis-in-Morocco.pdf.

Ojeda García, Raquel / Suárez Collado, Ángela (2015): The project of advanced regionalisation in Morocco: analysis of a Lampedusian reform. *British Journal of Middle East Studies*, 42(1): pp. 46–58. https://doi.org/10.1080/13530194.2015.973187.

Oxfam (2019): *Un Maroc égalitaire, une taxation juste* [An egalitarian Morocco, fair taxation]. 29 April. www.oxfam.org/fr/publications/un-maroc-egalitaire-une-taxation-juste.

Reporters Without Borders (2019): *Maroc: Hajar Raissouni, nouvelle victime de l'acharnement judiciaire contre les journalistes* [Morocco: Hajar Raissouni, new victim of judicial harassment against journalists]. Paris: Reporters sans frontières. https://rsf.org/fr/actualites/maroc-hajar-raissouni-nouvelle-victime-de-lacharnement-judiciaire-contre-les-journalistes.

Sefrioui, Rahim (2020): Justice. Un an de prison ferme pour le cheikh salafiste Abou Naim [Justice. One year in prison for Salafist sheik Abu Naim]. *Le 360*, 4 April, https://fr.le360.ma/societe/justice-un-an-de-prison-ferme-pour-le-cheikh-salafiste-abou-naim-212467.

Szmolka, Inmaculada (2021): Bipolarisation of the Moroccan political party arena? Refuting this idea through an analysis of the party system. *The Journal of North African Studies*, 26(1): pp.73–102. https://doi.org/10.1080/13629387.2019.1673741

Taureck, Rita (2006): Securitization theory and securitization studies. *Journal of International Relations and Development*, 9(1): pp. 53–61. https://doi.org/10.1057/palgrave.jird.1800072.

Tomé Alonso, Beatriz / García de Paredes, Marta (2020): Vingts ans de règne: Mohammed VI, à la recherche de l'occasion perdue [Twenty years of reign: Mohammed VI, in search of the lost opportunity]. *L'Année du Maghreb*, 23: pp. 245–68. https://doi.org/10.4000/anneemaghreb.6741.

UNDP (1994): *Human Development Report 1994: New Dimensions of Human Security*. New York: United Nations Development Programme, www.hdr.undp.org/en/content/human-development-report-1994.

UNDP (2019): *Human Development Report 2019. Beyond Income, beyond averages, beyond today: Inequalities in human development in the 21st century*.

New York: United Nations Development Programme, http://hdr.undp.org/sites/default/files/hdr2019.pdf.

Xinhua (2020): Spotlight: Africa on alert of 2nd wave as COVID-19 cases top 2 million. *MoroccoNews.com*, 19 November. www.morocconews.net/news/267023723/spotlight-africa-on-alert-of-2nd-wave-as-COVID-19-cases-top-2-million.

Zaireg, Reda (2020): *Sans échappatoire: Etat d'urgence en vulnérabilité sociale. Intensification des inégalités et aggravation de l'exclusion* [No escape: state of emergency in social vulnerability. Intensification of inequalities and deepening exclusion]. Rabat: Heinrich Böll Stiftung. https://ma.boell.org/fr/2020/06/04/sans-echappatoire-etat-durgence-en-vulnerabilite-sociale-intensification-des-inegalites.

6 Status-seeking in times of a global pandemic
The United Arab Emirates' foreign policy during COVID-19

Alexander Lohse

6.1 Introduction

In December 2019, while the Chinese city of Wuhan was experiencing a suspicious rise in cases of pneumonia with an unknown cause (WHO, 2020a), the leadership of the United Arab Emirates (UAE) announced the upcoming year 2020 to be 'the year of preparations for the next 50 years' (UAE, 2020a). Heading for the 'Golden Jubilee of the Union' in 2021, after fifty years of independence, the UAE was about to complete its long-term development plan, Vision 2021. However, only one month after the announcement, the novel coronavirus reached the UAE – the first country in the Middle East and North Africa (MENA) region to be hit. When the World Health Organization (WHO) declared COVID-19 to be a global pandemic in March 2020, the global crisis that the virus had caused threatened to destroy many of the achievements the UAE's leadership was planning to celebrate in 2021.

The COVID-19 crisis especially hit those sectors that were part of the UAE's diversification strategies for a post-oil economy, as outlined in Vision 2021: tourism, trade, aviation and logistics, as well as real estate and construction. Combined with a collapsing oil market, the resulting 'twin crises' (Young, 2020) severely affected the UAE's economy. However, a decade after its launch, Vision 2021 had already yielded some results. The UAE had extended its capacities in artificial intelligence (AI), health and other sectors that helped the government to handle this crisis. The authoritarian technocratic governance structure and status as a rentier state that had produced the financial leeway to remain flexible in times of economic recession also enabled a rapid and comprehensive domestic response to the pandemic.

Thus, whereas domestic crisis management entirely occupied many states around the globe, the UAE took advantage of the situation and embarked on a foreign policy strategy that aimed to improve its international status. For more than a decade, the UAE had continuously improved its regional standing, setting the state on track to become a regional power. As laid out in Vision 2021, the UAE wanted 'to be among the best countries in the world by 2021' (UAE, 2014: preface). As international status and reputation have

DOI: 10.4324/9781003240044-8

become essential preconditions for recognition as a regional power, Vision 2021 made the UAE's 'prestige as a regional and international role model [and] developing sectors of excellence and national champions' (UAE, 2014: 12; own addition) top foreign policy priorities. With little time left until the 'Golden Jubilee', the COVID-19 crisis set the stage for the UAE to work towards achieving this goal.

This chapter will point out the economic and societal impact of the COVID-19 crisis in the UAE and the Emirates' strategy to cope with it. Building on the growing International Relations (IR) literature on international status and status-seeking strategies, it will show how the Emirati leadership turned the global crisis into an opportunity to raise its international status. Firstly, the UAE started a humanitarian aid initiative reaching more than seventy countries in the first months of the pandemic, claiming to be the most active provider of COVID-19 assistance in the world in early 2020 (UAE Ministry of Foreign Affairs and International Competition, 2020). During this campaign, the UAE also offered help to developed countries such as Italy, Greece and the USA, as well as to regional opponents like Iran or Bashar al-Assad's Syria (UAE Federal Competitiveness and Statistics Authority, 2020: 183–98). Secondly, the UAE reconfigured its international relations, establishing cooperation with regional and global powers to improve its standing in prestigious areas such as high-tech and vaccine research and to extend the number of states that recognise the UAE's status. However, as will be shown, while the UAE's status-seeking strategies facilitated in cases such as Israel or Syria improving bilateral ties, it complicated reconciliation with fellow Gulf Cooperation Council (GCC) member Qatar.

6.2 The impact of the COVID-19 pandemic on the UAE's economy and society

The global economic repercussions of the COVID-19 pandemic had severe implications for vital sectors of the UAE's economy. As 30% of its gross domestic product (GDP) depends on the oil sector, the crash of oil markets in early 2020 severely affected the country. When Organisation of the Petroleum Exporting Countries (OPEC) countries and Russia were unable to compromise on oil production cuts in March 2020, a price war between the Kingdom of Saudi Arabia and Russia ensued. While the global oil demand was collapsing due to the pandemic, OPEC's crude production surged more than it had for almost thirty years (Smith, 2020). Anticipating the troubles arising from oil dependency, the UAE had started to develop other sectors of the economy in the 1980s, making it the most diversified economy of all GCC states. Trying to capitalise on global economic developments, the UAE concentrated its efforts on becoming a hub of globalisation (Guéraiche, 2017: 77ff.). Today, the most important non-oil sectors of the UAE's economy include trade, construction, transportation, finance and real estate (UAE Ministry of Economics, 2020: 26f.). This, however, has led to an extreme dependency on the free movement of goods and money. Therefore, when countries around the globe responded to the pandemic by closing borders and limiting trade and travel, the economic situation in the UAE deteriorated.

Having said that, the achievements since the launch of Vision 2021 have helped the UAE to cope with the repercussions of the crisis. In making a knowledge-based economy, a first-rate education system and a world-class healthcare system three of the six pillars of Vision 2021's National Agenda, the UAE has been focusing on improving these sectors for several years (UAE, 2018). Therefore, the UAE was the only country in the MENA region besides Israel that the WHO placed into the highest category of states in terms of preparedness for COVID-19 in February 2020 (WHO, 2020b). As Mohammed bin Rashid, the ruler of Dubai and prime minister of the UAE, pointed out in March 2020, the UAE's preparedness was a direct result of reforms since 2010: 'Over the past 10 years, we have invested in smart learning, electronic and smart services to enhance our readiness for emergencies and disasters. Today we are reaping the fruits of our strenuous efforts' (cited in Emirates News Agency, 2020a).

Besides good preparation, the efficient technocratic administration and the authoritarian rule in the UAE helped to handle the pandemic domestically (Lynch, 2020: 3). In response to the global COVID-19 crisis, the UAE continued its efforts to strengthen governance capabilities in vital sectors. In this regard, the prime minister announced a review of the UAE's government structure, resulting in a cabinet reshuffle that put a stronger focus on economic planning, food and water security, and advanced technology (Soubrier, 2020a: 11). The measures, which also included streamlining and downsizing the administration, were aimed at creating 'a government that is more agile, flexible and fast to maintain its pace with new and different priorities', according to Mohammed bin Rashid (cited in ASG, 2020: 1).

Key factors in the UAE's strategy to limit infections with and fatalities from COVID-19 were massive disinfection and testing campaigns and surveillance of its citizens. Starting in March, the UAE's government implemented strict public movement restrictions as part of its 'National Disinfection Programme'. Surveillance technologies, introduced originally to strengthen the ruling monarchy's hold on power, played a central role in the enforcement of these restrictions. In Dubai, the government was able to detect any unauthorised public movement by linking biometric data with phone numbers and car number plates. Tracking the movement of its citizens, the authorities sanctioned anyone who went out without an official permit (Hedges, 2020: 35f.; see also Chapter 2 by Demmelhuber, Gurol and Zumbrägel in this volume). In addition, the UAE used its expertise in technology for innovative solutions, such as COVID-19 detection helmets (Soubrier, 2020a: 12f.). In October, the UAE became the first country in the world to conduct more COVID-19 tests than the number of inhabitants (Emirates News Agency, 2020b). Thus, the UAE's focus on areas stretching from technology to health during the last ten years have helped to prepare the country for the COVID-19 crisis. Regarding the economic repercussions of COVID-19, the UAE implemented stimulus packages totalling nearly $35 billion to stabilise the economy (UAE, 2020b). Other measures included $70 billion to increase bank liquidity and ease lending restrictions as well as $76 billion to support the private sector (Young, 2020: 484). Whereas the full consequences of the crisis are still uncertain, the UAE's economy appears to be more stable than a decade ago. During the financial crisis of 2007–9, the near-bankruptcy of several government-related companies in Dubai, first of all Dubai World, brought Dubai's economy to the brink of collapse. In contrast to the situation back then, Dubai World was even able to repay $8.2 billion of its debt stemming from the financial crisis in the middle of the COVID-19 crisis in 2020 (Mogielnicki, 2020a: 11). As Dubai and Abu Dhabi turned to international markets in 2020 to finance their COVID-19 measures, the demand for those bonds exceeded the offer many times over, hinting at the continued reliance of investors on the UAE's economic stability (Mogielnicki, 2020b). Thus, although the world was facing the most significant recession since World War II, the UAE's economy seemed more resilient than a decade ago. For the time being, the financial resources from its extractive industries, which fed into sovereign wealth funds with an estimated value of more than $1 trillion, gave the UAE the leeway to handle the global crisis (O'Driscoll et al., 2020: 37). Accordingly, the UAE's prime minister expressed the goal 'to restore the UAE to its pre-Covid-19 glory "faster than any other country in the world"' (cited in Gibbon, 2020).

However, several long-term challenges remain. Borrowing money at times of growing budget deficits will present the UAE with significant challenges in the future. The UAE has been trying to increase its financial stability for some time, for example imposing a value-added tax in 2018 as an additional source of income. Considering the uncertain global demand for oil in the future, this combination might destabilise the UAE's rent-based economy and social contract (Mogielnicki, 2020b). In case of government spending reductions, the UAE will have to weigh different policy options also regarding their impact on regime stability. Thus, fiscal belt-tightening will likely not only cause reduced funds in social spending and the public sector, but will certainly also limit funds for foreign policy (Young, 2020: 482–4). As foreign and humanitarian aid and prestigious events can be costly, this might impair the UAE's status-seeking strategies and, consequently, its endeavour to become a regional power. Although these are relatively long-term considerations, the UAE's foreign policy during the COVID-19 crisis has provided the first impression of the consequences of budgetary restraint.

6.3 Status-seeking strategies

Although IR scholars have long regarded international standing as one of the driving forces of states' foreign policies (e.g. Galtung, 1964; Gilpin, 1981), approaches of international status have only gained a new impetus in IR during the last two decades. Rising powers in particular, such as China, Russia or Brazil, have been prominent examples of the interplay of power accumulation and status-seeking as a means to improve a state's global or regional ranking (e.g. Paul, Welch Larson and Wohlforth, 2014; Welch Larson and Shevchenko, 2019). According to Ward (2017: 3),

> as states become more powerful, their foreign policies often express not only a desire for more power and wealth, but also [...] ambitions for higher status. The drive for international status takes the form of policies aimed at acquiring markers of high status – like advanced technology, military victories and institutional reforms – along with demands that other states behave in ways that recognise the rising state's new position and the rights and privileges it entails.
>
> (own omission)

Welch Larson, Paul and Wohlforth (2014: 7) define international status as 'collective beliefs about a given state's ranking on valued attributes (wealth, coercive capabilities, culture, demographic position, socio-political organisation and diplomatic clout)'. In this view, status refers to the position a state occupies within a social hierarchy, which can be either membership in an esteemed club of states (e.g. the G7 or the UN Security Council) or the ranking within a group (Ward, 2017: 35). This position, however, fundamentally depends on recognition by others. A state can achieve a certain status only if other actors recognise its standing in a specific hierarchy. Correspondingly, it is not the mere possession of a valued attribute, but the perception and interpretation of those attributes by others that confer status (Welch Larson, Paul and Wohlforth, 2014: 7f.; Welch Larson and Shevchenko, 2019: 4).

In order to persuade other actors to recognise a specific status, states resort to signalling strategies. These comprise 'an assertive type of information transmission whereby the seeking state undertakes to attract other states' attention through diplomatic activity, repeated proclamations, ample use of rhetoric and acquisition of status symbols' (Carvalho Pinto, 2019: 350). As status signalling needs to go along with a high degree of visibility and a lack of ambiguity (Welch Larson, Paul and Wohlforth, 2014: 11f.; Renshon, 2017: 24), status symbols form an integral part of most signalling strategies. Some of the most common status symbols include space programmes, high-tech weaponry, leading positions in international organisations, hosting international events such as summits or sporting events or heading important statistics, e.g. economic growth rates. Such assets of a state represent manifestations of its status ambitions. In turn, status-conferring actors can make their recognition evident through status markers, such as accepting a state to a high-status group or consulting it on vital regional or global issues, but also through positive mentions in speeches and state visits (Welch Larson, Paul and Wohlforth, 2014: 10ff.; Ward, 2017: 35–41).

Not all states, however, are equally important in the recognition of another state's international status. Accordingly, the status-seeking strategies of any state are targeted at a specific peer group. Whereas recognition by established great powers is the precondition for access to the great power club, the peer group of a rising regional power includes global major powers as well as other established powers in the region (Ward, 2017: 39f.). Besides factors such as power and geographical proximity, activity in similar areas of international politics also determines which states are part of a peer group. Such similar states matter for status recognition whilst competing for status in the same policy fields, such as humanitarian politics or mediation (Wohlforth et al., 2017: 527ff.; Renshon, 2017: 22f.). Thus, as the UAE desires recognition as a regional power, it has to direct its status-seeking strategies above all towards the global powers China, Russia and the USA, as well as influential regional states such as Iran, Israel and Saudi Arabia. However, Qatar – as an important regional player and a very similar state – also forms a central part of the UAE's reference group. As Qatar has occupied the same foreign policy niches that are vital areas of the UAE's status-seeking strategies, the resulting status rivalry has rendered the conflict between the two states even more complicated (Khorrami, 2020).

6.4 Status-seeking in times of a global pandemic

The UAE is the best illustration of the assumption that status-seeking strategies need to be visible and unambiguous. As Carvalho Pinto has shown on the example of gender equality and women's participation in the Emirati workforce, the UAE has become sophisticated in turning 'cases and information that underlie the signalling strategy into spectacular media affairs' (Carvalho Pinto, 2019: 351). In so doing, the UAE at times diverts its audience from actual shortcomings in the respective area of status-seeking. Whereas the UAE's gender equality record is rather poor in a global comparison, the Emirati administration publicises the relatively favourable regional comparison and highlights supposed improvements by pointing to Emirati role models such as Mariam al-Mansouri, the first Arab female fighter pilot (ibid.: 353–5). Besides women's rights, sustainability and renewable energy, technology and science, as well as humanitarianism and tolerance are central issues in the UAE's status-signalling. Some examples of publicised achievements in those areas include the opening of the International Renewable Energy Agency (IRENA) in Masdar City in 2009 as the first international agency in the MENA region (Al Nowais, 2013), sending the first Arab astronaut to the International Space Station in 2019 (Asharq Al-Awsat, 2019) and the first visit of a Pope to the Arabian Peninsula in 2019 (UAE Embassy in Washington, 2020). The UAE has thereby been trying to project an image as a role model and leader of Arab and (less often) Muslim or Persian Gulf countries in terms of issue areas directed at a mostly American audience (Carvalho Pinto, 2019: 350). Taking a leading position not only globally, but also within the MENA region, the

USA has been the primary addressee of the UAE's status-seeking policies (ibid.: 351).

However, the COVID-19 pandemic has accelerated global and regional dynamics. While the USA has been on the retreat since at least the presidency of Barack Obama, China and Russia have been busy trying to fill that void in international politics. On a regional level, the disengagement of the USA has set the stage for stirring up rivalries between regional states in conflicts spanning from Libya to the Eastern Mediterranean, Syria and Yemen. Although the Trump administration reinvigorated US relations with Arab Gulf states, it continued to refrain from direct involvement in regional conflicts (Krieg, 2020a). Against this background, COVID-19 has profoundly affected the UAE's status-seeking strategies, as will be shown below. For one, it has added China, Russia and Israel to the states that recognise the UAE's rising status, propelling its ambitions as a leading regional state. Furthermore, the pandemic has also opened a window of opportunity for the UAE to reshape its regional relations and improve its international status by focusing on established issue areas of status-seeking, e.g. high technology and AI, humanitarianism and tolerance.

6.4.1 Humanitarianism

Since it was founded in 1971, the UAE has supported mostly Arab and Muslim states through deliveries of aid (Ziadah, 2019: 1689–92). Since then, it has continued to institutionalise its aid policies and has framed it in a discourse of 'humanitarian diplomacy'. This is evident, for example, in the 2017 Soft Power Strategy, which put humanitarian diplomacy at the top of a list of pillars that aim to strengthen the UAE's 'reputation as a modern and tolerant country' (UAE, 2020c).

Building on this approach, the UAE responded very early to the deteriorating situation in several countries around the world during the COVID-19 crisis. As Iran became the worst-affected country in the MENA region during the first weeks of the pandemic, the UAE sent urgently needed medical supplies to its regional rival in March 2020. First, the UAE dispatched a military transport aircraft to bring a WHO team and 7.5 tonnes of medical equipment from its humanitarian logistics hub International Humanitarian City (IHC) in Dubai to its neighbour. A few days later, the UAE sent 32 tonnes of medical supplies from Abu Dhabi (Fakhro, 2020: 32; Galeeva, 2020: 39). In addition, Emirati Foreign Minister Abdullah bin Zayed called his Iranian counterpart to express the UAE's solidarity with Iran. This assistance is especially remarkable as tensions with Iran had been rising after Iran had allegedly attacked oil tankers off the Emirati coast in 2019 (Fattah, 2020). In June 2020, the UAE's ambassador to the USA, Youssef al-Otaiba, stressed that the UAE's COVID-19 assistance to Iran and other countries should not be regarded as a political issue. Instead, it was a response 'at a very human level' without considering the bilateral relationship (Al-Monitor, 2020). By seemingly de-politicising the assistance, al-Otaiba framed the act as a purely humanitarian issue.

Besides Iran, the UAE sent COVID-19 relief to the Chinese province of Hubei and started the initiative 'Homeland of Humanity', through which the UAE repatriated people of different nationalities from China's hotspot province. Other early aid recipients included EU members such as Greece, Cyprus and Italy, as well as Somalia and Afghanistan (Galeeva, 2020: 39). Also in March, the crown prince of Abu Dhabi and strongman of the UAE, Mohammed bin Zayed, called Syrian President Bashar al-Assad. As bin Zayed wrote on Twitter, he had

> discussed with Syrian President Bashar al-Assad updates on COVID-19 [and ...] assured him of the support of the UAE and its willingness to help the Syrian people. Humanitarian solidarity during trying times supersedes all matters, and Syria and her people will not stand alone.
> (bin Zayed, 2020; own addition and omission)

Offering to dispatch aid to the war-torn country in March, the UAE had delivered at least 30 tonnes of food supplies by May 2020 (UAE Federal Competitiveness and Statistics Authority, 2020: 188).

Overall, the UAE announced by the end of June 2020 that it had provided assistance to more than one million medical workers worldwide by sending 1,000 tonnes of supplies to seventy countries. This supposedly made the UAE the 'most active provider of foreign COVID-19 assistance in the world' (UAE Ministry of Foreign Affairs and International Competition, 2020). However, a closer look into the UAE's COVID-19 aid statistics shows that 475 tonnes of those deliveries to thirty countries were 'food supplies consisting of dates', with Germany and the UK receiving fifteen tonnes each, and the USA twenty tonnes (UAE Federal Competitiveness and Statistics Authority, 2020: 188f.). This is precisely the amount of dates that the Khalifa bin Zayed Foundation had delivered to mosques and Islamic institutions in thirty countries on the occasion of Ramadan in May 2020 (Emirates News Agency, 2020c). For several years, the foundation had done so and delivered even more dates to more countries in the previous year (Emirates News Agency, 2019). Thus, regardless of the COVID-19 assistance it has provided in other instances, the UAE has also rebranded charity donations as COVID-19-related aid to embellish its aid statistics and claim the position as a global leader during the COVID-19 crisis without having to increase public spending.

In addition to bilateral supplies, the UAE played a central role in the WHO's response to COVID-19. During the first months of 2020, about 80% of the personal protective equipment (PPE) the WHO dispatched worldwide originated from the IHC in Dubai (IHC, 2020). Founded in 2003 by UAE Prime Minister bin Rashid, the IHC had developed into one of the most important logistical hubs for humanitarian non-governmental organisations

(NGOs) and international agencies, profiting from Dubai's position in global supply chains. With the arrival of the COVID-19 crisis, the importance of the IHC grew further. By August 2020, the WHO had already processed more shipments through their facilities in Dubai than in the previous five years combined (IHC, 2020).

In the realm of humanitarian diplomacy, COVID-19 has caused, or reinforced, two significant developments. Firstly, the direction of the UAE's humanitarian initiatives has changed. While Arab and Islamic countries used to be the main recipients of Emirati aid in earlier decades, during the COVID-19 crisis the UAE seemed to try to reach as many states as possible, claiming the position of a global aid provider. Notwithstanding its embellishing of statistics by pre-existing charity donations, the UAE's actual medical aid reached dozens of countries worldwide within the first months of the pandemic.

Secondly, the UAE has also been able to expand the scope of recognition for its humanitarian efforts. In addition to US and Western donors, international organisations and other global powers have started to credit the UAE for its humanitarian approach. In March, Tedros Adhanom Ghebreyesus, the director-general of the WHO, lauded the UAE's supplies to Iran; again in April he praised Emirati deliveries to African countries (Soubrier, 2020b). After the UAE had delivered polymerase chain reaction (PCR) COVID-19 test kits with a value of $10 million in June, Ghebreyesus affirmed the WHO's recognition of the UAE's increased international status as a humanitarian power. Thus, he stressed that

> the UAE is a strategic global partner to WHO, and we are deeply grateful to His Highness Sheikh Mohammed bin Zayed Al Nahyan [...] for his continued support for our shared mission to suppress and control COVID-19 globally.
> (cited in UAE Government, 2020; own omission)

The Chinese foreign ministry, for its part, included the UAE in a list of twenty-one countries that had provided support and friendly understanding to China during the first weeks of the pandemic, recognising the UAE's role as a friendly nation but also as a humanitarian actor (Fulton, 2020). In a similar vein, Iran's then Foreign Ministry Spokesman Sayyid Abbas Mousavi announced via Twitter that his country was 'sincerely thankful for these humanitarian efforts and will never forget the way they stood with #Iran in hard times' (Mousavi, 2020). Thus, providing aid globally generated public statements acknowledging the UAE's status as an important global humanitarian actor.

6.4.2 Reconfiguration of regional and global relations

Taking the global changes due to the COVID-19 pandemic as an opportunity, the UAE expanded its cooperation with several major regional and global powers. As a central pillar of the UAE's domestic COVID-19 response had been the surveillance of its citizens, the UAE cooperated closely with experienced actors in this field. Using their know-how from China, Chinese technology companies helped the UAE to limit the spread of the virus domestically. In so doing, 'Beijing has become a role model for Abu Dhabi to remote control the public through surveillance and monitoring tools relying on artificial intelligence and big data exploitation' (Krieg, 2020a; see also Chapter 2 by Demmelhuber, Gurol and Zumbrägel in this volume).

The second field of cooperation was the development of a vaccine against the novel coronavirus with the telling name '4humanity'. While the state-owned Chinese company Sinopharm supervised the first phases of its development, the UAE's company G42 Healthcare was responsible for large-scale phase III trials (G42, 2020a). In its relations with Russia, as well, technology and health were the central factors throughout 2020. Phase III trials for the Russian vaccine Sputnik V also took place in the UAE, making it the third country after Russia and Belarus to participate in the development (Reuters Staff, 2020). Thus, in the course of the COVID-19 pandemic, sophisticated technology and health have become central areas of cooperation between the UAE and major powers China and Russia.

Additionally, the UAE found a regional partner to cooperate with in these sectors. COVID-19 brought to the surface what had been a badly kept secret for years: the UAE's relationship with Israel. The first direct flight between the UAE and Israel carried COVID-19 relief for Palestinians in June 2020. Announcing the cooperation between the two countries in the same month, Benjamin Netanyahu (2020) stressed that Israel's 'ability to act against the corona pandemic could also serve the entire region, and is also creating for us the opportunity for open cooperation, which we have hitherto not had, with certain countries in the region'. In the following months, G42 continued to deepen its engagement with different Israeli firms and revealed its plans to open an international office in Israel (G42, 2020b). Technologies in the area of AI and surveillance as well as health were central aspects in the UAE's decision to formalise its relationship with Israel (Ibish, 2020). Thus, the UAE took advantage of the global pandemic to start the normalisation process and to boost cooperation in precisely those fields with the technologically most advanced nation in the region. Overall, the COVID-19 crisis encouraged the Emirati leadership to enhance its international reputation as a savvy, high-tech nation focusing on AI, big data and health.

However, making its collaboration with Israel public held even greater rewards for the UAE. Above all, this was the US gratitude and public recognition for being the leading Arab state and a role model for Muslim and Arab countries. Throughout the Abraham Accords signing ceremony, US President Donald Trump praised the UAE and its leadership, stressing that 'more Arab and Muslim countries will follow the United Arab Emirates' lead' (White House, 2020a). Furthermore, the president confirmed that the UAE is a great country with a great leader and a warrior, and smart. Respected all over the world. […] And I will say, because of your leadership and because of the fact that you are leading the way, we have many countries in your region and your part of the world that will be very quickly signing up also. […] And this can really lead to peace – real peace in the Middle East for the first time.

(White House, 2020b; own omissions)

UAE Foreign Minister Abdullah bin Zayed responded to these compliments, stressing that amid the COVID-19 pandemic, the UAE had 'reinforced its humanitarian commitments established by our nation's founding father, Sheikh Zayed' (White House, 2020c). He added that the UAE had managed to send a probe to Mars, launch a nuclear power plant and bring the prospects of peace to the region through the Abraham Accords (ibid.). Therefore, when the president of a major global power recognised the UAE's leading rank in the MENA region, Foreign Minister bin Zayed reaffirmed the main achievements of the UAE's status-seeking strategies in the year 2020.

However, in contrast to the Trump administration's positive stance, some US decision-makers view the UAE more critically. The war in Yemen in particular provoked sentiments in Washington that condemned the UAE's role in human rights violations. As this endangered its reputation as a supporter of Western values and a peaceful nation, the UAE announced to withdraw its troops from the war in 2019 (Al-Monitor, 2020). Therefore, the normalisation agreement with Israel helped improve the UAE's standing throughout US political circles, given their pro-Israel consensus. As all three parties involved stated that the Abraham Accords signified a unique chance to bring peace to the Arab–Israeli conflict, the UAE intended to (re-)establish its reputation as a regional mediator and peace-seeking nation (Ibish, 2020).

Regarding another relationship in the region, however, the impact of the global COVID-19 crisis has been ambiguous. Ties between Qatar and its fellow GCC states remained tense throughout 2020, with initially only minor signs of thawing relations as ministers from all GCC states met in virtual meetings to discuss common countermeasures to the pandemic in March and April (Soubrier, 2020a: 14). In 2017, the UAE, Saudi Arabia and other regional states had blockaded Qatar based on allegations of cooperation with regional Islamists and Iran (Dihstelhoff and Lohse, 2020: 49ff.). However, considering the diminished role of Political Islam in regional politics in 2020 and the UAE's own dialogue with Iran, a central reason for the continued conflict has been the status rivalry between the UAE and Qatar. Besides similarities in size, population and economy, a very striking concordance exists in the two states' areas of status-seeking. Both want to develop into global logistical hubs, investing heavily in national ports, airlines and airports and trying to attract global events. Also, both countries have been active in mediation efforts and peacekeeping as well as humanitarian aid (Khorrami, 2020). Accordingly, it was a Saudi initiative, supported by the USA, which succeeded in ending the GCC rift after three and a half years. The UAE, in contrast, remained absent from preceding negotiations, hinting at the Emirati leadership's reluctance to reconcile with Qatar as the underlying causes for the two states' rivalry, particularly competition over international status and contrary positions on regional politics, remain unresolved (Krieg, 2020b).

Altogether, the UAE has managed to reconfigure its regional and global relations as a result of the worldwide pandemic. For one, cooperation with China, Russia and Israel has greatly increased in areas that are not only focal points of Vision 2021, but which also serve the UAE's status-seeking strategies. However, although ending the GCC rift has become a vital issue due to the COVID-19 crisis, the status competition between the UAE and Qatar remains an obstacle to comprehensive reconciliation.

6.5 Conclusion

Not knowing that a virus was about to strike the world, the leadership of the UAE declared the year 2020 to be the year of preparation for the next fifty years. One year later, it is no exaggeration to say that the Emirati rulers have succeeded in this, more so than they could have imagined in 2019. The achievements based on Vision 2021 had already put the UAE in a comparatively good position when the COVID-19 pandemic hit the MENA region. Therefore, the UAE has been able to take advantage of international and regional reconfigurations caused by the global crisis. Continuing on its path towards becoming a regional power, the UAE used status-seeking as a means to improve its international standing. Signalling strategies included extending its humanitarian aid approach and embellishing statistics to portray itself as the most active provider of humanitarian aid early on in the pandemic, as well as raising its international profile in status-seeking areas like AI, health, humanitarianism and tolerance.

Whereas COVID-19 did not fundamentally alter the UAE's foreign policy, it did cause changes to its status-seeking strategies. Firstly, the UAE applied a global humanitarian aid approach. Before the pandemic, the recipients of the UAE's humanitarian aid were mostly Arab or Muslim countries. In 2020, the UAE sent medical supplies to dozens of countries worldwide, rich and poor, Muslim and non-Muslim, Arab and non-Arab. At the same time, the embellishment of its aid statistics hints at the UAE's future need for budgetary restraint in its humanitarian aid policies that was reinforced by the COVID-19 crisis. Nonetheless, international organisations like the WHO and global and regional powers recognised its position as a leading country of humanitarian aid. Thus, the UAE successfully signalled its higher status as a global humanitarian power throughout the COVID-19 pandemic.

Secondly, the UAE managed to enhance its relationships with global and regional powers. Together with China and Russia, the UAE is supporting research on vaccines and other COVID-19-related innovations. Phase III trials for the two most important non-Western vaccines will take place in the

UAE. The pandemic also facilitated the normalisation of ties with Israel, which started with aid deliveries to Palestine and cooperation in COVID-19 research. Through enhanced cooperation during the COVID-19 pandemic, the UAE improved its standing in the status-relevant issue areas of health, AI and technology, especially with regard to important regional and global powers. At the same time, the USA remains a central reference point for the UAE's status-seeking. The clearest recognition from Washington came in the course of the Abraham Accords, when the UAE was described as a leading nation and a role model for Arab and Muslim countries. Applying an international status approach has revealed the role of status-seeking strategies in the UAE's foreign policy. Reducing the normalisation agreement with Israel to hard-power explanations misses the value of international recognition and cooperation in vital areas of status-seeking for a state on its way to becoming a regional power. Besides, the status rivalry between Qatar and the UAE is essential in explaining the UAE's reluctance to end the GCC rift.

Overall, the COVID-19 pandemic enabled the UAE to expand its status-seeking strategies in several issue areas and to garner recognition from all major global powers as well as some regional states and international organisations. Therefore, it seems that the UAE will not only cope with the COVID-19 crisis, but that the pandemic will even strengthen the UAE's international standing and boost its drive to become a regional power. Seeking enhanced reputation has been particularly important as the UAE has been trying to divert international attention from less favourable incidents. Cooperation with Israel, China and Russia played a central role not only in the fight against COVID-19 but also in the establishment of a sophisticated surveillance state, that will further limit the freedoms of its citizens and migrant workers (see Chapter 8 by Hassan in this volume). Furthermore, although it has officially withdrawn from Yemen, Emirati troops remain in the country and support allied Yemeni groups that have been involved in abuses in previous years. In Libya, the UAE has repeatedly violated the UN Security Council's arms embargo, as evidenced by the UN Panel of Experts on Libya (HRW, 2021: 681–6). Thus, the UAE's status-seeking strategies during the COVID-19 crisis served to direct international attention to the Emirates' international achievements rather than misconduct. This is all the more important as the UAE stood for election as a non-permanent member of the UN Security Council in June 2021, just six months before the 'Golden Jubilee' of the Union. Positively evaluated, they indeed assumed their seat at this influential club of countries on 1 January 2022.

References

Al-Monitor (2020): UAE ambassador Yousef Al-Otaiba talks about COVID-19, the region, and prospects for governance in the post-pandemic future. *Al-Monitor Podcast*, 2 June. www.al-monitor.com/pulse/podcasts/2020/06/uae-ambassador-yousef-al-otaiba-talks-about-covid-19-the-region.html#ixzz6ftH5MhMt.

Al Nowais, Shireena (2013): 'Sheikh Abdullah's drive won us Irena', says team behind the lobby. *The National*, 30 June. www.thenationalnews.com/uae/environment/sheikh-abdullah-s-drive-won-us-irena-says-team-behind-the-lobby-1.286758.

ASG (2020): *UAE government reshuffle – priorities and new directions*. Washington: Albright Stonebridge Group. www.albrightstonebridge.com/files/ASG%20Analysis%20-%20UAE%20Government%20Reshuffle.pdf.

Asharq Al-Awsat (2019): First Arab set for ISS says voyage will make 'history'. *Asharq Al-Awsat*, 24 September. https://english.aawsat.com/home/article/1917026/first-arab-set-iss-says-voyage-will-make-history.

bin Zayed, Mohammed (2020): I discussed with Syrian President Bashar Alassad. *Twitter post*, 27 March. https://twitter.com/MohamedBinZayed/status/1243619459186733056.

Carvalho Pinto, Vania (2019): Signalling for status: UAE and women's rights. *Contexto Internacional*, 41(2): pp. 345–63. https://doi.org/10.1590/S0102-8529.2019410200006.

Dihstelhoff, Julius / Lohse, Alexander (2020): Political Islam as an ordering factor? The reconfiguration of the regional order in the Middle East since the 'Arab Spring'. In: Amour, Philipp O. (ed.): *The regional order in the Gulf region and the Middle East: regional rivalries and security alliances*. Basingstoke: Palgrave Macmillan, pp. 29–59. https://doi.org/10.1007/978-3-030-45465-4.

Emirates News Agency (2019): Khalifa Foundation conducts Ramadan campaign across 59 countries. *Emirates News Agency*, 5 June. http://wam.ae/en/details/1395302766515.

Emirates News Agency (2020a): UAE cabinet approves additional AED16 billion stimulus package. *Emirates News Agency*, 22 March. http://wam.ae/en/details/1395302832332.

Emirates News Agency (2020b): UAE first country where number of COVID-19 tests exceeded population: official spokesman. *Emirates News Agency*, 16 October. www.wam.ae/en/details/1395302875264.

Emirates News Agency (2020c): Khalifa Foundation distributes 475 tonnes of dates to 30 countries. *Emirates News Agency*, 7 May. https://wam.ae/en/details/1395302841290.

Fakhro, Elham (2020): COVID and Gulf foreign policy. In: POMEPS (ed.): *The COVID-19 pandemic in the Middle East and North Africa*. Washington: Project on Middle East Political Science, pp. 32–4. https://pomeps.org/wp-content/uploads/2020/04/POMEPS_Studies_39_Web.pdf.

Fattah, Zeinab (2020): UAE condemns Iranian scientist's slaying as threat to peace. *Bloomberg*, 30 November. www.bloomberg.com/news/articles/2020-11-30/uae-condems-iranian-scientist-assassination-as-threat-to-peace.

Fulton, Jonathan (2020): *China's soft power during the coronavirus is winning over the Gulf states*. Washington: Atlantic Council. www.atlanticcouncil.org/blogs/menasource/chinas-soft-power-during-the-coronavirus-is-winning-over-the-gulf-states.

G42 (2020a): *G42 healthcare COVID-19 vaccine trials expand to Egypt*. Press release, 17 September. https://g42.ai/news/healthcare/g42-healthcare-covid-19-vaccine-trials-expand-to-egypt.

G42 (2020b): *G42 to open international office in Israel*. Press release, 10 September. https://g42.ai/news/g42/g42-to-open-international-office-in-israel.

Galeeva, Diana (2020): Small states response to COVID-19: view from the UAE. In: POMEPS (ed.): *The COVID-19 pandemic in the Middle East and North Africa*.

Washington: Project on Middle East Political Science, pp. 38–40. https://pomeps. org/wp-content/uploads/2020/04/POMEPS_Studies_39_Web.pdf.

Galtung, Johan (1964): A structural theory of aggression. *Journal of Peace Research*, 1(2): pp. 95–119. https://doi.org/10.1177%2F002234336400100203.

Gibbon, Gavin (2020): Recovery plan: Sheikh Mohammed issues challenge to restore UAE economy post-Covid-19. *Arabian Business*, 11 May. www.arabianbusiness. com/politics-economics/446457-recovery-plan-sheikh-mohammed-issues-challenge-to-restore-uae-economy-post-covid-19.

Gilpin, Robert (1981): *War and change in world politics*. Cambridge: Cambridge University Press.

Guéraiche, William (2017): *The UAE: geopolitics, modernity and tradition*. London: I. B. Tauris. http://dx.doi.org/10.5040/9781350989320.0007.

Hedges, Matthew (2020): Surveillance: authoritarian exploitation of COVID-19 in the GCC. In: POMEPS (ed.): *The COVID-19 pandemic in the Middle East and North Africa*. Washington: Project on Middle East Political Science, pp. 35–7. https://pomeps.org/wp-content/uploads/2020/04/POMEPS_Studies_39_Web.pdf.

HRW (2021): *World report 2021. Events of 2020*. New York: Human Rights Watch. www.hrw.org/sites/default/files/media_2021/01/2021_hrw_world_report.pdf.

Ibish, Hussein (2020): *What motivated the U.S.-brokered UAE–Israel agreement?* Washington: The Arab Gulf States Institute. https://agsiw.org/what-motivated-the-u-s-brokered-uae-israel-agreement.

IHC (2020): *The International Humanitarian City in Dubai's response to the COVID-19 pandemic*. Dubai: International Humanitarian City. www.ihc.ae/the-international-humanitarian-city-in-dubais-response-to-the-covid-19-pandemic.

Khorrami, Nima (2020): *Qatar blockade. How competition over status has fuelled the Gulf crisis*. Milan: Istituto per gli Studi di Politica Internazionale. www.ispionline. it/en/pubblicazione/how-competition-over-status-has-fuelled-gulf-crisis-27313.

Krieg, Andreas (2020a): The UAE's tilt to China. *Middle East Eye*, 1 October. www. middleeasteye.net/opinion/why-security-partnership-between-abu-dhabi-and-beijing-growing.

Krieg, Andreas (2020b): Qatar blockade: the war of narratives is far from over. *Middle East Eye*, 6 January. www.middleeasteye.net/opinion/qatar-blockade-middle-east-vision-war-far-over.

Lynch, Marc (2020): The COVID-19 pandemic in the Middle East and North Africa. In: POMEPS (ed.): *The COVID-19 pandemic in the Middle East and North Africa*. Washington: Project on Middle East Political Science, pp. 3–6. https://pomeps.org/wp-content/uploads/2020/04/POMEPS_Studies_39_Web.pdf.

Mogielnicki, Robert (2020a): *Is this time different? The Gulf's early economic policy response to the crises of 2020*. Washington: The Arab Gulf States Institute. https://agsiw.org/wp-content/uploads/2020/08/Mogielnicki_Economic-Policy-Response_ONLINE.pdf.

Mogielnicki, Robert (2020b): *Debt maturities loom as Gulf states sell more bonds*. AGSIW Blog Post, 15 September 2020. Washington: The Arab Gulf States Institute. https://agsiw.org/debt-maturities-loom-as-gulf-states-sell-more-bonds.

Mousavi, Sayyid Abbas (2020): Tones of medical equipments [sic] just received. *Twitter post*, 16 March. https://twitter.com/SAMOUSAVI9/status/1239603004904558593.

Netanyahu, Benjamin (2020): *Speech to IAF pilots' course graduation ceremony*. Tel Aviv: Ministry of Foreign Affairs, 25 June. https://mfa.gov.il/MFA/PressRoom/2020/Pages/PM-Netanyahu-addresses-IAF-pilots-course-graduation-ceremony-25-June-2020.aspx.

O'Driscoll, Adylan / Bourhrous, Amal / Maddah, Meray / Fazil, Shivan (2020): *Protest and state–society relations in the Middle East and North Africa.* Stockholm: Stockholm International Peace Research Institute. www.sipri.org/sites/default/files/2020-10/sipripp56.pdf.

Paul, Thazha Varkey / Welch Larson, Deborah / Wohlforth, William (eds.) (2014): *Status in world politics.* Cambridge: Cambridge University Press. https://doi.org/10.1017/CBO9781107444409.

Renshon, Jonathan (2017): *Fighting for status: hierarchy and conflict in world politics.* Princeton: Princeton University Press.

Reuters Staff (2020): UAE to host second human trial abroad of Russia's COVID-19 vaccine. *Reuters*, 12 October. www.reuters.com/article/uk-health-coronavirus-russia-vaccine-emi-idUKKBN26X1FM.

Smith, Grant (2020): OPEC output surged most in 30 years during price war last month. *Bloomberg*, 1 May. www.bloomberg.com/news/articles/2020-05-01/opec-output-surged-most-in-30-years-during-price-war-last-month.

Soubrier, Emma (2020a): *Redefining Gulf security begins by including the human dimension.* Washington: The Arab Gulf States Institute. https://agsiw.org/wp-content/uploads/2020/11/Soubrier_Gulf-Human-Security_ONLINE.pdf.

Soubrier, Emma (2020b): *UAE security apparatus central to its pandemic response.* Washington: The Arab Gulf States Institute. https://agsiw.org/uae-security-apparatus-central-to-its-pandemic-response.

UAE (2014): *Vision 2021. United in ambition and determination.* www.vision2021.ae/docs/default-source/default-document-library/uae_vision-arabic.pdf?sfvrsn=b09a06a6_6.

UAE (2018): *Vision 2021. National agenda.* www.vision2021.ae/en/national-agenda-2021.

UAE (2020a): *Announcement of 2020: Towards the next 50.* https://u.ae/en/about-the-uae/the-uae-government/2020-towards-the-next-50/announcement-of-2020-towards-the-next-50.

UAE (2020b): *Economic support of the federal government.* https://u.ae/en/information-and-services/justice-safety-and-the-law/handling-the-covid-19-outbreak/economic-support-to-minimise-the-impact-of-covid-19/economic-support-of-the-federal-government.

UAE (2020c): *The UAE soft power strategy.* https://u.ae/en/about-the-uae/strategies-initiatives-and-awards/federal-governments-strategies-and-plans/the-uae-soft-power-strategy.

UAE Embassy in Washington (2020): *Tolerance and inclusion.* www.uae-embassy.org/about-uae/tolerance-inclusion.

UAE Federal Competitiveness and Statistics Authority (2020): *The UAE government's initiatives to combat the COVID-19 crisis.* Abu Dhabi: Federal Competitiveness and Statistics Authority. https://fcsc.gov.ae/en-us/Lists/D_Reports/Attachments/49/UAE%20Gov%20Initiatives%20to%20Combat%20Covid-19%20-%20En.pdf.

UAE Government (2020): *UAE contributes 500,000 COVID-19 testing kits worth USD 10 million to World Health Organization.* https://reliefweb.int/report/united-arab-emirates/uae-contributes-500000-covid-19-testing-kits-worth-usd-10-million-world.

UAE Ministry of Economics (2020): *Annual economic report 2019.* Abu Dhabi: Ministry of Economics. www.economy.gov.ae/EconomicalReportsEn/MOE_Annual%20Economic%20Report_2019_.pdf.

UAE Ministry of Foreign Affairs and International Competition (2020): *UAE affirms commitment to strengthening international cooperation with provision of COVID-19 aid and PPE to 1 million medical professionals worldwide*. Press release, 29 June. Abu Dhabi: Ministry of Foreign Affairs and International Cooperation. www.mofaic.gov.ae/en/mediahub/news/2020/6/29/29-06-2020-uae-aid.

Ward, Steven (2017): *Status and the challenge of rising powers*. Cambridge: Cambridge University Press. https://doi.org/10.1017/9781316856444.

Welch Larson, Deborah / Paul, Thazha Varkey / Wohlforth, William (2014): Status and world order. In: Paul, Thazha Varkey / Welch Larson, Deborah / Wohlforth, William (eds.): *Status in world politics*. Cambridge: Cambridge University Press, pp. 3–29. https://doi.org/10.1017/CBO9781107444409.

Welch Larson, Deborah / Shevchenko, Alexei (2019): *Quest for status. Chinese and Russian foreign policy*. New Haven: Yale University Press. https://doi.org/doi:10.1017/slr.2020.74.

White House (2020a): *Remarks by President Trump announcing the normalization of relations between Israel and the United Arab Emirates*. 13 August 2020. www.whitehouse.gov/briefings-statements/remarks-president-trump-announcing-normalization-relations-israel-united-arab-emirates.

White House (2020b): *Remarks by President Trump and Minister bin Zayed of the United Arab Emirates before bilateral meeting*. 15 September 2020. www.whitehouse.gov/briefings-statements/remarks-president-trump-minister-bin-zayed-united-arab-emirates-bilateral-meeting.

White House (2020c): *Remarks by President Trump, Prime Minister Netanyahu, Minister bin Zayed, and Minister Al Zayani at the Abraham Accords signing ceremony*. 15 September 2020. www.whitehouse.gov/briefings-statements/remarks-president-trump-prime-minister-netanyahu-minister-bin-zayed-minister-al-zayani-abraham-accords-signing-ceremony.

WHO (2020a): *Pneumonia of unknown cause – China* . Geneva: World Health Organization. www.who.int/csr/don/05-january-2020-pneumonia-of-unkown-cause-china/en.

WHO (2020b): *COVID-19 strategic preparedness and response plan. Country preparedness and response status for COVID-19*. Geneva: World Health Organization. www.who.int//docs/default-source/coronaviruse/covid-19-sprp-country-status.pdf.

Wohlforth, William C. / de Carvalho, Benjamin / Leira, Halvard / Neumann, Iver B. (2017): Moral authority and status in international relations: good states and the social dimension of status seeking. *Review of International Studies*, 44(3): pp. 526–46. https://doi.org/10.1017/S0260210517000560.

Young, Karen E. (2020): Twin crises deepen Gulf states' policy competition and independence. *Global Discourse: An interdisciplinary journal of current affairs*, 10(4): pp. 481–7. https://doi.org/10.1332/204378920X16015780589771.

Ziadah, Rafeef (2019): Circulating power: humanitarian logistics, militarism, and the United Arab Emirates. *Antipode*, 51(5): pp. 1684–702. https://doi.org/10.1111/anti.12547.

Part III
Social response

7 Religion and pandemic

State, Islam and society in Saudi Arabia and Iran during the coronavirus crisis[1]

Noël van den Heuvel and Ulrike Freitag

7.1 Introduction

In the midst of the events of the current pandemic, taking only a cursory glance one can get the impression that (medical) scientific rationalism and 'religious irrationalism' once again stand in opposition to each other: While recalcitrant religious communities are accelerating the spread of the virus, scientific epistemology proves its superiority (Boaz, 2020: 2–3; Meyer, 2020; Wildman et al., 2020). However, to date, most religious groups rose to the task to prove both assumptions wrong. Religious organisations still are the biggest actors in international crisis relief, including the current pandemic. Many of them managed to continue their services while respecting healthcare guidelines, thus providing much-needed solace to their members (Karam, 2020; Meyer, 2020). Nonetheless, other congregations continued to hold events in person that acted as important vectors for the virus. In South Korea, one Christian church sparked the country's earliest cluster with around 5,000 cases (Kim, 2020). In New York and Israel, the COVID-19 case numbers were particularly high among ultra-orthodox Jews (Benmeleh, 2020). There seems to be an especially high number of victims among evangelical Christians in the USA after pastors called upon their flocks to continue coming together to pray (Woodward, 2020). In Pakistan, certain religious groups and organisations refused to close mosques during Ramadan (Ahmed, 2020). This argument could be supported further by examples from other religious communities. The spectrum of religious responses from relief work over compliance to unruliness indicates that this pandemic is once again a time of renegotiation of the relation between religion, science and politics (Meyer, 2020). This process, along with the question of how religion shapes the public understanding of this virus and this crisis, merits closer investigation (Meyer, 2020; Toniol, 2020). The complex nature of these different relationships will be investigated further through two cases of decidedly Islamic states, Iran and Saudi Arabia.

Both Iran, with its majority Shi'ite population, and Saudi Arabia, where the Wahhabi[2] interpretation of Sunni Islam dominates, define themselves as Islamic states.[3] However, their pandemic and religious policies could not have been more different at the beginning of the pandemic. In Saudi Arabia, the

DOI: 10.4324/9781003240044-10

Umrah, or minor pilgrimage to Mecca, was suspended just two days after the first case appeared in the country. The major pilgrimage, the Hajj, took place at the end of July with only 1,000 pilgrims chosen from the country's residents (Hubbard and Walsh, 2020). In contrast, over a month passed before Iran's most important shrines were closed, and then only for a relatively short time (MEE Staff, 2020a; Nirumand, 2020). In August 2020, large gatherings for the important festival of Ashura were allowed, limited only by minor social distancing and mask-wearing rules (Esfandiari, 2020; RFE/RL, 2020).

This article aims at understanding the different ways in which religiously legitimised states and religious authorities have responded to the pandemic, taking two different Islamic states as examples. We argue that the different strategies pursued are not specifically 'Islamic' but point to wider tendencies among religious forces. In the same vein, one cannot speak of a unified relationship between 'Islam' and the pandemic. Religion is a complex, multifaceted phenomenon which shows, moreover, great diversity within and between traditions. Beyond the need to reflect on different understandings of the relationship between the individual and divine manifestations, and hence the ways in which science can or cannot intervene in human destiny, we show that the specific configurations of state, religious establishment and population are also important to understand the different responses. We argue that it is a complicated mix of these factors which account for the different state actions, as well as the public responses and/or the compliance with governmental measures. Thereby, the coronavirus pandemic offers a useful lens for understanding both the differences in religious tendencies and the differing relations between state, religion and society in Iran and Saudi Arabia.

Given the impossibility of conducting research in Iran or Saudi Arabia during the pandemic, the primary material for this article consists of publicly accessible material, mostly news items and comments on social media in English and Arabic. This was analysed and contextualised in a historical perspective and on the basis of relevant research literature.

7.2 Islam, pilgrimage and disease

In January 2020, the journal *Foreign Policy* reported on the spread of the pandemic with a play on China's New Silk Road project, using the headline 'Welcome to the Belt and Road Pandemic' (Garrett, 2020). In contrast, a Turkish subheading reflected the dominant regional historical experience: 'COVID-19 will travel pre-modern pilgrimage routes and invoke postmodern conspiracy theories' (Al Marashi, 2020). Whereas the virus likely reached Iran and Abu Dhabi directly from China, the first Saudi victim was infected in Iran (Reuters Staff, 2020). Similarly, the first infected Kuwaitis are thought to have caught the virus on a pilgrimage to the shrine of Imam 'Ali Rida in Mashhad (Al Marashi, 2020; Turak, 2020). In the collective memory of the region, however, multiple epidemics have left their marks, not only the recent severe acute respiratory syndrome (SARS) (2002) and

Middle East respiratory syndrome (MERS) (2012) outbreaks, but also the plague and cholera epidemics of the nineteenth century. These haunted the region in the yearly rhythm of the Hajj and were fought from the middle of the century onward by concerted international cooperation, involving health conferences, quarantine installations, the provision of health services and sanitary inspections (Chiffoleau, 2012).

Given this context, attention has turned primarily to pilgrimages and their important element of physical closeness, in addition to regular communal religious practices, particularly joint prayer (Eshagi, 2020a). Whereas Saudi Arabia rigorously banned pilgrimages and communal prayer, the Iranian government reacted with significantly more hesitation. Most likely in an attempt to avoid compromising the celebrations of the anniversary of the state's founding on 11 February or the parliamentary elections on 21 February 2020, it initially waited until 19 February before announcing that the first cases had been detected within the country (Nirumand, 2020: 4). On 26 February, a week after the first two COVID-19 deaths in Iran, President Rouhani assured Iranians that there were no plans to isolate regions affected by the virus, although this resulted in pilgrims to Qom spreading the virus. Ten days later, parliamentarians requested that Tehran, Qom and other cities be placed under quarantine, which was rejected. On 13 March, religious leader Ayatollah Khomeini announced a nationwide curfew. It was only on 16 March, after 853 people had already died, that the holy shrines in Qom, Mashhad and Tehran were closed. Although the government urged Iranians to stay home over the (pre-Islamic) new year's holiday on 20 March, it did not issue a travel ban, meaning that more than 1.2 million people travelled during the holiday period. True travel bans were only issued on 25 March. Many of the measures were revoked again at the beginning of April (Alastia, 2020; Nirumand, 2020: 4). International air travel also continued, even to Wuhan, China – the epicentre of the new disease – possibly facilitating the spread of the virus across the Middle East (Ibrahim, Pinnell and Ganguly, 2020).

In Saudi Arabia, the Grand Mufti, Shaykh 'Abdulaziz Bin 'Abdullah Al al-Shaykh, in his capacity as the highest religious authority, immediately lent his support to the stringent measures instituted by the government. With the argument that 'protecting human life and bodily health' belongs to the teachings of Islam, he called upon the population to cooperate with the government (Saudi Gazette, 2020a). The domestic media extensively cited religious authorities who all expressed a similar message (Saudi Gazette, 2020b). A line was added to the call to prayer, telling the faithful to pray at home (Kalin, 2020). It is supposed to have come from the traditions of the Prophet Muhammad and the commentary of his closest companions, and was thus said to be based on the second-most important source of Islamic law, after the Qur'an. The recourse to this source demonstrates the state's efforts to use Islamic legal reasoning to justify the pandemic-related measures. The director of the mosques of Mecca and Medina emphasised in a statement after the nightly prayer on 6 April that the protection of health and human life is one of the most important tasks of any regime based on the Shariah. Thus, it was mandatory to follow the measures taken by the Saudi government, which were based on the advice of health experts (haramaininfo, 2020).

In Iran, in contrast, there were furious protests against the closure of holy places, even leading to a short-term occupation of the shrine in Qom (Fazeli, 2020). The director of the shrine, Mohammad Saeedi, even called upon the faithful on 26 February to continue with their pilgrimages to the shrine. In a video, he proclaimed: 'We view this shrine as a site of healing. That means that people should come here to heal themselves of spiritual and physical afflictions' (*Middle East Monitor*, 2020).

The divergent religious policies continued: mosques in Iran reopened on 12 May despite rising rates of infection so as to allow people to engage in collective prayer during the last fifteen days of Ramadan, even if under relatively strict guidelines. In contrast, Saudi Arabia issued a five-day lockdown extending from the final day of Ramadan and through Eid al-Fitr (MEE Staff, 2020b, 2020c). In July and August, in Iran, tense discussions emerged about the holiday of Muharram, which is one of the most important Shi'i festivals. Even though some limitations were put in place, gatherings of mourners were eventually allowed and even publicly supported by Rouhani (Esfandiari, 2020; RFE/RL, 2020).

Why was the de facto cancellation of the most important Islamic pilgrimage met with approval in Saudi Arabia, while the closure of Shi'i shrines and the cancellation of the Ashura festival in Iran were met with resistance? To understand this, a brief digression is necessary on the meaning of pilgrimages in Islam and, more specifically, on the respective religious traditions of Saudi Arabia and Iran. Pilgrimages in Islam, as in Christianity, are a central component of religious practice. Performing the pilgrimage rites in the holy city of Mecca is obligatory for every Muslim who is able to do so. Depending on the route, other holy places can be visited along the way. In Shi'a Islam, in addition to the tomb of the Prophet and his descendants, the tombs of the early Shi'i imams are especially venerated. As descendants of the Prophet and bearers of the divine light, they occupy a prominent position. Like prophets, they are said to be able to intercede for the faithful on the Day of Judgement (Halm, 1988: 177).

In both Sunni and Shi'a belief, the idea of such intercession is widespread. The graves of miracle-working saints are therefore often sought out by people needing help in times of crisis. Some of these sites even attract more pilgrims than the hajj (Bhardwaj, 1998). Touching and kissing the thresholds, gates and columns or clinging to the grids surrounding the tombs are common practices. To this day, many believers combine modern medical treatments with visits to shrines in the hope of optimising their chances of being healed (e.g. for more on the treatment of infertility, see Naef, 2017: 18–22). However, this veneration of the graves of saints is theologically highly controversial in Sunni Islam, where it was primarily popularised by mystics. This different approach can be traced back to diverging conceptions of Wahhabis (and other Salafis and Sunni reformists) and Shi'ites (as well as Sufis) regarding the nature of God.

The Sufi scholar and philosopher Ibn 'Arabi, who died in 1240 and whose views had great influence on the Shi'i theological tradition, held the view that God is both transcendent and immanent in creation, which means that people can also experience God within creation (Halm, 1988: 94, 118; Ende, 2010: 58). The Prophet, as a perfect human being, is understood as a carrier of the divine light and thus plays a special role. With the Shi'ites, this is continued by the imams descending from the Prophet. Thus, Qom and its shrines were regarded by many as being 'insulated against epidemics and other disasters' (Gambrell, 2020). For the Sunni-Hanbali scholar Ibn Taymiyya, on the other hand, who died in 1328 and whose writings constitute a major source of Islamic legal thinking for the Wahhabis, God is a transcendent being that humans must submit to by interpreting the Qur'an and prophetic tradition as literally as possible. Although he also recognised saints, through whose miracles God manifested himself, he condemned visiting their graves – and especially seeking their intercession with God – as an act of polytheism (Sharify-Funk, Dickson and Xavier, 2018: 1–31; Nakash, 1995: 158–62). Consequently, the Wahhabis, ever since their appearance in the mid-eighteenth century, have insisted on destroying the graves of saints and other places considered holy by Islamic mystics. In addition to the Mosque of the Prophet's descendant Husayn in Kerbela, Iraq – which is of particular importance for Shi'ites – numerous burial domes in Mecca and Medina have been affected (Vassiliev, 2000: 96–8). Since then, there have also been regular clashes between Saudi guards and Shi'ite pilgrims during the hajj (Steinberg, 2004: 161–7).

Due to its rejection of the belief in the superhuman capabilities of people, or in places with special auras and more generally of practices deemed 'magical' or 'superstitious', Wahhabi Islam can be considered a religious tendency that advocates a demystification of the world in the Weberian sense, comparable with early Protestantism (e.g. Kugle, 2007: 280). On the basis of this dogma, Wahhabis have historically suppressed many indigenous healing practices and advocated the use of modern medicine. An anti-magical explanation of health and disease, as offered by scientific medicine, is a much better fit for the transcendental understanding of God held by the Wahhabis. They also ask God for healing, but he no longer extends it through holy places and holy people as a matter of course. With regard to ritualistic healing practices, only the words of the Qur'an continue to be attributed with a curing and prophylactic effect. Related older practices, however, such as healing with the saliva of a believer who often recites the Qur'an, are rejected (Doumato, 1989: 268). However, professionalised versions of Islamic or alternative medicine that do not heal through the blessings of saints or holy places remain popular (Ibrahim et al., 2017).

This abstention from the use of symbols also has aspects which are relevant to the pandemic. The founder of the Wahhabiyya, Muhammad Ibn 'Abd al-Wahhab (1703–92), emphasised that prayer is not connected with a specific place, but can reach God from anywhere (Saud, 2013: 89); this position took hold in Iran much later (Bozorgmehr, 2020). The Wahhabi's rather literalist approach to religious interpretation contrasts with the more allegorical and esoteric understanding of religion held by mainstream Sunni, but particularly Sufi-inspired or Shi'ite, scholars (for modern Salafi-Wahhabi literalism, but also its limitations, see Gleave, 2012: 175–84, 194–6; Delong-Bas, 2004; for allegory in Shi'a, see Poonawala, 2012). One can assume that this theology facilitates a greater acceptance of pragmatic restrictions on religious practice for the sake of health. However, this should in no way be equated with secularisation: Abd al-Rahman al-Sudais, the person responsible for the Saudi holy sites, repeatedly emphasised in his address to the faithful that the coronavirus pandemic had been sent by God (haramaininfo, 2020).

It is difficult to assess the extent to which the notion of a God-sent plague is shared by Muslims in Saudi Arabia and elsewhere – insofar as they already view religion and medicine as separate spheres. For example, the leader of the Saudi-based Muslim World League, Muhammad Ibn 'Abd al-Karim al-'Isa, was challenged by an irritated reader: if many scholars emphasised that the virus was sent by God, they also said that believers who succumbed to it would be martyrs. Was this true, and if so, why then view the virus as a serious threat? Al-'Isa had supported the Saudi government's strict measures which, to this reader at least, seemed highly contradictory (Raval, 2020).

7.3 State and religion

The preceding section has already made clear that the centralised policies in Saudi Arabia – in contrast with Iran – were in line with the advice of scientific experts. In contrast, in Iran, there are various centres of power struggling to gain the political upper hand. This contrast is interesting in that both states legitimise themselves in Islamic terms. In order to understand the dramatic differences, it is necessary to take a short look at the states' respective justifications for Islamic rule.

In Saudi Arabia, the Qur'an and the tradition (Sunna) of the Prophet hold constitutional rank, according to the Basic Law of Governance (Basic Law, Ch. 1, Art. 1). However, since God has not regulated all human affairs, and since there is also a need to ensure that divine law is observed, a worldly power is needed that acts as the representative of God on earth. It is a religious obligation to obey it, but it is the duty of religious scholars to advise the ruler. Believers are obliged to follow all royal decrees and regulations, even if they are not based on Shariah – with the exception of those that obviously contradict religious law. Insofar as the scholars have a different opinion than the ruler, they are obliged to discreetly notify the ruler of this discrepancy. Since the 1970s, the Saudi government has created religious bodies that are a part of the state bureaucracy. At the same time, new educational and judicial institutions were created by the state, limiting the position of the scholars. It is therefore not surprising that since the founding of the Saudi state, conflicts have arisen time and again about the respective roles of rulers and scholars. Although the scholars lost their independence, their integration into state institutions provided them with new spheres in which they could act, primarily in the education and justice ministries. For this reason, al-Atawneh describes the Saudi system as a 'theo-monarchy' in which there is an 'extended compromise between the two main authorities' (religious institutions and the monarchy; al-Atawneh, 2009: 733).

A political/social modernisation project had already begun under King Abdullah (2005–15) and has particularly taken hold under his successor, Salman. It has increasingly taken on centralising tendencies, and the scholars have had to accept further restrictions on their room for manoeuvre (for a euphemistic view of these developments, see Kéchichian, 2019: 54–65; for a critical view, see Amnesty International, 2019). Opposition of any kind is rigorously suppressed. To name just two examples from the coronavirus crisis: when the prominent Hadith scholar Shaykh 'Abdullah al-Sa'd expressed the view that community prayer in mosques – and especially Friday prayer – should continue even during the pandemic, he was summarily arrested. Even constructive proposals, such as the release of prisoners, were severely punished (Prisoners of Conscience, 2020; Wash Sālifat al-Hāshtāq?, 2020).

In Shi'ite Islam, scholars have played a prominent role since the late eighteenth century. These *mujtahid*s, due to their education, have the authority to independently conduct a rational and scientific interpretation of the law. The most prominent among them hold the rank of an Ayatollah (literally 'miraculous sign of God'), with the most respected among them considered the highest religious authority. Such a rank is not awarded, but is an expression of religious recognition by other *mujtahid*s as well as by ordinary believers (Ende, 2005: 79–88). Ayatollah Khomeini used this as a foundation for the concept of the 'guardianship of the Islamic jurist' (velāyat-e faqīh), anchored in the country's constitution. Alongside this 'revolutionary leader', the constitution also provides for a Council of Guardians consisting of clergymen and jurists to monitor the work of the (elected) parliament to ensure that laws conform to Islam. It holds responsibilities that would otherwise belong to a constitutional court. In this way, a type of parallel structure emerged. On one side are the elected institutions such as the president, parliament and a council of expert scholars. On the other side are the Islamic (revolutionary) leader, to whom the armed forces, judiciary and an arbitration council are subordinate. While Khomeini's authority as a religious leader was uncontested, this became more complicated under his successors, who were less prominent in terms of both religious qualifications and charisma. Recent constitutional changes that strengthened the president and no longer required the Islamic leader to be the most recognised cleric must be seen in this context. However, profound differences also arose within the clergy over issues of a sociopolitical nature, which were able to be aired publicly, especially under the presidency of Mohammad Khatami (1997–2005; Steinbach, 2005).

Against this background, the reaction to the coronavirus pandemic, which often appears chaotic, becomes understandable. Different factions of the state fought over the proper response to the crisis, betraying an internal power struggle (Fassihi, 2020). Furthermore, there have been domestic political disputes for years. Young urbanites, in particular, have been demonstrating against religious restrictions as well as against the increase in petrol prices and economic problems (Fassihi and Gladstone, 2019). The social tensions which were expected because of the already difficult economic situation – which is at least partly due to the crushing international sanctions – were another reason for the Iranian government not to impose an excessively harsh lockdown (Bozorgmehr, 2020; Kabir, 2020). At the same time, it was only able (or willing, depending on the reading) to provide minor financial relief to its population (Galestan, 2020; Kabir, 2020). Former president Khatami predicts the resurgence of violent protests in the country, although whether or not this will occur, and induce change in the foreseeable future cannot be predicted (Yücesoy, 2020). All of this stands in stark contrast to the situation in Saudi Arabia, where the government was able to provide considerable support to private companies and individuals, albeit at the cost of incurring a massive deficit (KPMG, 2020).

In this already tense political situation, the question of whether or not to close the shrines in Mashhad and Qom and whether or not to quarantine the cities (a move 90% of the population approved, according to one study, cf. Tamimi Arab, 2020) posed a dilemma to the state. After all, Qom is considered to be 'the most sacred and holiest place in Iran, the centre of Shiite scholarship and the backbone of the Islamic Revolution' (Jazi, 2020) and Mashhad comes close to its ranks in this regard (Bozorgmehr, 2017). Defining them as centres of the pandemic could have made the disease look like a supernatural punishment for the religious establishment, or even the state itself. Quarantining the cities and closing their sacred sites could have appeared like an undermining of their sanctity, which could have harmed the legitimacy of the regime (Jazi, 2020). The following half-hearted closure of the shrines alienated the strictly religious social basis of the regime. After all, it is a majority of these Iranians who believe in the healing powers of the shrines. The closure of mosques and the ban on communal Friday prayers and visits to holy sites had never occurred before in the history of the Islamic Republic (Knipp, 2020; Zamirirad, 2020). To some, this action, when it was finally taken, appeared like a punishment of the religious Shi'ite current and its institutions by the state. Furthermore, the regime found itself under strong pressure from scholars because the religious economy of Iran's pilgrimage sites differs from that of Saudi Arabia. Not only do scholars in Iran have greater political power, they are also influential economic players. The shrines are centres around which a variety of other businesses are organised (Higgins, 2007). When they were closed, these businesses faced economic difficulties as well (Bozorgmehr, 2020; Fassihi, 2020). In contrast, the religious sites in

Mecca and Medina are under state control, which allowed the government to implement its policies without discussion.

Favouring religious (or religio-economic) sentiments over necessary healthcare measures, however, resulted also in further disapproval by a majority of Iranian society (Tamimi Arab, 2020). The partly politically motivated claim by Islamic leader Ayatollah Ali Khamenei, that evil spirits and enemies of Iran were working together in the pandemic and that the shrines had to be closed therefore, was allegedly meant to convince people to refrain from their religious rituals (Knipp, 2020). However, it subjected the regime to further ridicule by other Iranians. A study showing that 60% of Iranians have little or very little trust in the handling of the crisis while 90% favour quarantining cities indicates clearly that with the initial policy decisions, the state chose catering to its specific religious basis rather than the general public (Tamimi Arab, 2020).

In contrast to earlier historical periods and despite the initial policies in Iran, the key question in both countries was not whether religion or politics would take the lead in combatting the pandemic; neither state promoted the primacy of ritualistic responses to the crisis such as fasting (Phillips, 2020: 438). The focus was rather on the search for the best policy option and a struggle over who was to determine it. The primacy of politics on the Arabian Peninsula had, in fact, already been established in the middle of the nineteenth century. At that time, the Ottoman government increasingly introduced quarantine and hygiene measures along the hajj routes to combat the spread of disease. The British, French and Dutch, from whose empires many pilgrims hailed and who feared the transmission of diseases to Europe, urged the Ottomans to enforce internationally agreed hygiene measures in Hejaz and to monitor pilgrims. These included sanitary measures and improvements to the water supply, as well as room occupancy limits.

Locally, these measures, which restricted trade and pilgrimage, often spawned resentment. Both the Ottoman government and the local people took note of how Europeans combined their concern for the health of pilgrims with the gathering of news about Muslim resistance in the colonies. However, there was also a great deal of friction between the Arab elites of Mecca and the Ottomans. In 1895, all this came to an explosive head: Bedouins and city dwellers banded together to destroy steam disinfection machines and a hospital. In Jeddah, the British vice-consul, who had long observed the hajj as a doctor, was assassinated, and sporadic unrest continued in the region for weeks. Rumours allegedly circulated that the foreign doctors had brought cholera with them and that patients in the hospital were being systematically killed (Low, 2008; Freitag, 2020: 249–67). Religious arguments and political motives were closely linked in the resistance to government measures. Overall, however, the combination of European and Ottoman pressure won the day. When Ibn Sa'ud established his rule in the Hejaz, he took care to cooperate with the European powers and the new international institutions in order to prevent new outbreaks by imposing quarantines and, later, vaccinating pilgrims. This served to make the pilgrimage safer, which was important for his legitimacy; it also secured exclusive Saudi control over the health regime applicable for pilgrims in 1957. Current Saudi policies must be seen against this background (Chiffoleau, 2015: 193–200). In recent years, Saudis experienced MERS – also a coronavirus – that probably originated in camels and began to spread among humans. So far, most outbreaks of MERS have taken place in Saudi Arabia and just a few cases have been detected in Iran (WHO, 2019; ECDC, 2020).

The situation in Iran, dominated by the Russians and the British, was similarly conflict-ridden. There, too, the population's attitude toward hygiene measures was characterised by a reluctance to accept foreign influence and by the obstruction of religious practices. Initially, quarantine was known primarily from entry into the Ottoman Empire, where it was perceived as a harassment of Shi'ites by the Sunni Ottomans (Burrell, 1979: 143–8; Pistor-Hatam, 1991: 232). Within the country itself, disease control was promoted primarily by European advisors and often interpreted as being directed against Islam. Certainly, the clerics, who had recently emerged from the cholera epidemic of 1892 with newly won powers, held this position. They had become leaders of the masses in protests against foreign economic influence, such as a highly unpopular tobacco monopoly held by British merchants (Jazi, 2020). The influence of the clerics and their conflict with the state and foreign powers is exemplified in an episode from the cholera epidemic of 1903. This epidemic spread from the Ottoman-controlled Shi'ite pilgrimage centre of Kerbela. The Iranian authorities quickly set up a quarantine station at the border and had it run by Belgian customs officials. This triggered local outrage, and religious dignitaries are said to have even called for the murder of the station's director. A large group of pilgrims led by a religious scholar finally broke through the border and brought cholera into the country (Burrell, 1979: 143–8). By the time of the Spanish flu (1918–20), the hostility between religious institutions and epidemic measures had already diminished, and the director of the Imam Reza Shrine in Mashhad was willing to cooperate with the authorities in fighting the epidemic. Among other things, the burial of people from surrounding areas at the shrine was prohibited. Nevertheless, the measures were not far-reaching enough, so that pilgrims spread the disease throughout the country (Spinney, 2018: 134–43). A few years after, in a parallel development with Saudi Arabia, Reza Shah further developed governmental responses to cholera outbreaks. Iran's borders were closed, professional quarantine measures were developed and – with the help of Germany – in 1927, Iran began to develop its own vaccines (Davar, 2020).

Over the course of the century, Iran developed a professional modern healthcare system and was able to contain several endemic diseases by inoculation such as the plague and fend off recurring outbreaks of different infectious diseases (Parhizgari, Gouya and Mostafavi, 2017; Pietromarchi, 2019). However, it seems like this time, the clerics are not able to gain political capital from the pandemic. In combination with the already low approval of the regime, many Iranians see an inherent contradiction between science and religion. This sentiment is further invigorated by the statements and actions of the state and its representatives (Jazi, 2020; Tamimi Arab, 2020; Zamirirad, 2020).

7.4 Conclusions

The comparison of the Saudi Arabian and Iranian responses to the coronavirus pandemic illustrates that there are widely different perspectives on how religious and scientific prescripts relate to one another. It also shows that in both countries, the Islamically legitimated governments decided to follow scientific advice, albeit with varying stringency and success. This, we argue, is largely the result of the different political systems which afford religious institutions and authorities more or less autonomy.

In Saudi Arabia, the initial alliance between the founder of the dynasty and the charismatic initiator of a new interpretation of Islam, renewed several times over Saudi history, has long given way to a preponderance of the state. This increased over the course of the second half of the twentieth century through oil-driven modernisation. State power was further centralised since the latest change in rulership in 2015 when formerly semi-autonomous branches of the royal family were submitted to that of the king and his heir apparent in 2017. In the process, other claims to independent societal positions, be it from among the clergy or civil society, were also eliminated. This allowed the government to disregard possible objections by scholars, and the few who allowed themselves an independent opinion immediately faced draconian punishment. It is possible that the pandemic has even reinforced the authoritarian tendencies of recent years (Pétriat, 2020). Because of the international significance of the Saudi pilgrimage sites, it was extremely important for the Saudi leadership to quickly receive support from international Islamic bodies that are conveniently located within the country (Muslim World League, 2020; OIC, 2020).

In contrast, the history of the Iranian revolution has led to the establishment of a range of relatively autonomous and competing institutions., thus potentially limiting the state's room for manoeuvre. This existence of several poles of power in Iran made a certain plurality possible, even if the country is not exactly known for freedom of opinion. In fact, there was a crackdown on 'fake news' about actual coronavirus numbers in the country (von Hein, 2020; Yücesoy, 2020; see also Chapter 4 by Richter et al. in this volume). Furthermore, the pandemic occurred at a time when the state was already faced with a legitimacy crisis.

While the history of the Islamic Republic goes some way towards explaining the differences, one should not dismiss the divergent theologies and resultant meanings of collective rituals in explaining why the Saudi clergy were more willing to accept the restrictions in the context of the pandemic than the Shi'ite clergy in Iran. This is of course not to say that there are no internal debates within Shi'ite Islam, which can be illustrated by a quick glimpse at neighbouring countries. In the discussion of whether to publicly celebrate Ashura in 2020, the influential Iraqi Shi'ite Ayatollah 'Ali al-Sistani argued against such celebrations in order to avoid large crowds, while Qom-based Ayatollah Makarem Shirazi weighed in by emphasising that commemorating Ashura is a religious duty: 'We have some principles that we cannot give up at all, including mourning in Muharram' (Esfandiari, 2020; Eshagi, 2020b; RFE/RL 2020). Thus, no pandemic response can be inferred from religious orientation alone. A second important factor for the religious response to the pandemic, as we have shown, is the institutionalisation of religion, or rather, how institutionalised religion relates to the state. The clergy in the Islamic Republic of Iran continue to occupy important institutions, whereas they are now clearly subordinate to political power in the Saudi monarchy.

Despite all the differences in detail, the same range of reactions can be found in other religions. As in Iran, some Pentecostal preachers in the USA have openly called upon their congregants to disregard public health regulations (Wildman et al., 2020). Pentecostals, like the Iranian Shi'ites, emphasise the experience of God, either mediated by the blessings of the saints or through a direct experience of the Holy Spirit. In such a context, it is difficult to refrain from partaking in the healing power inherent in such rituals. Representatives of puritanical currents that emphasise divine transcendence seem to find this a bit easier (for more on transcendence and prayer in Wahhabism, see Saud, 2013: 89; for the experience of God in Pentecostalism, see Hovi, 2011: 131).

However, most religions have one element in common: they form communities that practise their religion together. This does not correspond to the logic of physical distancing as recommended by epidemiologists. It is therefore not surprising that communal worship, pilgrimages and religious festivals across religions and world regions remain problematic from a virological point of view. However, this should, Meyer reminds us, not be taken as proof for a privileged responsibility of religion for the pandemic but rather as a reminder 'of the potential for infection to occur in any social relation' (Meyer, 2020). Moreover, a longing for community and reassurance by everyone, particularly vis-à-vis this invisible danger, has not just become evident in secular rituals such as collective clapping or singing from the balconies. It has also manifested itself in an actual worldwide increase in religiosity (Bentzen, 2020; Meyer, 2020; Taylor, 2020).

Notes

1 This is an expanded version of the German-language article from 2020 entitled 'Religion und Pandemie. Staat, Religion und Gesellschaft in Saudi-Arabien und Iran in der Coronakrise', *Geschichte und Gesellschaft*, 46(3), pp. 494–506. We would like to thank Dr Kamran Arjomand, Dr des. Besnik Sinani and Peyman Eshagi for their very helpful notes and comments.

2 'Wahhabi' is here understood as a shorthand for a mostly Hanbali interpretation of Islam which is based on Muhammad b. Abd al-Wahhab's understanding of a mostly literalist Islam which favours in particular the interpretations of Ibn Taymiyya and Ibn Qayyim al-Jawziyya. While Wahhabi was initially a term used by Ibn Abd al-Wahhab's opponents, it has since become a reference to this particular strand of monotheistic Islam giving primacy to the pious ancestors, while being differentiated from other Salafi trends by its history, its particular emphasis on doctrinal purity and its political quietism with regard to the family of Al Saud (e.g. Commins, 2006: 215; Lacroix, 2011: 52).
3 Although the focus in this article is on religion, it is important to note that in a 2012 study, 19% of Saudis indicated that they are not religious and 5% that they are atheists (WIN-Gallup International, 2012: 16), while in Iran, in a 2020 study just 32% identified as Shi'i Muslims while the rest adhered to other religions or were unreligious (Maleki and Tamimi Arab, 2020: i).

References

Ahmed, Imran (2020): The politics of congregational prayer. Trust, public health, and religious authority in Pakistan. *Journal of Law, Religion and State*, 8(2/3): pp. 251–71. https://doi.org/10.1163/22124810-2020015.

Alastia, Sanaz (2020): The Iranian legal response to Covid-19. A constitutional analysis of coronavirus lockdown. *verfassungsblog.de*, 24 April. https://verfassungsblog.de/the-iranian-legal-response-to-covid-19-a-constitutional-analysis-of-coronavirus-lockdown.

Al-Atawneh, Muhammad (2009): Is Saudi Arabia a theocracy? Religion and governance in contemporary Saudi Arabia. *Middle Eastern Studies*, 45(5): pp. 721–37. https://doi.org/10.1080/00263200802586105.

Al Marashi, Ibrahim (2020): The coronavirus and biosecurity in the Middle East. *TRT World*, 4 March. www.trtworld.com/opinion/the-coronavirus-and-biosecurity-in-the-middle-east-34289.

Amnesty International (2019): *Saudi Arabia 2019*. www.amnesty.org/en/countries/middle-east-and-north-africa/saudi-arabia/report-saudi-arabia.

Benmeleh, Yaacov (2020): One community, 6,000 miles apart, is wracked by coronavirus. *Bloomberg*, 2 April. www.bloomberg.com/news/articles/2020-04-02/virus-outbreak-spurs-near-sealing-of-israeli-ultra-orthodox-city.

Bentzen, Jeanet (2020): Rising religiosity as a global response to COVID-19 fear. *VoxEU*, 9 June. https://voxeu.org/article/rising-religiosity-global-response-covid-19-fear.

Bhardwaj, Surinder (1998): Non-hajj pilgrimage in Islam. A neglected dimension of religious circulation. *Journal of Cultural Geography*, 17(2): pp. 69–87. https://doi.org/10.1080/08873639809478321.

Boaz, Danielle N. (2020): Between 'essential services' and culpable homicide. State responses to religious organisations and the spread of the novel coronavirus in 2020. *Journal of Law, Religion and State*, 8(2/3): 129–51. https://doi.org/10.1163/22124810-2020008.

Bozorgmehr, Najmeh (2017): Iranian hardliners take a stand in Islamic Republic's second city. *Financial Times*, 13 January. www.ft.com/content/da7e7704-d1c1-11e6-b06b-680c49b4b4c0.

Bozorgmehr, Najmeh (2020): How Iran's clergy fought back against coronavirus. *Financial Times*, 17 June. www.ft.com/content/8e9b50bb-ebf7-4702-9894-1f2081ae869a.

Burrell, Robert Michael (1979): *Aspects of the reign of Muzaffar al-Dīn Shāh of Persia. 1896–1907* (doctoral dissertation). London: University of London.

Chiffoleau, Sylvia (2012): *Genèse de la santé publique internationale. De la peste d'Orient à l'OMS* [Genesis of international public health. From the Oriental plague to the WHO]. Rennes: Presses Universitaires de Rennes. https://doi.org/10.4000/books.pur.117311.

Chiffoleau, Sylvia (2015): *Le voyage à La Mecque. Un pèlerinage mondial en terre d'Islam* [The travel to Mecca. A global pilgrimage to the land of Islam]. Paris: Belin.

Chiffoleau, Sylvia (2016): Des pèlerins et des épidémies. Recomposition des flux « dangereux » sur la mer Rouge et le Golfe [Pilgrims and epidemics. Reorganising 'hazardous' flows on the Red Sea and the Gulf]. *Arabian Humanities*, 6(6). https://doi.org/10.4000/cy.3051.

Commins, David (2009): *The Wahhabi mission and Saudi Arabia*. London: I. B. Tauris. https://doi.org/10.1017/S0020743808081543.

Davar, Faramarz (2020): How did Iran fight a deadly virus 100 years ago? *Iranwire*, 11 March. https://iranwire.com/en/features/6803.

Delong-Bas, Natana J. (2004): *Wahhabi Islam. From revival and reform to global jihad*. Oxford: Oxford University Press.

Doumato, Eleanor (1989): *Arabian women. Religion, work, and cultural ideology in the Arabian Peninsula from the nineteenth century through the age of 'Abd al-Azīz* (doctoral dissertation). New York: Columbia University.

ECDC (2020): *Geographical distribution of confirmed MERS-CoV cases by country of infection and year*, 4 September. Solna: European Centre for Disease Prevention and Control. www.ecdc.europa.eu/en/publications-data/geographical-distribution-confirmed-mers-cov-cases-country-infection-and-year.

Ende, Werner (2005): Der schiitische Islam. In: Ende, Werner / Steinbach, Udo (eds.): *Der Islam in der Gegenwart*. Munich: C. H. Beck, pp. 70–89.

Ende, Werner (2010): Shi'i Islam. In: Ende, Werner / Steinbach, Udo (eds.): *Islam in the world today. A handbook of politics, religion, culture, and society*. Ithaca: Cornell University Press, pp. 51–69. https://doi.org/10.7591/9780801464836.

Esfandiari, Golnaz (2020): To weep or not to weep: Iran debates holding Muharram during pandemic. *Radio Free Europe/Radio Liberty*, 3 August. www.rferl.org/a/iran-debates-holding-muharram-ceremonies-during-pandemic/30763494.html.

Eshagi, Peyman (2020a): 'Social distance' against 'closeness': reconsidering the issue of closeness in the Shiite Islam festivals under the Covid-19 pandemic. *The Open University*. https://fass.open.ac.uk/festivals-research/blogs/as-close-as-possible.

Eshagi, Peyman (2020b): To do or not to do? Internal discussions on holding the religious festivals of Shiite Islam in 2020 during the Covid-19 lockdown. *The Open University*, 30 July. https://fass.open.ac.uk/festivals-research/blogs/to-do-or-not-to-do.

Fassihi, Farnaz (2020): Power struggle hampers Iran's coronavirus response. *New York Times*, 17 March. https://nyti.ms/2Wl1ARZ.

Fassihi, Farnaz / Gladstone, Rick (2019): With brutal crackdown, Iran is convulsed by worst unrest in 40 years. *New York Times*, 1 December. https://nyti.ms/2Yd2bUM.

Fazeli, Yaghoub (2020): Iranian religious fanatics protest closure of Shia shrines due to coronavirus. *Alarabiya*, 16 March. https://english.alarabiya.net/en/News/middle-east/2020/03/17/Iranian-religious-fanatics-protest-closure-of-Shia-shrines-due-to-coronavirus.

Freitag, Ulrike (2020): *A history of Jeddah. The gate to Mecca in the nineteenth and twentieth centuries.* Cambridge: Cambridge University Press. https://doi.org/10.1017/9781108778831.

Galestan, Mansoureh (2020): *Iran regime's denials regarding coronavirus are persistent, but faltering.* London: National Council of Resistance of Iran. www.ncr-iran.org/en/news/iran-regimes-denials-regarding-coronavirus-are-persistent-but-faltering.

Gambrell, Jon (2020): 'Virus at Iran's gates': how Tehran failed to stop outbreak. *abc News,* 17 March. https://abcnews.go.com/International/wireStory/virus-irans-gates-tehran-failed-stop-outbreak-69635940.

Garrett, Laurie (2020): Welcome to the Belt and Road pandemic. *Foreign Policy,* 24 January. https://foreignpolicy.com/2020/01/24/wuhan-virus-china-belt-and-road-pandemic.

Gleave, Robert (2012): *Islam and literalism. Literal meaning and interpretation in Islamic legal theory.* Edinburgh: Edinburgh University Press.

Halm, Heinz (1988): *Die Schia* [The Shi'a]. Darmstadt: Wissenschaftliche Buchgesellschaft.

Haramaininfo (2020): 6 April 2020 message from Shaikh Sudais after 'Isha'. *YouTube,* 6 April. www.youtube.com/watch?v=ZORg0q63sGM.

Higgins, Andrew (2007): Inside Iran's holy money machine. *The Wall Street Journal,* 2 June. www.wsj.com/articles/SB118072271215621679.

Hovi, Tuija (2011): Praising as bodily practice. The neocharismatic culture of celebration. *Scripta Instituti Donneriani Aboensisi,* 23: pp. 129–40. https://doi.org/10.30674/scripta.67384.

Hubbard, Ben / Walsh, Daclan (2020): The hajj pilgrimage is canceled, and grief rocks the Muslim world. *The New York Times,* 23 June. https://nyti.ms/2NqCI5I.

Ibrahim, Nagwa / Al Alwan, Ashraf / Al Eid, Ahmed / Al Ghawa, Yazeed / Al Ghalbi, Maram (2017): Traditional Islamic medicine utilization among adult patients with cancers in Saudi Arabia. *EC Pharmacology and Toxicology,* 4(5): pp. 171–82.

Ibrahim, Nader / Pinnell, Owen / Ganguly, Manisha (2020): Coronavirus by air: the spread of Covid-19 in the Middle East. *BBC,* 5 May. www.bbc.com/news/av/world-middle-east-52537663.

Jazi, Arash (2020): The facial crisis of Shiite Iran. *Religious matters in an entangled world,* 7 April. https://religiousmatters.nl/the-facial-crisis-of-shiite-iran.

Kabir, Marmar (2020): Iran in the time of corona. *Le Monde Diplomatique,* 24 March. https://mondediplo.com/outsidein/iran-in-the-time-of-corona.

Kalin, Stephen (2020): Saudi Arabia closes mosques, calls G20 leaders to meet over coronavirus. *Reuters,* 17 March. www.reuters.com/article/us-health-coronavirus-saudi/saudi-arabia-closes-mosques-calls-g20-leaders-to-meet-over-coronavirus-idUSKBN2143DH.

Karam, Azza (2020): Religion & the pandemic: a call beyond the here & now. *Inter Press Service,* 4 August. www.ipsnews.net/2020/08/religion-pandemic-call-beyond-now.

Kéchichian, Joseph A. (2019): *Saudi Arabia in 2030. The emergence of a new leadership.* Seoul: Asan Institute for Policy Studies. http://en.asaninst.org/contents/saudi-arabia-in-2030-the-emergence-of-a-new-leadership.

Kim, Min Joo (2020): Churches have become South Korea's coronavirus battleground. *The Washington Post,* 17 September. www.washingtonpost.com/world/asia_pacific/churches-coronavirus-south-korea-religion/2020/09/17/6ea63912-f6fd-11ea-85f7-5941188a98cd_story.html.

Knipp, Kersten (2020): How the coronavirus has altered Iranian's view of faith. *Deutsche Welle,* 23 April. https://p.dw.com/p/3bHsW.

KPMG (2020): *Kingdom of Saudi Arabia. Government and institution measures in response to COVID-19*. London: KPMG International. https://home.kpmg/xx/en/home/insights/2020/04/saudi-arabia-government-and-institution-measures-in-response-to-covid.html.

Kugle, Scott Alan (2007): *Sufis and saints' bodies. Mysticism, corporeality and sacred power in Islam*. Chapel Hill: The University of North Carolina Press. https://doi.org/10.5149/9780807872772_kugle.

Lacroix, Stéphane (2011): *Awakening Islam. The politics of religious dissent in contemporary Saudi Arabia*. Cambridge, MA: Harvard University Press.

Low, Michael Christopher (2008): Empire and the hajj. Pilgrims, plagues, and pan-Islam under British surveillance, 1865–1908. *International Journal of Middle East Studies*, 40(2): pp. 269–90. https://doi.org/doi:10.1017/S0020743808080549.

Maleki, Ammar / Tamimi Arab, Pooyan (2020): *Iranians' attitudes toward religion: a 2020 survey report*. The Hague: The Group for Analyzing and Measuring Attitudes in IRAN (GAMAAN). https://gamaan.org/wp-content/uploads/2020/09/GAMAAN-Iran-Religion-Survey-2020-English.pdf.

MEE Staff (2020a): Coronavirus. Saudi Arabia bans all umrah pilgrimage to Mecca. *Middle East Eye*, 4 March. www.middleeasteye.net/news/coronavirus-saudi-arabia-bans-umrah-pilgrimage-residents-and-citizens.

MEE Staff (2020b): Coronavirus. Saudi Arabia to go under full lockdown during Eid holiday. *Middle East Eye*, 13 May. www.middleeasteye.net/news/coronavirus-saudi-arabia-full-lockdown-eid-holiday-ramadan.

MEE Staff (2020c): Iran to reopen mosques on Tuesday despite uptick in coronavirus cases. *Middle East Eye*, 11 May. www.middleeasteye.net/news/iran-reopen-mosques-tuesday-despite-uptick-coronavirus-cases.

Meyer, Birgit (2020): Studying religion in times of corona. *Religious Matters in an Entangled World*, 21 April. https://religiousmatters.nl/studying-religion-in-times-of-corona.

Middle East Monitor (2020): Iran cleric encourages visitors to Qom religious sites, despite coronavirus fear. *Middle East Monitor*, 27 February. www.middleeastmonitor.com/20200227-iran-cleric-encourages-visitors-to-qom-religious-sites-despite-coronavirus-fears.

Muslim World League (2020): *Twitter post*. 20 March. https://twitter.com/MWLOrg_en/status/1241012872362278914.

Naef, Shirin (2017): *Kinship, law and religion. An anthropological study of assisted reproductive technologies in Iran*. Tübingen: Narr Francke Attempto.

Nakash, Yitzhak (1995): The visitation of the shrines of the Imams and the Shi'i mujtahids in the early twentieth century. *Studia Islamica*, 81, pp. 153–64. https://doi.org/10.2307/1596023.

Nirumand, Bahman (2020): *Iran-Report 04/20*. Berlin: Heinrich Böll Stiftung. www.boell.de/de/2020/04/02/iran-report-0420.

OIC (2020): *Al-Othaimeen: news agencies in OIC member countries refute fake news on the coronavirus pandemic*. Press release, 16 May. Jeddah: Organisation of Islamic Cooperation. www.oic-oci.org/topic/?t_id=23419&t_ref=14010&lan=en.

Parhizgari, Najmeh / Gouya, Mohammad Mehdi / Mostafavi, Ehsan (2017): Emerging and re-emerging infectious diseases in Iran. *Iranian Journal of Microbiology*, 9(3): pp. 122–42. www.ncbi.nlm.nih.gov/pmc/articles/PMC5719507.

Pétriat, Philippe (2020): The painful history of epidemics in Saudi Arabia. *Orient XXI*, 21 May. https://orientxxi.info/magazine/the-painful-history-of-epidemics-in-saudi-arabia,3895.

Phillips, Howard (2020): '17, '18, '19. Religion and science in three pandemics, 1817, 1918, and 2019. *Journal of Global History*, 15(3): pp. 434–43. https://doi.org/10.1017/S1740022820000315.

Pietromarchi, Virginia (2019): Iran's healthcare system threatened by US sanctions: rights group. *Aljazeera*, 29 October. www.aljazeera.com/economy/2019/10/29/irans-healthcare-system-threatened-by-us-sanctions-rights-group.

Pistor-Hatam, Anja (1991): Pilger, Pest und Cholera. Die Wallfahrt zu den Heiligen Stätten im Irak als gesundheitspolitisches Problem im 19. Jahrhundert [Pilgrims, plague and cholera. Pilgrimage to the holy places in Iraq as a health problem in the nineteenh century]. *Die Welt des Islams*, 31(2): pp. 228–45. https://doi.org/10.1163/157006091X00083.

Poonawala, Ismail (2012): Ta'wīl. In: Bearman, P. / Bianquis, T. / Bosworth, C. E. / van Donzel, E. / Heinrichs, W. P. (eds.): *Encyclopaedia of Islam*. Second edition. http://dx.doi.org/10.1163/1573-3912_islam_SIM_7457.

Prisoners of Conscience (2020): *Twitter post*. 21 March. https://twitter.com/m3takl_en/status/1241482984269795329?s=12.

Raval, Preet (2020): *Twitter post*. 21 March. https://twitter.com/ravalpreet222/status/1241265112356274176.

Reuters Staff (2020): Saudi Arabia announces first case of coronavirus. *Reuters*, 2 March. www.reuters.com/article/us-health-coronavirus-saudi-idUSKBN20P2FK.

RFE/RL (2020): Iran scales back Ashura commemoration amid pandemic. *Radio Free Europe/Radio Liberty*, 31 August. www.rferl.org/a/iran-religion-ashura/30812705.html.

Saud, Laith (2013): Islamic political theology. In: McCloud, Amina Beverly / Hibbard, Scott W. / Saud, Laith (eds.): *An introduction to Islam in the 21st century*. Chichester: Wiley-Blackwell, pp. 81–108.

Saudi Gazette (2020a): Measures to combat coronavirus are for people's safety: Grand Mufti. *Saudi Gazette*, 16 March. https://saudigazette.com.sa/article/590962/SAUDI-ARABIA/Measures.

Saudi Gazette (2020b): Itikaf suspended at two holy mosques. *Saudi Gazette*, 21 April. https://saudigazette.com.sa/article/592122/SAUDI-ARABIA/Itikaf-su.

Sharify-Funk, Meena / Dickson, William Rory / Xavier, Merin Shobhana (2018): *Contemporary sufism. Piety, politics and popular culture*. Abingdon: Routledge.

Spinney, Laura (2018): *Die Welt im Fieber. Wie die Spanische Grippe die Gesellschaft veränderte* [The world in fever. How the Spanish flu changed society]. Munich: Hanser, pp. 134–43.

Steinbach, Udo (2005): Iran. In: Ende, Werner / Steinbach, Udo (eds.): *Der Islam in der Gegenwart*. Munich: C. H. Beck, pp. 246–63.

Steinberg, Guido (2004): *Saudi-Arabien. Politik, Geschichte, Religion* [Saudi Arabia. Politics, History, Religion]. Munich: C. H. Beck.

Tamimi Arab, Pooyan (2020): On secularisation and the coronavirus in Iran. *Religious Matters in an Entangled World*, 29 March. https://religiousmatters.nl/on-secularization-and-the-coronavirus-in-iran.

Taylor, Alan (2020): Music and encouragement from balconies around the world. *The Atlantic*, 24 March. www.theatlantic.com/photo/2020/03/music-and-encouragement-from-balconies-around-world/608668.

Toniol, Rodrigo (2020): Temporalities of the pandemic and a proposed research agenda about religion. *Religious Matters in an Entangled World*, 4 May. https://religiousmatters.nl/temporalities-of-the-pandemic-and-a-proposed-research-agenda-about-religion.

Turak, Natasha (2020): First Middle East cases of coronavirus confirmed in the UAE. *CNBC*, 29 January. www.cnbc.com/2020/01/29/first-middle-east-cases-of-coronavirus-confirmed-in-the-uae.html.

Vassiliev, Alexei (2000): *The history of Saudi Arabia*. London: Saqi Books.

von Hein, Shabnam (2020): Iran's coronavirus strategy divides health experts, government. *Deutsche Welle*, 2 October. https://p.dw.com/p/3jJ5V.

Wash Sālifat al-Hāshtāq? (2020): *Twitter post* [in Arabic]. 28 March. https://twitter.com/AbtWhaat/status/1243981574661713920.

WHO (2019): *Middle East respiratory syndrome coronavirus (MERS-CoV)* 11 March. Geneva: World Health Organization. www.who.int/news-room/fact-sheets/detail/middle-east-respiratory-syndrome-coronavirus-(mers-cov).

Wildman, Wesley J. / Bulbulia, Joseph / Sosis, Richard / Schjoedt, Uffe (2020): Religion and the COVID-19 pandemic. *Religion, Brain & Behavior*, 10(2): 115–17. https://doi.org/10.1080/2153599X.2020.1749339.

WIN-Gallup International (2012): *Global index of religiosity and atheism 2012*. Press release. Vienna: Gallup International. https://sidmennt.is/wp-content/uploads/Gallup-International-um-tr%C3%BA-og-tr%C3%BAleysi-2012.pdf.

Woodward, Alex (2020): A phantom plague. America's bible belt played down the pandemic and even cashed in. Now dozens of pastors are dead. *The Independent*, 2 April. www.independent.co.uk/news/world/americas/bible-belt-us-coronavirus-pandemic-pastors-church-a9481226.html.

Yücesoy, Vahid (2020): Iran's coronavirus response: a lesson in what not to do. *Bulletin of the Atomic Scientists*, 29 May. https://thebulletin.org/2020/05/irans-coronavirus-response-a-lesson-in-what-not-to-do.

Zamirirad, Azadeh (2020): *Drei Folgen der Coronakrise in Iran* [Three consequences of the corona crisis in Iran]. Berlin: Stiftung Wissenschaft und Politik. www.swp-berlin.org/publikation/drei-folgen-der-coronakrise-in-iran.

8 'On the horns of a dilemma'

Human traffickers, the COVID-19 pandemic and victims of trafficking in Khartoum

Manara Babiker Hassan

8.1 Introduction

Samasra (سماسرة [brokers] sg. *samsar*) are the main proponents of the trafficking business in Sudan. They make their money by collecting 'transportation fees' and they further exploit their 'clients' through sexual abuse, insufficient provision of food and medication during the journey and forced labour. During their temporary stay in Khartoum – the capital of Sudan and an important hub for irregular migration in East Africa – women are very often employed as domestic workers.

Women from Ethiopia are the prime group of concern in this regard. In contrast to other foreigners who often work in domestic employment, such as Filipinos, Ethiopian women and girls can be easily employed without the need for official recruitment processes and – in contrast to women from Sudan or South Sudan – they work seven days a week without interruption. Therefore, they are a popular resource among the rich families of Khartoum who often need even more than one housemaid to keep their villas and gardens in good order.

In this chapter, I analyse how the recent political and economic changes in Sudan and Ethiopia have helped the *samasra* to extend their business further. When South Sudan became independent from Sudan in 2011, the number of South Sudanese people living in Khartoum decreased drastically due to the return of many citizens to the newly founded state. Most Sudanese families instead turned to Ethiopian workers, whose situation suddenly became even more dramatic in 2013, when the Ethiopian government banned all further labour migration to the Middle East for humanitarian reasons after cases of exploitation in the Gulf became public. However, for those Ethiopian women and girls already in Khartoum and waiting for their onward journey, this ban meant an indefinite interruption of their travels; therefore, they needed to find income to finance their prolonged stay and they became easy prey for the exploitative informal networks between the *samasra* as suppliers and rich Sudanese families as consumers.

DOI: 10.4324/9781003240044-11

The *samasra* exploited this situation by demanding higher wages for the girls they 'supplied' to the market, often increasing their salary to SDG 450–600 (Sudanese pounds) a week, instead of the SDG 40–60 that was the usual price per week for South Sudanese housemaids before 2011. These increased sums – equal to not more than $8–11 according to the official exchange rates, but still a significant amount of money for Khartoum's poorest, especially when considered against the informal exchange rates which are significantly higher – are however still cheaper than the estimated SDG 1,500–2,000 that a South Sudanese housemaid would typically demand per week. The sums paid for Ethiopian housemaids are often forwarded in full to the *samasra* as repayment of outstanding debts for the 'trafficking service'. However, after the girls have paid all their dues back to the *samasra* they are not able to stop working, and as they can neither proceed further to Europe or the Persian Gulf nor return to Ethiopia without the help of the *samasra*, they often remain at the *samsar*'s disposal and are thus prone to further exploitation.

Although South Sudanese people started to return to Khartoum after the war escalated in South Sudan in 2013, and the Ethiopian government lifted their travel ban for Ethiopian nationals visiting Middle Eastern (MENA) countries in 2013, this encouraged the *samasra* to increase their activities throughout Khartoum. Many Ethiopian girls stopped working and started initiatives to continue their application process for a visa, preferably in Dubai, to continue their journey towards the Arab Gulf states. Those who kept working did so only under the condition of much higher wages, now reaching SDG 5,000–7,000 (approx. $90–120), so only wealthy families in Khartoum continued to employ them. The outbreak of uprisings against the authoritarian regime of Omar al-Bashir that started in Khartoum and other Sudanese cities in late 2018 meant a unique 'window of opportunity' for the *samasra* to continue their activities and to further use Khartoum as a transit hub, since the authorities were increasingly busy following the protesters and not them as criminal networks – after many of Sudan's police and security forces were already involved as beneficiaries in the trafficking business, or at least they were too weak to take action against them effectively (Abdel Ati, 2017: 1).

When COVID-19 reached Sudan and the government announced a countrywide lockdown in March 2020, many Sudanese families welcomed the offer from the *samasra* to employ young domestic workers even more, as this enabled them to isolate themselves better. Khartoum's rich families thus became one of the cornerstones for the *samasra* to continue their trafficking business even when public life, and the prospects for international travelling, came to a far-reaching halt.

Whilst the COVID-19 pandemic has created specific challenges for the *samasra*, this chapter shows that, overall, they have successfully developed strategies that allow them to continue their trafficking of girls from Ethiopia, and the Horn of Africa in general, towards the Arab Gulf. Such methods commence at the Sudanese–Ethiopian border – involving the security forces in their illegal activities – continue with logistics and exploitation in Sudan and along the way towards the Arabian Peninsula and include arranging accommodation for girls in Khartoum in ways that hide them from the authorities when they overstay their entry visa.

The crucial aspect that this study points out is the *samasra*'s exploitation of Ethiopian women and girls attempting to achieve a better life through convincing them that travel is the easiest way to fulfil their desires. This makes the girls fully submissive to them, and they endure their brutal treatment out of fear of missing the chance to escape home, accepting their plight living under the full control of the *samasra* and being forced to work for food and shelter regardless of their human and legal rights to a decent life. They are on the 'horns of a dilemma' here: staying under the *samasra*'s exploitative control is no option, but working without payment in – sometimes no less exploitative – Sudanese families for food and shelter is not a promising possibility either. The complete closure of most businesses and public life in Khartoum during the COVID-19 pandemic has made their already dramatic situation even worse, and they have become more vulnerable to their brokers' abuses of power.

The research included in this chapter builds on fourteen interviews conducted in Khartoum during 2020, thus in the midst of the COVID-19 pandemic. Those included two with *samasra* and ten with trafficked women and girls between 17 March and 4 July 2020. Known as 'Dubai girls' (بنات دبي, Banat Dubai), they now work for free in private households, yet are barred from even leaving the house in order to put the family at ease that they will not contract the virus and bring it into the house. Given the proximity of Ramadan, some families agreed in spring 2020, when the pandemic's first wave hit Khartoum, to employ two housekeepers. I was allowed to interview the girls employed by my friends and relatives in their houses. However, since all women and girls who told me their stories continue to be in vulnerable positions most likely also in the foreseeable future, I keep their identities private throughout the whole chapter to ensure their absolute anonymity. Those interviews had to be held in secrecy, i.e. without the knowledge of the *samasra*, since all the women and girls contacted for this study were afraid of potential punishment or even the cancellation of their further travel towards Dubai. Additionally, I conducted two interviews with a civil society representative and a political decision-maker (see the list of interviews at the end of this chapter).

I added the insights from these personal encounters to the existing literature on irregular migration from the Horn of Africa to the Gulf, including some recent articles on the impact of COVID-19 in the region. Some local scholars from Ethiopia and Sudan have published studies on the *samasra* and their business, so I triangulated their findings with official reports, common knowledge of Khartoum citizens about the situation of Ethiopian women in Sudan's capital and my own research resulting from my PhD project.

8.2 Trafficking as a flourishing business at the Ethiopia–Sudan border

Sudan's land border extends over more than 6,000 kilometres, plus the 870 kilometres of coastline along the Red Sea. The sheer length of the border, in combination with the often deserted and inhospitable landscape, makes it difficult to manage them effectively, and the lack of cooperation with any of the neighbouring governments (Egypt, Eritrea, Ethiopia, South Sudan, Central African Republic, Chad and Libya) does not alleviate that at all. While the Government of Sudan (GoS) has invested in modern technical infrastructure such as Geographical Information Systems and Remote Sensing technology, irregular border crossings are still frequent and largely uncontrolled. The economic deprivation of most of Sudan's border regions and the overall weakness of local security institutions, in combination with the traditional means of securing the Sudanese border and the diminishing influence of traditional leaders on border societies, have led local citizens to cooperate with smugglers and traffickers (Interview 1).

Sudan holds a very poor record in regional cooperation with its neighbours. Although the country has been run by a military-based authoritarian regime for decades, cross-border cooperation in the area of security and the control of human smuggling and trafficking has been limited. This weakness is one of several factors that have created an environment where smuggling and trafficking flourish. Regional tensions and ethnic and tribal conflicts, as well as economic disparities and social injustices, have led to thousands of young men and women crossing the border from Ethiopia to Sudan every month. Most of them use Khartoum as a stepping stone and proceed toward the Middle East or Europe (Ayalew, Adugna and Deshingkar, 2018). Sudan issues temporary visas to foreigners who intend to enter Sudanese territory and allows foreigners with a valid visa for a third country to travel through its ports. This is the legal stipulation that perfectly plays into the hands of the *samasra*: it allows them to continue their activities in trafficking, as the GoS – after issuing temporary visas – does minimal follow-up or monitoring of the further presence of such foreigners in the country and their whereabouts in case they overstay their visa. Likewise, there is no firm penalty for the 'guarantor' under whose name the girls were brought to Sudan (Interview 2).

The main route that links Ethiopia and Sudan begins in Addis Ababa and passes north-west through the towns of Bahir Dar, Gondar and the border town Metema, which is a conglomerate with its Sudanese twin city of Gaballat. From here, the way toward Khartoum passes through al-Qadarif and Wad Madani. From the beginning, *samasra* from Ethiopia and Sudan manage the smuggling and trafficking process, including the undocumented crossing of the border (Ayalew, Adugna and Deshingkar, 2018). The migrants who use this route mainly come from Ethiopia, Eritrea and Somalia; following this path has become their only alternative, especially once the Ethiopian government restricted direct internal travel toward the Middle East. Besides, most of them lack the necessary travel documents, so they pay the *samasra* to arrange their passing, either through formal channels by using fraudulent documents or through irregular border crossings.

Figures from the United Nations High Commissioner for Refugees (UNHCR) and other organisations illustrate the importance of this route as passage for irregular migrants, and likewise as a lucrative source of profit for smugglers and traffickers. This importance increased after the Ethiopian government banned labour migration to Saudi Arabia and the Gulf in 2013 in response to growing concerns about the human rights violations of Ethiopian migrant workers there (Tinti, 2017: 10–11). Until that time, more than 400 employment agencies had arranged Ethiopian migrants' regular travel options to the Gulf states, but after the ban more Ethiopian women sought to reach the labour markets in the Gulf through illegal employment agencies or directly through the *samasra*, who promised flights from Sudan to the Gulf. This way seemed preferable to many, despite its risks and potential for exploitation – even though possibilities for direct, safer and cheaper ways of obtaining plane tickets from Bole International Airport in Addis Ababa toward Dubai or other destinations in the Middle East were made available again in 2015 (Busza, Teferra, Omer and Zimmerman, 2017: 2).

The work of the *samasra* mainly depends on their interpersonal and managerial skills. In their illegal activities, they need to be skilled at communicating, persuading and resisting the various stress and risk factors. In particular, they need to keep their networks undetected, as they must not be discovered by the police or by potential competitors. To this end, they need to protect their reputation within their local communities, so that locals do not disclose their activities to the authorities. There is also strong competition among them, so that they sometimes even use their own money to avoid migration failures, in an effort to keep their good reputation and credentials inside their networks. *Samasra* need to please their leaders who control the trafficking from the place of origin to the destination; they have 'the ability to establish strong networks with hard-working, smart and trustworthy individual smugglers along the transit route' (Adunga, Deshingkar and Ayalew, 2019: 15).

Individual *samasra* along the route have their own local structure and personnel with specific jobs. They usually do not know the respective 'mastermind' (boss) behind the networks. Despite their different nationalities, they cooperate effectively to achieve their goals. Ethiopian *samasra* pass through villages and towns and convince young men and women to make the journey; the ones at the border (on both the Ethiopian and Sudanese sides) assist in crossing the border through informal methods, including bribing border guards and local representatives. They decide on the appropriate time, conditions and means of transportation. They continuously develop their methods to avoid being followed (ibid.: 5).

Without doubt, *samasra* are highly professional individuals who are fully aware of the existing gaps in the laws and treaties which protect trafficked people. They earn this awareness through years of working with corrupt security authorities, who protect them from any deterrent penalties – despite the fact that trafficking is recognised globally as criminal conduct and a series of international treaties have been adopted to stifle trafficking and bring the perpetrators to justice, the most prominent among them being the Palermo I Protocol. However, some governments still seem to understand trafficking as a crime in which the trafficked persons are regarded as the criminals (Gebreegziabher, 2013) – thus, the victims are treated like the perpetrators. The *samasra*, meanwhile, benefit from the weak presence of the security forces: in case they are arrested, they are often professional enough to obscure their deeds in a way that the authorities are unable (or unwilling) to prove their illegality. The fact that the women and girls are pressured to admit that they fully intended to emigrate and paid the cost of the journey often leads the authorities to dismiss the charges against the *samasra*.

That most women and girls have indeed formally consented to the 'service' of the *samasra* to facilitate their travels from Addis Ababa to Dubai and that this resulted from their very own desire to have the *samasra* help them quickly and easily find a better life make it difficult to prove that they were subjected to coercion. As 'Abdu',[1] an Ethiopian *samsar* working in Khartoum, stated:

> I have worked as a *samsar* for seven years, and recently I went to work to send girls to Dubai via Khartoum after my brother opened an office to bring girls to work in Dubai. We help those girls to make a better life for themselves and their families and we facilitate work opportunities there for an amount of money – about $1,000 – to cover the costs of their cross-border deportation and their stay in Khartoum until their entry visas for Dubai are issued. My mission is to secure housing and subsistence for girls, whose numbers reach about 70 to 100, and to reconcile their legal status to live in Khartoum until they can travel further. Their travel is done in small groups that do not exceed ten girls on the trip to avoid any suspicion. We are doing humanitarian work by helping those girls travel with less than the costs of formal immigration to Dubai from Addis directly. We do not ask for specific conditions for girls such as those required by official immigration: a sufficient level of education, language competence, age, etc. We bear a lot of pressure and costs to carry out this work. Sometimes we use our own money to deport girls so that our mission does not fail.
>
> (Interview 3; translated from Arabic by the author)

Abdu's statement shows the typical absence of awareness among *samasra* that smuggling and trafficking are illegal acts. Instead they see themselves as 'helpers' or 'service providers' who help girls from Ethiopia in the realisation of their dream of a better life in Dubai. However, their behaviour proves that they are fully aware that their deeds are illegal. Respective signs can be observed by the indirect and often hidden ways they transport girls to Khartoum, and by their eagerness to avoid any suspicions about large numbers of girls travelling through Khartoum Airport. During COVID-19, their system of 'work for food and shelter', as they call it, has become another indication of their ability to obscure their business and to hide it from the Sudanese state authorities, the Ethiopian embassy in Khartoum, certain non-governmental organisations (NGOs) and even the families who employ the girls. They all fail, and sometimes willingly refuse, to identify these actions as what they are: criminal deeds intended to exploit vulnerable women and girls. This means that unless the victims proactively contact the authorities and indicate that they are being exploited by the *samasra*, they will not receive any help from them.

8.3 Trafficked women and girls in Khartoum: some examples

Fadila is a 22-year-old woman who speaks Arabic with some fluency and a bit of English. She said that coming to Khartoum was not her first attempt: in the second half of 2019 she paid a *samsar* approximately ETB 17,000 (Ethiopian Birr; approx. $600) to take her to Beirut, where she stayed for six months, before deciding to return because of the tough nature of her work. She waited until she had saved up enough money to pay off her loans, and when she heard about the 'magical livelihood' in Dubai, she got excited to try anew, especially when she heard that the trip would be cheaper this time. As Fadila recounted during our interview her shock in finding herself in Khartoum instead of Dubai, she broke into tears. Now she is forced to work in a private household despite the lockdown for an indefinite period to come. She lost her phone during the 'death trip', as she described the route from Ethiopia to Khartoum; she also lost her money and her golden ring. She could not contact her family until she was able to find a job, when the *madame* she is now working for provided her with a telephone. She does not know anyone apart from the *madame* and the *samsar*, who occasionally calls and sometimes visits the girls working in his area.

Jiwar is a 19-year-old girl who finds speaking Arabic difficult, so she was accompanied during the interview by her cousin, who can speak Arabic and a bit of English. The two were obliged by the *samsar* to work together in the same household. She said that the work was not physically difficult, but they were prohibited from contacting anyone and of course they did not have phones. When she decided to leave Ethiopia and put her fate into the hands of the *samasra*, she had no idea about the poor conditions of the trip to Khartoum. Her brother-in-law, who works as a *samsar*, persuaded her to travel to Dubai, where she was promised a better livelihood and from where she could help her family back in Ethiopia. He loaned her the travelling expenses and promised her that no one would ever know about her decision. Now she finds herself working for only room and board; watching TV is her only leisure time activity. She feels that her residence is like a prison for her, as there is no possibility for her to go anywhere else.

The 25-year-old Zinnet is not in Khartoum for the first time. In 2011, a *samsar* had promised to transport her to Saudi Arabia, but she found herself working in Khartoum until 2015, when she was eventually informed that there was no way to travel onward. She decided to return to Ethiopia, but needed to work another year to save up enough money for her trip back to her home country. Back in Ethiopia, another *samsar* soon promised to help her reach Dubai, so her journey started anew. Now she finds herself for the first time working for free. Upset about the unbearable conditions at work, she tried to escape from her workplace and to continue her travel with the help of another *samsar*. When her first *samsar* heard from her *madame* about her plans, he calmly told her that he had no problem returning her passport to her, so long as she paid back the sums he had paid for her visa application; of course she did not have this amount and had to agree to return to work. The *samsar* refused to leave her with the *madame* whose house she fled, instead taking her with him and obliging her to serve him until she receives her visa – a very typical behaviour by many *samasra* (Adugna, Deshingkar and Ayalew, 2019: 10).

8.4 The 'pandemic paradox' in trafficking: effects of COVID-19 on processes, perpetrators and victims

The COVID-19 pandemic has dramatically worsened the circumstances for those in trafficking processes: the victims, naturally, but also in a way the perpetrators. Effective protection against coronavirus infection in trafficking situations is a challenging, if not impossible, task. Victims of trafficking have little access to personal protective equipment (PPE), can hardly decide to wear masks and are even less able to insist that others around them do, especially in situations of sexual exploitation. Women and children are more vulnerable than men in this regard. Physical distancing is generally difficult in such settings. Trafficked individuals usually live in neglected neighbourhoods and in very poor conditions. Physical space is limited, and hygienic standards are insufficient. In consequence, the rates of infection are usually very high. Sadly, exact numbers are non-existent because of the victims' lack of access to medical treatment and thus proper documentation (Todres and Diaz, 2020).

However, in a way the situation has also improved for at least some of the trafficked girls in Khartoum. When Sudan's Security and Defence Council declared a state of health emergency on 16 March 2020, the government closed all airports and land and sea border crossings. On 26 March 2020, the authorities announced a total lockdown in the country and stopped all intrastate transportation. Trafficked girls who had already reached Khartoum were unable to predict for how long and under what conditions they would now need to survive in this intermediate location. However, their insufficient living conditions in overcrowded places made the *samasra* look for ways to avoid any possible infection with the virus, since they feared additional costs for medical treatment, if not the death – and thus 'loss' – of one or more of the girls, which would likely also bring them into contact with the authorities. For those reasons, the *samasra* undertook some efforts to distribute girls into private houses for work.

At the same time, the *samasra* were keen to reduce the costs they had to pay for the food and accommodation for the girls. Typically, they pay SDG 5,000–7,000 per month for two-room houses in which they place at least thirty girls (fifteen girls residing in one room of approx. sixteen square metres). Lacking proper beds, the girls sleep on simple plastic quilts and they share a pit-latrine in a covered area for bathing and cooking in a separate corner; there is a water-cooled air conditioner, a fan and a lamp in each room. The house owners – typically older Ethiopian women who came to Khartoum decades ago and now benefit from the trafficking business – are responsible for their food, which is paid for by the *samasra*. In better, but also more expensive, houses with three-room flats, the *samsar* usually resides in one room and packs the other two with girls – albeit only eight in total, because the building owners usually do not allow more than that in the flat. While these houses offer more comfort, especially an individual bed for each girl, a local *samasra* helper and guard at a mosque, 'Zien Eldeen', admitted that these houses are less preferred by the *samasra* due to the higher costs (Interview 4).

Facing the outbreak of COVID-19, the *samasra* adopted a new system of distributing the girls for working in houses for food and shelter. This new system looked like a good solution for the *samasra*, as it helped them to get rid of potential additional costs. Also, for some of the girls, it meant a release from the overcrowded houses. However, it also strengthened a typical feature of trafficking, namely, obliging the victims to work under very hard conditions without payment or any protection from potential exploitation, in exchange for bearable living costs and the provision of core sustenance.

In summary, COVID-19 did not hinder the *samasra* in continuing their activities, but it obliged them to reduce their costs related to the girls' room and board. Despite the increased risk of infection, the lockdown improved their working conditions, not only because less public life meant more activities out of sight, but also because rich families were more eager to get their own 'Dubai girl' and keep them in their house as a private servant.

For the victims, little has changed in their overall exploitative situation, but one of the repercussions of the pandemic was that despite all the exploitation, their living conditions in the private households are still better than in their former *samasra* houses. The direct contact with Sudanese families during the lockdown may have also allowed them to improve their Arabic, which would certainly help in their eventual destination country in the Persian Gulf. There, for now, the COVID-19 pandemic has already worsened the situation of migrants tremendously (Alsharif and Malit, 2020: 10–13). In various Gulf Cooperation Council (GCC) countries, voices have become vocal that demand 'to take the COVID-19 crisis as an opportunity to permanently reduce the share of migrants in the overall population' (Woertz, 2020: 759). If that became reality, it would clearly dim the prospects also for female migrant workers in domestic workplaces.

8.5 Government responses: tackling trafficking effectively?

The profound regime changes in Ethiopia and Sudan in 2018 and 2019, respectively, have fostered hope for better policies to control trafficking as well. However, the faltering democratisation processes in both countries, the worsening economic crises and the resurgence of violent clashes in Ethiopia's northern province of Tigray allow nagging doubts that such expectations might turn true any time soon.

8.5.1 The Ethiopian government: ongoing failure in border control despite increased efforts

Until recently, the government of Ethiopia (GoE) did not pay adequate attention to human trafficking, despite Ethiopia being an important source country for young women who are subjected to forced labour and sexual exploitation in various destination countries around the globe. Busza et al., (2017: 2) estimated that 170,000–180,000 Ethiopian women depart each year towards the Middle East and the Gulf states, among whom 60–70% are estimated to be irregular migrants – thus, an estimated 100,000 women are potential prey for the *samasra* every year. These numbers illustrate the high incentives for local citizens to get involved in the lucrative trafficking business, either as an active contributor or at least as 'silent approvers'.

The Ethiopian penal code of 1957, which was in force until 2004, contained no provisions on human trafficking. The law failed to deal with the matter adequately, as it left out various issues associated with human trafficking. Over time, the seriousness of the problem forced the government to look for mechanisms to strengthen the legal framework. In June 2012, it acceded to the Palermo I Protocol and promulgated Proclamation 909/2015 on the prevention and suppression of trafficking in personal smuggling in August 2015. This proclamation criminalised sex and labour trafficking, prescribing penalties of fifteen to twenty-five years' imprisonment and fines of ETB 150,000–300,000 (approx. $3,800–7,600) for offences involving an adult male victim and twenty-five years to life imprisonment and fines of ETB 200,000–500,000 (approx. $5,000–12,600) for those involving an adult female or child victim.

This was followed by Proclamation 923/2016, when the GoE determined that regulating the employment of Ethiopian nationals in foreign states would greatly contribute to preventing the problem of trafficking and irregular migration by minimising the vulnerabilities of such individuals to human trafficking. It started to oversee recruitment agencies better, although weaknesses continued to exist, not least in the legal prosecution of ongoing non-compliance (U.S. State Department, 2020).

Those efforts by the GoE to combat human trafficking and to formulate a legal framework to criminalise trafficking and define penalties for perpetrators came after the humanitarian conditions of trafficking victims worsened, and the traffickers increasingly escaped legal control, which reduced the effectiveness of the existing laws and further weakened its already weak implementation. The GoE had banned outgoing labour migration to the Gulf in 2013, in response to growing incidents of human rights violations against labour migrants in Saudi Arabia and other Gulf countries. This led to a termination of the activities of more than 400 employment agencies which arranged travel for Ethiopian migrants. These agencies were waiting for a new law to be passed after bilateral labour agreements with the receiving countries, and in 2015 it was eventually announced. However, working with the new laws was not completely accepted by all agencies; only twenty were fully *bona fide*, while others became increasingly involved in irregular migration instead. In consequence, the options to look for irregular emigration paths widened even further (Tinti, 2017: 11). The north-western route via Sudan and towards Europe became especially popular; smugglers and traffickers diversified their migration facilitation and new actors joined the business. This confirmed the overall observation that the closure of legal paths of migration does not necessarily trigger a lasting reduction in absolute emigration numbers (Völkel, 2017: 87–8). Instead, stricter limits for legal migration and more complicated procedures through regular air or land routes have not stemmed clandestine migration, but have rather increased the costs and risks for those intending to leave, therefore increasing the number of migration facilitators, who can dynamically and creatively develop new routes and strategies to overcome the barriers.

The GoE intensified the border control regulations following increased media coverage of the suffering of Ethiopian migrants en route, backed by the EU and its overall policies of externalising border control (Ayalew, Adugna and Deshingkar, 2018).[2] In numerous initiatives, most notably the 'Khartoum Process' (Weber, 2018: 49–51), the EU has begun to persuade African governments, including the GoE, to introduce pre-emptive measures in order to deter their citizens from irregular emigration to Europe. In exchange, the EU extended various promises including development aid, trade facilitation, foreign investment and other advantages (Koch, Weber and Werenfels, 2018). The GoE has made great efforts in all areas to combat trafficking in persons, including criminalising the brokers and portraying migrants as victims. It established anti-human-trafficking task forces within its border control units in 2011, and set up checkpoints along the main migration routes (Ayalew, Adunga and Deshingkar, 2018). However, despite all these efforts the GoE has not yet fully met the minimum standards for eliminating trafficking, as analysed by the U.S. State Department (2020).

Controlling the borders is the main pillar of combating trafficking in persons in Ethiopia; however, a number of studies have indicated that there is a certain level of corruption and a lack of professionalism in the work of the security forces in border cities such as Metema (Bakewell et al., 2020: 24). This leads to the obstruction of the enforcement of laws and regulations set by the GoE to reduce smuggling and trafficking operations. Instead, corruption helps to boost the collective work of brokers and smugglers, who meet the new regulations with more changes that help keep them working and prevent them being tracked.

With his takeover in 2018, new Prime Minister Abiy Ahmed made some attempts to acknowledge the insufficient humanitarian situation in Ethiopia as a major source of human trafficking and smuggling, and he tried to bring the business of the *samasra* under better control. Despite his attempts, however, the current crisis in Tigray threatens the success of any political initiative: the recent outbreak of fights has already created huge numbers of new refugees arriving at the Ethiopia–Sudan border, expected to reach as many as 200,000 people, according to the UNHCR (Nebehey and Farge, 2020).

8.5.2 Sudan's government: the old regime is gone, but the uncertainties remain

Due to its geographic location between Sub-Saharan Africa and the Middle East – in particular along the Nile, a truly international waterway – Sudan has become a major transit country for irregular migrants heading toward Europe and the Persian Gulf. Widely perceived as a pariah regime, cooperation in migration was one of a few areas where former President Omar al-Bashir could show some willingness for cooperation, if often only on paper. The 'Khartoum Process', the EU's attempt to manage migration in East Africa better, has become the most visible sign of this (albeit still limited) cooperation (Reitano, 2016).

However, in response to notable European pressure, the GoS has taken several measures to combat trafficking and smuggling. At the international level, it acceded to the Palermo I Protocol in 2014, yet without any further steps toward ratification so far. Regionally, it initiated cooperation with neighbouring countries, not least in the framework of the Intergovernmental Authority on Development (IGAD) – the regional organisation at the Horn of Africa that Sudan co-founded in 1985 and which has been serving as a rare international channel for Sudan's diplomacy after its exclusion from the African Union in June 2019 – and the far-reaching sanctions imposed by the international community against the (former) regime of Omar al-Bashir (Atta-Asamoah and Mahmood, 2019: 12–13). Locally, the GoS has implemented some actions against smugglers and brokers in Khartoum, Kassala and those states that are most active in the trafficking process (Abdel Ati, 2017: 43–4).

The GoS created a National Committee for Combating Human Trafficking (NCCHT) in 2014, tasked with systematising reports from the authorities and developing solutions for the driving causes behind human trafficking. However, as in other countries such as Egypt (Völkel, 2020), it also served as a focal point for international donors such as the UNHCR or the EU Emergency Trust Fund for Africa (Weber, 2018: 53), which is meant to generate income for the regime under the umbrella of humanitarian purposes. During the al-Bashir regime, the NCCHT faced some obstacles affecting its performance: it lacked a budget and physical work space, there was no consistency among its members and its influence was thus very limited (Abdel Ati, 2017: 41–2).

Some analysts argue that the previous regime of Omar al-Bashir dealt with the Khartoum Process as a means of improving Sudan's position in European political negotiations, capitalising on the EU's desperate desire to curb illegal migration from Africa towards Europe (Völkel, 2020: 12). However, reports exist that much of the EU's support – equipment that is used for better border control – has also been used for the surveillance and suppression of ordinary citizens; not least, the Janjaweed – the militia that was accused of being the main traitor behind the genocidal cruelties in Sudan's deplored Darfur province in the 2000s (Peter and Strazzari, 2016: 1542–3) – has started to benefit from EU support as well after their eventual inclusion in the formal Sudanese armed forces (Yahya, 2020: 4). This all puts into question the EU's credibility as well, as it apparently turned a blind eye to the Janjaweed's war crimes and the Sudanese authorities' questionable record overall. However, the Khartoum Process could lead to a radical change in the GoS's methods to curb illegal migration, especially if a more democratic regime eventually takes power in Sudan. Unless this happens, the difference of expectations between the two sides with regard to migration cooperation will lead to misunderstanding and discontent (Weber, 2018), which will hinder its actual implementation. The current crisis in Tigray could become a serious challenge for Sudan's current regime 'in the making', should a huge number of refugees indeed arrive in the border state of al-Qadarif, straining Sudan's budget and occupying additional security and administrative personnel amidst the ongoing COVID-19 pandemic and an already extremely difficult economic crisis.

Irrespective of external conditions, the establishment of the civilian-led transitional government in September 2019 hampered Sudan's ability to maintain consistent anti-trafficking efforts due to high turnover rates within the state's administration. Besides organisational deficits, officials are insufficiently trained on the identification, investigation and prosecution of trafficking crimes. The current regime has expressed its keenness to improve current standards, and approved in March 2020 the NCCHT's 2020–2 National Action Plan. Now concrete actions need to follow. However, the unstable conditions in politics and the economy, plus the socioeconomic hardships triggered by the COVID-19 pandemic, render any quick successes unrealistic.

8.6 Conclusion

This chapter analysed the impact of COVID-19 on trafficked women and girls during their intermediate stay in Khartoum along their intended journey from Ethiopia towards the Gulf countries, especially Dubai. Given the lucrative nature of their business, the *samasra* have proven successful in further developing their methods of bringing women and girls from Ethiopia to Sudan despite the governmental methods of trying to combat their deeds. They have also found ways to adapt to the coronavirus crisis, such as primarily extending their 'work for food and shelter' system. Thus, like in a game of cat-and-mouse, the more the governments of Ethiopia and Sudan develop their legal methods to combat human trafficking, the more methods and tricks the *samasra* devise to ensure the continuation of their work.

COVID-19 may affect the performance of some authorities responsible for combating human trafficking, leading to reduced screening and registering of irregular migrants, not to mention caring about them. There are, however, no visible signs yet that the networks of the *samasra* will be noticeably affected. In contrast, as long as the governments of Sudan and Ethiopia barely cooperate and the economic and security situation in the Horn of Africa remains as fragile as it has been the last few years, the *samasra* will continue to enjoy perfect conditions for their illegal, but thriving, business. The trafficked women in Khartoum are meanwhile trapped and on the horns of a dilemma, being transferred from the *samasra* to Sudanese families where they are in a safer place than before but work for free indefinitely. Only a lasting improvement in the economic and overall security situation – which would palpably enhance the social reality for Ethiopians and the Sudanese – plus the further opening of legal migration channels could reduce the exploitative risks connected to trafficking in the Horn of Africa.

Notes

1 All names of interview partners mentioned in this chapter have been changed for the purpose of anonymisation.
2 However, it should be acknowledged that the EU has suspended migration cooperation with Sudan in 2019, in response to the 'Sudan uprisings' in that year, suspecting that EU money could be used to suppress the protesters (Wills, 2019).

References

Abdel Ati, Hassan A. (2017): *Human smuggling and trafficking in Eastern Sudan*. Bergen: Christian Michelsen Institute. www.cmi.no/publications/file/6325-human-smuggling-and-trafficking-in-eastern-sudan.pdf.

Adugna, Fekadu / Deshingkar, Priya / Ayalew, Tekalign (2019): *Brokers, migrants and the state: Berri Kefach 'door openers' in Ethiopian clandestine migration to South Africa*. Falmer, Brighton: University of Sussex. http://sro.sussex.ac.uk/id/eprint/87061/1/WP56_Adugna_2019_Brokers%20migrants%20and%20the%20state.pdf.

Alsharif, Fahad L. al-Ghalib / Malit, Froilan T. Jr. (2020): *Migration and the COVID-19 pandemic in the Gulf: a study of foreign expatriate worker communities' coping attitudes, practices, and future prospects in Dubai and Jeddah*. Amman: Konrad Adenauer Stiftung. www.kas.de/documents/286298/8668222/Policy+Report+No+15+Migration+and+The+COVID-19+Pandemic+in+the+Gulf.pdf/87dd88bd-ed47-41c7-be23-48c5a5eb8d7c?version=1.0&t=1603448109241.

Atta-Asamoah, Andrews / Mahmood, Omar S. (2019): *Sudan after Bashir: regional opportunities and challenges*. Addis Ababa: Institute for Security Studies. https://issafrica.s3.amazonaws.com/site/uploads/ear-23.pdf.

Ayalew, Tekalign / Adugna, Fekadu / Deshingkar, Priya (2018): Social embeddedness of human smuggling in East Africa: brokering Ethiopian migration to Sudan. *African Human Mobility Review*, 4(3): pp. 1333–58. http://sro.sussex.ac.uk/id/eprint/83454/3/83454.pdf.

Bakewell, Oliver / Gezahegne, Kiya / Ali, Kelklachew / Sturridge, Caitlin (2020): *Migration and migration management on the Ethiopia–Sudan border: research from Metema*. London: EU Trust Fund for Africa (Horn of Africa Window) Research and Evidence Facility. https://blogs.soas.ac.uk/ref-hornresearch/files/2020/03/Migration-Management-Metema-final-Mar-2020.pdf.

Busza, Joanna / Teferra, Sehin / Omer, Serawit / Zimmerman, Cathy (2017): Learning from returnee Ethiopian migrant domestic workers: a qualitative assessment to reduce the risk of human trafficking. *Globalization and Health*, 13(71): pp. 1–9. https://doi.org/10.1186/s12992-017-0293-x.

Gebreegziabher, Shewit (2013): *The situations of trafficking women from Ethiopia to Sudan: the case of Metema route* (master thesis). Addis Ababa: Addis Ababa University.

Koch, Anne / Weber, Annette / Werenfels, Isabelle (2018): *Profiteers of migration? Authoritarian states in Africa and European migration management*. Berlin: Stiftung Wissenschaft und Politik. www.swp-berlin.org/en/publication/profiteers-of-migration.

Nebehey, Stephanie / Farge, Emma (2020): U.N. plans for 200,000 Ethiopian refugees in Sudan. *Reuters*, 20 November. www.reuters.com/article/us-ethiopia-conflict-un/u-n-plans-for-200000-ethiopian-refugees-in-sudan-idUSKBN28010Q.

Peter, Mateja / Strazzari, Francesco (2016): Securitisation of research: fieldwork under new restrictions in Darfur and Mali. *Third World Quarterly*, 38(7): pp. 1531–50. https://doi.org/10.1080/01436597.2016.1256766.

Reitano, Tuesday (2016): *The Khartoum process: a sustainable response to human smuggling and trafficking?* Pretoria: Institute for Security Studies. https://issafrica.s3.amazonaws.com/site/uploads/policybrief93.pdf.

Tinti, Peter (2017) *Ethiopia country statement: addressing migrant smuggling and human trafficking in East Africa*. Paris: Expertise France. www.expertisefrance.fr/documents/20182/234347/AMMi+-+Country+Report+-+Ethiopia+copie.pdf/b9121722-aa7e-47e0-b359-065673391226.

Todres, Jonathan / Diaz, Angela (2020): COVID-19 and human trafficking – the amplified impact on vulnerable populations. *JAMA Pediatrics*, online first, https://jamanetwork.com/journals/jamapediatrics/fullarticle/2770536.

U.S. State Department (2020): *2020 Trafficking in Persons report: Ethiopia*. Washington: U.S. State Department. www.state.gov/reports/2020-trafficking-in-persons-report/ethiopia.

Völkel, Jan Claudius (2017): When interior ministers play diplomat: fatal ambiguities in Europe's securitised migration policy. In: Jünemann, Annette / Fromm, Nicolas / Scherer, Nikolas (eds.): *Fortress Europe? Challenges and failures of migration and asylum policies*. Wiesbaden: Springer, pp. 83–103. https://doi.org/10.1007/978-3-658-17011-0.

Völkel, Jan Claudius (2020): Fanning fears, winning praise: Egypt's smart play on Europe's apprehension of more undocumented immigration. *Mediterranean Politics*, online first. https://doi.org/10.1080/13629395.2020.1758450.

Weber, Annette (2018): Migration hub Sudan/Eritrea: disappointed expectations – conflicting interests. In: Koch, Anne / Weber, Annette / Werenfels, Isabelle (2018): *Profiteers of migration? Authoritarian states in Africa and European migration management*. Berlin: Stiftung Wissenschaft und Politik, pp. 44–55. www.swp-berlin.org/en/publication/profiteers-of-migration.

Wills, Tom (2019): EU suspends migration control projects in Sudan amid repression fears. *Deutsche Welle*, 22 July. https://p.dw.com/p/3MXbc.

Woertz, Eckart (2020): Wither the self-sufficiency illusion? Food security in Arab Gulf states and the impact of COVID-19. *Food Security*, 12: pp. 757–60. https://doi.org/10.1007/s12571-020-01081-4.

Yahya, Abdelmageed M. (2020): *Irregular migration or human trafficking? The realities of cross-border population mobility in Western Sudan*. Bergen: Christian Michelsen Institute, www.cmi.no/publications/file/7174-irregular-migration-or-human-trafficking.pdf.

List of interviews

1. Senior Supervisor, Higher Academy for Strategic and Security Studies, Khartoum, 5 October 2020.
2. Academic Supervisor, Police High Academy, Khartoum, 11 November 2020.
3. 'Abdu', Ethiopian *samsar*, Khartoum, 18 September 2020.
4. 'Zien Eldeen', Sudanese *samasra* helper, Khartoum, 25 December 2020.
5.–14. Ten trafficked Ethiopian women and girls in different households, Khartoum, 17 March–4 July 2020.

9 A paradoxical management of COVID-19 in Lebanon
Challenges and lessons learnt

Michèle Kosremelli Asmar and Joumana Stephan Yeretzian

9.1 Introduction

In its early days, the COVID-19 pandemic in Lebanon seemed to follow a similar trajectory to that of other countries in the Eastern Mediterranean region, with a slow transmission rate and a relatively low death rate (Al-Mandhari et al., 2020). As social measures were relaxed and the country came out of the imposed lockdown in July 2020, disease transmission accelerated. However, in contrast to its neighbouring countries, Lebanon – a small country with an estimated population of 6.8 million, an area of 10,452 km² and a population density of 653 inhabitants per square kilometre – has seen a traditional dominance of the private healthcare sector. Yet, paradoxically, the country's response to the COVID-19 pandemic was initiated, guided and controlled by the public sector, wherein lies the interest of delving into the Lebanese experience with COVID-19, especially in view of the existing contextual, health and governance characteristics.

Whereas the management of the COVID-19 pandemic has proved to be challenging for all nations worldwide, the task was even more daunting for Lebanon, a country already burdened by multiple economic, social, humanitarian and political difficulties. Consequently, dealing with COVID-19 has been a very complex endeavour in Lebanon which has highlighted the strengths and weaknesses of the Lebanese healthcare system and the preparedness, or lack thereof, of the government to face pandemics and other crises of a similar nature. The analysis of the Lebanese situation also emphasises the interdependence of context, health and governance in the management of a pandemic and stresses the need to apply holistic solutions that do not limit the pandemic to a health crisis but rather extend it to 'an economic crisis, a humanitarian crisis, a security crisis and a human rights crisis' (United Nations, 2020: 1), all rolled into one.

This chapter is based on a thorough review of published scientific and newspaper articles and reports and documentation found on official websites, and it benefits from the authors' own experiences in Lebanon's public healthcare sector. It starts with a discussion of the context of public health in Lebanon

DOI: 10.4324/9781003240044-12

prior to the COVID-19 pandemic. The chapter then goes on to describe the beginning of the pandemic and to analyse the steps taken by the government and the Ministry of Public Health (MoPH) to manage and control its spread. The chapter highlights the challenges faced in the Lebanese context and ends with the lessons learnt and some recommendations for moving forward.

9.2 Public health in the era dominated by the private sector

The civil war years (1975–89) saw the collapse of the public sector and the subsequent dominance of the private sector, which took control of the healthcare system in Lebanon (IGSPS, 2012). This led to an increase in both private hospitals offering secondary and tertiary care services and private dispensaries, mostly run by non-governmental or religious organisations and ensuring primary healthcare (PHC) services. The postwar period (1990s) witnessed a gradual renewal of control of the MoPH over the regulatory functions, thus balancing private and public healthcare facilities. The reform campaign conducted by the MoPH over the past three decades succeeded in replacing the laissez-faire and fragmented healthcare system with a collaborative governance strategy whose aim was to elaborate a national health policy, promote universal health coverage (UHC) and enforce emergency preparedness and health security (van Lerberghe, Mechbal and Kronfol, 2018).

Today, Lebanon's public healthcare system combines a centralised and decentralised administration under the responsibility of the MoPH. The system is a mixture of public and private components where the regulatory and financing functions are handled by the public sector, whilst service delivery functions are predominantly covered by the private sector. The role of the MoPH lies primarily in the governance of the system, mainly overseeing and steering its functioning and sharing evidence-based information. Lebanon has a relatively large and well-trained health workforce with a surplus of pharmacists and physicians, 70% of whom are specialists (IGSPS, 2012: 104). Healthcare is generally accessible, if expensive, although more than half of the population is not covered by health insurance. The MoPH provides a social safety net by covering around 54% of the uninsured population for hospitalisation and expensive treatments.

The main focus of the public healthcare system in Lebanon is on curative hospital care, with 166 hospitals, the majority of which are private (82%) and located in Beirut and Mount Lebanon. In fact, in contrast to the unspecified amount of spending on PHC, approximately 64% of the MoPH budget goes towards subsidising hospitalisations. The ratio of hospital beds per 1,000 population is estimated to be 3.5; approximately 85% of the beds are in private facilities. In general, hospitals offer secondary care with some selected tertiary care services. Tertiary care hospitals are rare, mostly limited to the six private university hospitals. Currently, intermediate care is provided through private home care companies; rehabilitative care relies solely on private physiotherapy centres and long-term rehabilitation institutions; and long-term care, mostly for the elderly, is covered in long-stay hospitals or nursing home facilities.

Private ambulatory care is well developed and is the main pillar of outpatient service provision, with a wide range of private clinics, pharmacies, diagnostic laboratories and other healthcare facilities managed by independent healthcare professionals. More recently, a primary healthcare network consisting of 229 primary healthcare centres (PHCC) was established by the MoPH through contracting services with multi-owners, mostly private-sector non-governmental organisations (NGOs), with the aim of reaching UHC. In addition, a comprehensive National Mental Health Programme was implemented in all PHCCs. The relation between PHC, secondary care and tertiary care is not well defined because of the absence of a national regulatory framework for the referral system.

At the onset of the COVID-19 pandemic, in addition to the weaknesses and fragmentations inherent in the system, the healthcare system in Lebanon faced several challenges on different levels. First and foremost was the high number of refugees coming into the country from Syria, which increased Lebanon's population by around 30% as the government estimates that there are around 1.5 million Syrian refugees in the country (914,848 registered with UNHCR). Besides, more than 200,000 Palestinians and an additional 17,000 refugees from Iraq, Sudan and other countries are currently in Lebanon (UNHCR, 2020). In global comparison, Lebanon currently hosts most refugees per capita; this has resulted in undue pressure on the infrastructure, service delivery, public finances and environment of the country. For example, although Lebanon is rich in rivers and water sources in comparison to neighbouring countries such as Jordan, Palestine/Israel and Syria, the influx of refugees in the country has reduced the amount of available renewable water to around 700 m^3 per person, a level that is below the threshold of water poverty (Vidal, 2016).

In fact, in the past years, Lebanon has had its share of environmental difficulties, ranging from problems with potable water supply to air pollution, the waste crisis and multiple periods of drought. Data from 2016 showed that only 36% of households reported access to potable water in that year (WHO and UNICEF, 2016). Moreover, the level of air pollution is high: a study from 2015 attested that the annual average concentration of pollutant markers $PM_{2.5}$ and PM_{10} in Beirut exceeded the limits of the World Health Organization (WHO) by 150% and 200%, respectively (Nakhlé et al., 2015). Other environmental problems in Lebanon include the waste crisis that triggered major protests in 2016 but remains unresolved (HRW, 2017) as well as the multiple drought periods, which are linked to climate change and are considered a health threat due to the destruction of agricultural resources and the onset of wild fires in vegetative regions (Verner et al., 2018).

Traditionally classified by the World Bank as an 'upper-middle-income country', Lebanon has recently been shifted to a fragile and conflict-affected country in view of the current economic crisis and long-term structural weaknesses in the system, including a weak infrastructure, poor service delivery, institutionalised corruption and bureaucratic over-regulation (World Bank, 2020). The severe economic, financial and social conditions were further highlighted by the 17 October 2019 popular uprising, which brought forth the reality of increased poverty levels and higher unemployment rates. The situation was further compounded by the COVID-19 pandemic and the explosion in Beirut's sea port on 4 August 2020 (WHO, 2020). The economic situation has led to problems with the retention of healthcare personnel, especially nurses, who were already in short supply, as well as a limited capacity for ensuring vital equipment and medication in the face of the collapse of the economy, the devaluation of the Lebanese pound (LL), bank constraints on the US dollar and unpaid government dues (DeJong, 2020). This has also engendered shortages in essential goods given Lebanon's history of heavy reliance on foreign supply chains and poor local manufacturing capacities (Khoury, Azar and Hitti, 2020).

9.3 COVID-19: a trigger for leadership of the health public sector

Upon the declaration of the first case of COVID-19 on 21 February 2020, the Lebanese government was quick to react (DeJong, 2020). It immediately proceeded to implement strict measures, in accordance with the recommendations of the US Centers for Disease Control and the WHO, which allowed it to contain the spread of the virus successfully in its early days.

The first sector to react was the educational sector, whereby the minister of higher education promptly ordered the closure of all schools and universities on 29 February 2020 (DeJong, 2020; see also Chapter 10 by El Hage and Yehya in this volume). The rest of the public institutions rapidly followed suit, as two weeks later, on 15 March 2020, the government declared a state of medical emergency and on 18 March 2020 Lebanon went into a full lockdown, with the airport, sea ports and all land borders being closed (Khoury, Azar and Hitti, 2020; Bizri et al., 2021; see also Chapter 3 by AbiGhanem in this volume). In addition, a daily nationwide curfew was put in place from 7 p.m. through 6 a.m.; during the day only food and health facilities were allowed to open. In parallel, testing, contact tracing, physical distancing, isolation and quarantine for suspected and confirmed cases were implemented. With limited resources, the national testing strategy targeted Lebanese repatriates and high-risk groups, such as refugees and migrant workers.

The MoPH established a call centre for the triage, referral and follow-up of patients and initiated testing, contact tracing and isolation of positive cases. Moreover, large media campaigns were developed to raise awareness of public health and preventive measures. A hotline was set up for self-reporting symptoms of suspected COVID-19 and for instructions on testing and home isolation measures.

Although the airport was closed to tourist activity, the Lebanese government had to repatriate citizens who were caught outside the country at the time of the lockdown and students who did not have the means to support themselves in these trying times (Khoury, Azar and Hitti, 2020). To mitigate the risks of infection, all incoming passengers were tested and quarantined pending the results of their polymerase chain reaction (PCR) tests. All positive cases were isolated.

These measures allowed Lebanon to contain the spread of the disease successfully in the first three months: there was a total of 1,220 cases and 27 deaths by 31 May 2020. The cases were concentrated in Beirut and Mount Lebanon, but there were fewer than expected and the hospitals were not overburdened (DeJong, 2020). In fact, the proportion of COVID-19 cases in Lebanon was 179 per 1 million population, with a mortality rate of 4 per 1 million, considerably lower than the global average infection and mortality rates of 989 per 1 million and 54.8 per 1 million, respectively (Bizri et al., 2021). These low rates could be explained by the fact that most reported cases were asymptomatic or mild (95%) and were concentrated in the 20–59-year age group (84%). The fact that the age distribution of the disease was different from that in more afflicted countries might also explain the lower mortality rate witnessed in the Lebanese population. In addition, 80% of the cases at the time were among Lebanese repatriates or due to community clusters and contact with an infected person. Moreover, all patients who tested positive, irrespective of the disease severity, were advised to be admitted to hospital by the MoPH. However, the lack of widespread testing at the time meant that most of the asymptomatic or unreported cases went undetected (DeJong, 2020).

The containment of the pandemic in Lebanon can be explained by the government's rapid response. One day after the confirmation of the first case, Prime Minister Hassan Diab established a National Committee for COVID-19 whose task was to oversee the national preparedness and response to the COVID-19 pandemic (Khoury, Azar and Hitti, 2020). At the same time, the MoPH mobilised the National Committee for Communicable Diseases to focus on and monitor the evolution and progress of the pandemic. This committee, which is chaired by the Director General of the MoPH, acts as a scientific advisory board to the minister of public health. In addition to representatives from the MoPH and the WHO, it includes scientific experts in infectious diseases, virology, laboratory medicine and public health.

At the start of the pandemic, patients were managed at the Rafik Hariri University Hospital (RHUH), a national reference hospital and laboratory. The RHUH lab was the only lab running reverse transcriptase-PCR (RT-PCR) tests for the diagnosis of COVID-19 until April 2020. The hospital contained 19 intensive care unit (ICU) beds, four isolation units with negative pressure, a molecular laboratory and a fully trained nursing and medical team. Since this was the only hospital actively engaged in the management of COVID-19 cases, all international and national resources were diverted towards supporting the RHUH COVID-19-designated activities (Khoury, Azar and Hitti, 2020; Bizri et al., 2021). In addition, the MoPH secured the support of four private university hospitals for case management and RT-PCR testing whilst additional public hospitals across Lebanon were prepared to receive COVID-19 cases in the event of a potential surge (Khoury, Azar and Hitti, 2020). The MoPH also established a list of private labs that were allowed to conduct RT-PCR testing on the condition that they report their results to the ministry through the automated reporting mechanisms which were set up to keep track of COVID-19 cases. However, although testing was available for free at RHUH, the private facilities charged a fee of 150,000 LL ($100 according to the official exchange rate; DeJong, 2020).

Several factors within the Lebanese context offered some hope that the country would continue to beat the odds in this pandemic (DeJong, 2020; Diwan and Abi-Rached, 2020; Bizri et al., 2021). These included the rapid and successful governmental response and the compliance of the population – in the beginning – with calls for social distancing and remaining at home. Moreover, the younger age of the Lebanese population, with around one-quarter (24.6%) of the population being below the age of 15 years and only 10% being over the age of 65 years, and the accessibility of healthcare – especially in urban areas, where almost 89% of the Lebanese population lives – and the availability of a relatively large and well-trained workforce probably played a positive role in mitigating the gravity of the crisis. Surprisingly, the paucity of public spaces and the scarcity of public transportation in the country were also seen as advantages in this case.

However, at the end of the lockdown and with the re-opening of the airport on 1 July 2020, the numbers rapidly multiplied to 4,555 cases and 61 deaths by the end of July. Due to the prevailing economic situation, the government was unable to provide stimulus packages to help the employed, the freelancers and the small business owners who were forced to close in order to comply with the national lockdown and curfew (Bizri et al., 2021). By the same token, the government was unable to offer the necessary support to equip hospitals with much-needed resources to fight the disease. In addition, decreasing trust in the government, perceived lack of transparency and the proliferation of messages on social media increased the people's psychological burden. This along with the inconsistent behaviour of politicians and the contradictory discourse of self-proclaimed experts potentially decreased the society's compliance with governmental and health recommendations. The situation was further exacerbated by the devastating effects of the 4 August 2020 sea port explosion in Beirut which resulted in more than 200 casualties, 6,500 injuries and around 300,000 displaced residents. Moreover, at least 15 medical facilities, including three major hospitals (two of which had COVID-19 units and provided testing) faced partial or heavy structural damage, resulting in the loss of 500 hospital beds (OCHA Lebanon, 2020; Orient-Le-Jour, 2020). By the end of August, the cumulative number of COVID-19 cases had increased to 17,308 with 167 deaths (WHO Brief, 31 August 2020) and an observed maximum of 689 new cases and seven deaths within a 24-hour period on 27 August (WHO Brief, 27 August 2020).

Nine months after the confirmation of the first case of COVID-19, the outbreak in Lebanon appears to be spiralling out of control (Lewis, 2020). With community transmissions well confirmed and the private sector reluctant to engage, the government is struggling to mitigate the spread of the disease while managing the overburdened healthcare sector and weighing the financial concerns of the citizens. On 30 November 2020, after a two-week lockdown, the country reported 1,000 cases (99% among residents) and fourteen deaths within a 24-hour period (WHO Brief, 1 December 2020). The cumulative number of cases amounted to 127,903, including 1,741 infected healthcare workers and 1,018 deaths. The proportion of cases per 1 million population rose to 18,738 with an average mortality of 149 per 1 million population. Slightly more than half of the cases were among men (54%); two-thirds were mild (66.5%) and 0.6% critical. The overall fatality rate was 0.8%, with an average local positive test rate over the past fourteen days of 15.3% (or 14.1% including testing at points of entry). A total of 905 regular beds and 456 ICU beds were designated for COVID-19 with occupancy rates of 72% and 78%, respectively (WHO Brief, 1 December 2020).

As a result, the government struggled between health and economy as the population attempted to adapt and introduce the necessary behavioural changes in lifestyle. Access to healthcare and availability of medication were threatened as the numbers of infected individuals rose, the few engaged hospitals became saturated and healthcare personnel became overburdened (Lewis, 2020). The various lockdowns, border closures and disruptions in transportation services threatened the financial viability of the population and the availability of medical supplies and other necessities, such as food and water. The prevailing economic and political situation in the country did not help matters and, as usual, the situation was worse for the more vulnerable elements of the population, highlighting the need for equity and a focus on gender and social inequalities (DeJong, 2020).

9.4 COVID-19 management: successes and pitfalls

The positive aspect of the Lebanese response lies primarily in the fact that it was led by the public sector, even though it is well recognised that the private sector is the actual backbone of the Lebanese healthcare system. Despite Lebanon's record of public mismanagement, the government's response to this crisis was rapid and efficient and was one of the reasons behind the initial control of the spread of the disease (Diwan and Abi-Rached, 2020). The containment measures implemented in Lebanon aligned with WHO recommendations and were similar to those implemented in other countries (Ministry of Public Health, 2020). A three-month action plan was developed and shared with all stakeholders to contain the pandemic. This action plan included several measures such as closing the borders, schools and nurseries, universities, restaurants and shopping centres and instituting curfews and an alternating traffic system (Diwan and Abi-Rached, 2020). Apart from that were the health initiatives that included thorough contact tracing of early COVID-19 cases and centralised management of hospital quarantining (Khalife, 2020). Moreover, the population was quick to react and adjust its behaviour to comply with the COVID-19 guidelines. Staying at home, avoiding crowded areas, reducing mass gatherings and applying social distancing criteria further contributed to slowing the progression of the virus and reducing contact and infection rates (Kharoubi and Saleh, 2020).

In addition, the pandemic afforded an opportunity to test the surveillance system that had been put in place by the MoPH over the past decade. The system was found to perform well, thus justifying the efforts and expenses of developing it. The MoPH's strategy to build up epidemiological surveillance in the country and enhance its response capacity has paid off and has allowed a highly skilled and capable team to be developed, which was vital in the detection and management of the COVID-19 pandemic in Lebanon. It also played an essential role in screening for and following up positive cases.

Moreover, at the beginning of the pandemic, the government appeared to be successful in organising the response (UN-Habitat, 2020: 9). The development of a national action plan, establishment of a national committee and engagement of expert committees already in place all facilitated the management and coordination of the pandemic. The aim was to provide a country-wide response through coordination, decentralisation and empowerment of health district offices, civil defence and local authorities. It was encouraging to see the engagement and collaboration of various sectors, especially those concerned with health, education and industry. The dedication of the MoPH staff and the mobilisation of first responder health workers and civil society groups helped in addressing major deficiencies or gaps in the system (DeJong, 2020). For example, the Lebanese Red Cross was actively involved in transporting suspected COVID-19 patients to hospitals. Initiatives from the private sector (universities, hospitals, NGOs, industry and concerned citizens) and the public sector (municipalities, ministries, universities, hospitals, etc.) resulted in the organisation of flu and mobile clinics, and the provision of personal protective equipment (PPE) and respirators (UNICEF, 2020: 17). Educational webinars and media campaigns helped raise awareness and spread information among the population.

In addition, a national strategic communication campaign was launched four days after the first case of COVID-19 was detected. The main strategy focused on using media – mainly television and radio – with the support of health professionals, to share important information with the general public.

Finally, the use of technology in fighting the pandemic was another breakthrough. The implementation of e-health, which was in its infancy at the start of the pandemic, was expanded during the crisis with the development of several applications and digital platforms to help track cases and disseminate information. Examples include the symptom tracker and the

COVID-19 dashboard, which were applications developed by the private sector for the MoPH. It is also noteworthy that healthcare workers made use of the WhatsApp platform to share information and knowledge quickly with each other.

Even though there is no doubt that the initial management of the pandemic was successful, the situation rapidly deteriorated after the end of the lockdown, particularly following the 4 August 2020 sea port explosion. As the pressure increased on all sides, the responses started to become more reactive than strategic and priorities shifted. Even though plans, measures, resources and tools were developed and implemented by the Lebanese government in its response to COVID-19, the major drawback was the continued absence of a comprehensive national strategy (Abi-Rached et al., 2020). This resulted in incoherent, non-contextualised decisions and actions, very often copied from other countries. The zoning strategy, for example, which could have been very effective, had a troubled rollout and consequently did not yield the expected results.

In this context, non-health constraints (economic, social, political, etc.) took precedence, impeding the containment of the virus and the efficiency of its management and putting the healthcare system under undue pressure. Moreover, it had to deal with pressures from economic, professional and industrial bodies and with lockdown fatigue in the population. The government was urged to take more lenient measures to allow the economy to pick up, and decisions consequently became more politically orientated and the government was put into a situation where it tried to please all political parties, mainly the more powerful ones.

From a public health perspective, it is clear that the COVID-19 response was not holistic. Partitioning between different healthcare fields (care, prevention, psychosocial, etc.) was a main flaw in the response; the focus was on the medical perspective, leaving little room for prevention or promotion. In fact, increasing the capacities of the hospital sector was the main concern of the government. However, in the midst of a crisis, focusing on the medical aspect along with repeated confinements is clearly not the most economical and cost-efficient strategy (Rozier, 2020).

As the crisis evolved, the decision-making process started to suffer because of the multiplicity of decision-making committees and the lack of coordination between them. In addition, there was a lack of evidence-based decisions even though daily briefs on case numbers, deaths, tests, etc. were reported from various agencies, namely, the MoPH, the WHO and the Disaster Risk Management Unit. The authorities quickly relaxed the pressure by focusing on the 'civility' of the population and thus did not persevere in the 'three T' strategy (tracing, testing and treating). They opted for a 'stop and go' strategy which alternated between periods of high restriction and relaxation. The alternative would have been a more comprehensive strategy, built on the confidence and buy-in of its people. Unfortunately, these are two major elements where the government response greatly failed (Rozier, 2020).

The lack of coordination between the various parties concerned also led to a duplication of efforts, with a concentration on certain issues while others remained unaddressed. Whereas the various committees and organisations were concerned with implementing the lockdown and establishing the rules and exemptions, there was little coordination for economic support, equipping hospitals, training human resources or setting up isolation facilities.

The communication strategy was also poor due to the absence of an official speaker and a formal communication mechanism (Lewis, 2020). Information and messages were shared by several experts, ministers and officials based on their own perception and interpretation of the situation. The same case prevailed with the media (Bizri et al., 2021). Therefore, instead of empowering the people with adequate information to make enlightened decisions, this left the population distrustful of the government's actions.

Moreover, as mentioned earlier, a pandemic is not only a health crisis (Bizri et al., 2021). It also includes other aspects that need addressing. Here the Lebanese government failed to implement any social or economic measures, such as enhancing production and business, encouraging agriculture, restructuring bank loans, freezing debt, reducing or exempting loan interest payments or alleviating the inequality in access to care for the most vulnerable. In essence, these vulnerable groups were left behind.

Finally, examples from other countries have shown that a successful strategy is also based on promptly discovering and strictly dealing with violations regarding COVID-19 prevention. Lebanon, because of political clientelism, economic pressures, disrupted social environment and a lack of human resources, was unable to control and apply such measures adequately.

The COVID-19 pandemic management in Lebanon had, as in almost all countries, positive and negative aspects. On the one hand, it has shed light on the complexity of the crisis, whilst on the other hand it has opened opportunities for meaningful changes through reforms. Historically, crises have always been double-sided and have always provided society with prospects for advancement. In the Lebanese case, the government missed several opportunities to improve the system. These included developing a recognised leadership and governance, building trust between the population and the government, improving health communication and promoting transparency and access to data. The government should have also invested in developing civic social responsibility among the population, promoting collaboration between all stakeholders and enhancing a collective perspective while increasing equity and access to care for vulnerable groups and establishing a 'bottom-up' approach leading to an alliance between community and government. Finally, they failed to recognise the importance of improving the social determinants of health and building human resources through the recruitment and training of personnel.

9.5 COVID-19 management and the impact of context, health and governance

Lebanon faced challenges due to the complex context and multiple crises that have been ongoing for the past few years. These had a major impact on the management of the pandemic and can be categorised in terms of context, health and governance, as summarised in Figure 9.1.

The prevailing problems in the Lebanese context only increased with the measures undertaken to limit the spread of the coronavirus. The various lockdowns and confinement strategies exacerbated the already precarious economic situation in the country and augmented social problems (Diwan and Abi-Rached, 2020). Bank restrictions were heightened; unemployment levels soared, as several businesses either closed or had to let people go; poverty levels rose as employees saw their salaries reduced or go unpaid, a result of people working alternate days or from home; small business owners lost business and prices escalated with the Lebanese pound losing its buying power on the unofficial market. The context was further complicated by the challenges of providing essential goods to displaced and other vulnerable populations and the difficulty of enforcing social distancing measures in camps and overcrowded urban beltways (UN-Habitat, 2020: 10; UNICEF, 2020: 12). In addition, there were issues of lax border controls and difficulties in containing mass gatherings and religious and cultural activities (Abi-Rached et al., 2020; WHO-EMRO, 2020).

The underlying health issues have also been discussed at length in earlier sections. These include the private nature of the health sector and the weak control of the public sector, as well as the traditional focus on curative rather

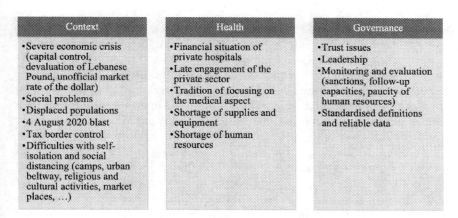

Figure 9.1 Challenges for the management of the COVID-19 pandemic in Lebanon (own compilation).

than preventive perspectives (Lewis, 2020). Private hospitals faced severe financial issues – especially in view of the failure of the MoPH to cover its dues for over a year. Monetary and liquidity problems also affected the healthcare sector, thus impacting the acquisition of, and resulting in shortages of, supplies and equipment. Add to that shortages in healthcare personnel due to lack of funds, infection or relocation, and the reluctance of the private sector to engage in the fight against COVID-19 can be raised.

Maybe the most important challenge related to the governance of the healthcare system is the lack of leadership and trust. The Lebanese population has lost faith in the governing body. It is suspected that trust issues were at the root of the population's non-compliance with the imposed measures. While 92% of polled Lebanese perceived COVID-19 as 'very' or 'somewhat serious' in late 2020, people perceived the government as completely detached from their struggles and concerns and felt that they had to make their own decisions and take matters into their own hands: only 18% attested that the government had done a 'good' or 'very good' job in fighting the pandemic (KAS, 2020: 7–8). The absence of a data-driven knowledge ecosystem that could feed a monitoring and evaluation system for better follow-up and improvement, as well as standardised definitions and coordinated, timely data shared between stakeholders would have provided inputs that could have improved the response towards the crisis and could have set the basis for future response mechanisms (Lewis, 2020).

9.6 Conclusion: lessons from Lebanon's 'paradoxical management' of COVID-19

The COVID-19 crisis in Lebanon is a pandemic of unforeseen proportions that has highlighted the deficiencies in the healthcare system's capacity to respond adequately in the long term. After Lebanon experienced a slow transmission rate during the early months of the pandemic, as social measures were relaxed and the country came out of the imposed lockdown, disease transmission accelerated from July 2020 on.

The containment of the COVID-19 pandemic has become a big challenge, especially for the public health sector, which was for a long time literally absent. In a country where the private sector occupies a preponderant place, the role of the public health sector in COVID-19 is certainly paradoxical and provides solid grounds for a new vision of the healthcare landscape in Lebanon.

The lessons learnt from managing the COVID-19 pandemic in Lebanon closely mirror those highlighted elsewhere in the world, and they offer opportunities for future endeavours and improvements to existing systems. First and foremost, the COVID-19 pandemic has shown again the importance of public health by placing this domain at the forefront of the fight against the pandemic and emphasising the need to support and fund public health initiatives (DeJong, 2020); strong public health agencies that can effectively assess and manage potential threats are also essential in future. In addition, the presence of a disaster readiness and preparedness cell where all public and private stakeholders are represented is key to ensuring successful crisis management.

Secondly, the pandemic underlined the need for good governance. Strong and empathic leadership is key in building trust between the government and the population, whilst transparent communication and clear messages are essential in inspiring confidence in governmental decisions and adherence to imposed measures (Abi-Rached et al., 2020). Furthermore, rapid and decisive government actions tailored for specific populations and based on cultural sensitivity and real-time data are key to successful strategies.

Thirdly, it quickly became clear that there is a need for a holistic approach that includes a global and comprehensive strategy going beyond the health component to encompass provisions for economic, social and humanitarian initiatives. Collaboration is required between the multiple stakeholders – including ministries, public and private hospitals, professional orders and syndicates, industries, civil societies and NGOs – to ensure a sound and efficient response (DeJong, 2020; Diwan and Abi-Rached, 2020). It is important to engage and coordinate their efforts to provide harmonised and complementary actions and to reduce redundancy and duplication. It is not enough to focus on physical health alone; a successful intervention needs to account for the population's mental health as well as other aspects of life, including the economy, education, trade and industry.

Finally, the pandemic stressed the importance of an empowered and informed population, since social responsibility and self-sufficiency are key factors in enhancing the response to a pandemic (Abi-Rached et al., 2020). The population should be empowered by providing them with accurate and timely information that will allow them to develop their personal skills and, therefore, become agents of change. Media training is essential to help in the delivery of news and to avoid the abundance of fake news and infodemics. Digital technologies and artificial intelligence analytical tools are also key to a successful response, as they allow better prevention and help in optimising treatments. In addition, populations should be encouraged to become self-sufficient and innovative and governments should provide opportunities for the development of local supply industries to respond to shortages in essential supplies and equipment. By the same token, the presence of trained and competent health human resources is essential in the fight against the pandemic. With that in mind, healthcare professionals should be nurtured and provided with incentives to remain in the country.

References

Abi-Rached, Joelle / Issa, Nahla / Khalife, Jade / Salameh, Pascale / Karra-Aly, Ayah / Kosremelli Asmar, Michèle (2020): *Towards a zero-COVID Lebanon: a call for action*. Paris: Arab Reform Initiative. www.arab-reform.net/publication/towards-a-zero-cOVID-lebanon-a-call-for-action.

Al-Mandhari, Ahmed Salim / Brennan, Richard J. / Abubakar, Abdinasir / Hajjeh, Rana (2020): Tackling COVID-19 in the Eastern Mediterranean region. *The Lancet*, 19 November. www.thelancet.com/journals/lancet/article/PIIS0140-6736(20)32349-7/fulltext.
Bizri, Abdul Rahman / Khachfe, Hussein H. / Fares, Mohamad Y. / Musharrafieh, Umayya (2021): COVID-19 pandemic: an insult over injury for Lebanon. *Journal of Community Health*, 46(3): pp. 487–93. https://doi.org/10.1007/s10900-020-00884-y.
DeJong, Jocelyn (2020): The challenges of a public health approach to COVID-19 amid crises in Lebanon. *Middle East Report Online*, 8 May. https://merip.org/2020/05/the-challenges-of-a-public-health-approach-to-covid-19-amid-crises-in-lebanon.
Diwan, Ishak / Abi-Rached, Joelle (2020): *Lebanon: managing COVID-19 in the time of revolution*. Paris: Arab Reform Initiative. www.arab-reform.net/publication/managing-covid-19-in-the-time-of-revolution.
HRW (2017): *Lebanon: waste crisis posing health risks*. Brussels: Human Rights Watch. www.hrw.org/news/2017/12/01/lebanon-waste-crisis-posing-health-risks.
IGSPS (2012): *National health statistics report in Lebanon*. Beirut: Saint Joseph University, Institute of Health Management and Social Protection. www.usj.edu.lb/intranet/annonce/files/pdf/175_pdf_1.pdf.
KAS (2020): *10 years after the Arab uprisings: where does public opinion in the region stand today?* Tunis: Konrad Adenauer Stiftung. www.kas.de/documents/252038/11055681/Where+does+Public+Opinion+in+the+Region+Stand+Today+-+10+Years+after+the+Arab+Uprisings.pdf/73611431-093a-3e69-8e5e-7811f1f153e9?version=1.0&t=1611755841567.
Khalife, Jade (2020): *An endgame for COVID-19 in Lebanon: a strategic overview*. COVID-19 Database, 17 April. https://covidaba.com/en/an-endgame-for-covid-19-in-lebanon-a-suppression-and-lift-strategy-crush-the-curve-don't-flatten-it/.
Kharroubi, Samer / Saleh, Fatima (2020): Are lockdown measures effective against COVID-19? *Frontiers in Public Health*, 8: pp. 1–4. https://doi.org/10.3389/fpubh.2020.549692.
Khoury, Petra / Azar, Eid / Hitti, Eveline (2020): COVID-19 response in Lebanon: current experience and challenges in a low-resource setting. *JAMA*, 324(6): pp. 548–9. https://doi.org/10.1001/jama.2020.12695.
Lewis, Emily (2020): How coronavirus is finally breaking Lebanon's neglected health care system. *L'Orient-Le-Jour*, 15 October. https://today.lorientlejour.com/article/1236587/how-coronavirus-is-finally-breaking-lebanons-neglected-health-care-system.html.
Ministry of Public Health (2020): *Coronavirus disease 2019 (COVID-2019) health strategic preparedness and response plan*. Beirut: Ministry of Public Health. www.moph.gov.lb/en/Media/view/27426/coronavirus-disease-health-strategic-preparedness-and-response-plan-.
Nakhlé, Myriam Mrad et al. (2015): Beirut air pollution and health effects – BAPHE study protocol and objectives. *Multidisciplinary Respiratory Medicine*, 10(1): pp. 21–3. https://doi.org/10.1186/s40248-015-0016-1.
OCHA Lebanon (2020): *Lebanon: Beirut port explosions situation report No. 3*. 10 August. https://reliefweb.int/report/lebanon/lebanon-beirut-port-explosions-situation-report-no-3-10-august-2020-enar.
Orient-Le-Jour (2020): Sur 55 structures évaluées plus de la moitié 'hors service' selon l'OMS [More than half of 55 evaluated structures are 'out of service', according to

the WHO]. *L'Orient-Le-Jour*, 12 August. www.lorientlejour.com/article/1229142/plus-de-la-moitie-des-hopitaux-de-beyrouth-hors-service-deplore-loms.html.

Rozier, Muriel (2020): COVID-19: Le Liban condamné au 'stop and go' [COVID-19: Lebanon condemned to 'stop and go']. *Commerce du Levant*, 20 November. www.lecommercedulevant.com/article/30135-covid-19-le-liban-condamne-au-stop-and-go-.

UN-Habitat (2020): *UN-Habitat Lebanon Unions of Municipalities' COVID-19 rapid assessment report*. Beirut: UN-Habitat. https://unhabitat.org/sites/default/files/2020/06/un-h_uoms_covid-19_rapid_assessment_report_2020.06.22_final.pdf.

UNHCR (2020): *Lebanon fact sheet*. www.unhcr.org/lb/wp-content/uploads/sites/16/2020/02/UNHCR-Lebanon-Operational-Fact-sheet-January-2020.pdf.

UNICEF (2020): *COVID-19: an unprecedented global crisis with widespread implications*. Beirut: United Nations International Children's Emergency Fund. www.unicef.org/lebanon/media/5616/file.

United Nations (2020): *United Nations comprehensive response to COVID-19: saving lives, protecting societies, recovering better*. New York: United Nations. https://unsdg.un.org/sites/default/files/2020-06/UN-Response-to-COVID-19.pdf.

van Lerberghe, Wim / Mechbal, Abdelhaye. / Kronfol, Nabil (2018): *The collaborative governance of Lebanon's health sector. Twenty years of efforts to transform health system performance*. Beirut: PSO. www.moph.gov.lb/en/Pages/131/18162/the-collaborative-governance-of-lebanons-health-sector.

Verner, Dorte et al. (2018): *Droughts and agriculture in Lebanon: causes, consequences, and risk management*. Washington: World Bank Group. http://documents1.worldbank.org/curated/en/892381538415122088/pdf/130405-WP-P160212-Lebanon-WEB.pdf.

Vidal, John (2016): Water supplies in Syria deteriorating fast due to conflict, experts warn. *The Guardian*, 7 September. www.theguardian.com/environment/2016/sep/07/water-supplies-in-syria-deteriorating-fast-due-to-conflict-experts-warn.

WHO (2020): *Lebanon explosion update for partners*. 18 August. Geneva: World Health Organization. www.who.int/emergencies/who-lebanon-partners-update-18august2020.pdf.

WHO Briefs (2020): 31 May, 27 August, 31 August, 1 December (unpublished).

WHO-EMRO (2020): *Statement by WHO's regional director on an upsurge in the number of COVID-19 cases in the Eastern Mediterranean region*. Press release, 3 September. Beirut: WHO Regional Office for the Eastern Mediterranean. www.emro.who.int/pdf/media/news/statement-by-whos-regional-director-on-an-upsurge-in-the-number-of-covid-19-cases-in-the-eastern-mediterranean-region.pdf?ua=1.

WHO and UNICEF (2016): *Lebanon water quality survey*. Beirut: WHO and UNICEF. www.unicef.org/lebanon/media/576/file/JMP%20Report.pdf.

World Bank (2020): *Classification of fragile and conflict-affected situations*. Washington: World Bank Group. www.worldbank.org/en/topic/fragilityconflictviolence/brief/harmonized-list-of-fragile-situations.

10 Digital learning under COVID-19

Challenges and opportunities – the Lebanese case

Fadi El Hage and Fouad Yehya

10.1 Introduction

The lockdowns in response to COVID-19 have interrupted physical learning in most of the educational institutions with a near-universal impact on learners and teachers at every level, from pre-primary to universities, adult learning and vocational skills training institutions. Maintaining learning continuity during this hard period relies on the concerted efforts of educational policymakers, universities, school leaders and communities to continue learning remotely, share resources and facilitate the teaching/learning process. This requires educators, particularly teachers, to adapt to new pedagogical concepts, approaches and strategies of teaching – for which they may not have been well trained – to overcome the lack of resilience, challenges of engagement and learners' risks of falling behind.

The Lebanese education system – with its highly structured and prescribed system that focuses on acquiring skills to pass high-stakes exams ('official exams') and a curriculum that has not been updated since 1997 – struggles to meet the demands of distance learning and the requirements of the twenty-first century.

This chapter will focus on the Lebanese situation since the researchers are dealing with the situation themselves and since Lebanon, as a multicultural and multiconfessional country and traditionally a 'regional champion' in education, can be considered a 'model' for other Arab countries in a double sense: it features elements that other countries should aspire to realise themselves, but it also shares deficiencies that other Arab countries suffer from as well. Therefore, analysing the challenges that the COVID-19 pandemic has brought to the Lebanese education system is illustrative also in a regional perspective.

Its main question will revolve around the implementation of information and communications technology (ICT) in the Lebanese educational system, asking, to what extent is it ready to adopt online learning possibilities to dampen the negative impacts of the COVID-19 pandemic on children's access to education and to avoid losing academic years and formal learning?

DOI: 10.4324/9781003240044-13

The first section of this chapter sheds light on the Lebanese educational status quo before the COVID-19 pandemic and the extent to which ICT had already been implemented in Lebanese schools and educational centres. The second section describes the challenges of distance learning, especially for school children, and the challenges that educators are facing in adopting online learning skills.

The third section focuses on the importance of using active teaching methods in distance learning, in order to shift from mastering digital tools to integrating a real remote pedagogy. The fourth section will emphasise the importance of teaching subjects from the humanities in the digital and robotics age in order to highlight the complexity of human beings and including their emotions and personal stories in any educational approach. Future teachers will need better competence in seeing their school students comprehensively as human beings with unique competences that machines and robots in the post-COVID-19 world cannot acquire. It is thus important that today's universities start to prepare the next generation of teachers in that spirit already.

10.2 The Lebanese educational status quo before COVID-19

The Lebanese education system, with its public and private sectors, is a five-cycle system: kindergarten, lower and upper elementary, intermediate and secondary levels adhering to the multilingual, cultural and gender diversity of the society (Baytiyeh, 2017). The Lebanese education system is centralised and all public education institutions are regulated by the Ministry of Education and Higher Education (MEHE), which manages the system through regional education offices. Both private and public schools follow the same national curriculum to achieve the same learning outcomes and skills that comply with those of the official exams; however, a tremendous gap persists between the private and public sector due to the substantial financing of the private sector (Ghamrawi, Ghamrawi and Shal, 2015: 132), especially in the domain of educational technology. According to Loo and Magazier (2017), around 75% of learners are enrolled in private schools, which may reflect the need of the Lebanese public education system to make substantial improvements in order to develop the system's capacity. Additionally, the Lebanese curriculum is far from the needs of today's learners in terms of success in modern life. It has not been reformed since 1997 and mainly relies on a teacher-centred approach whereby the teacher acts as the provider of information, mainly focusing on recall and memorisation. According to Jabbour (2013), very few Lebanese schools adopt a student-centred approach. This limits critical thinking, collaboration, communication and research skills whilst promoting short-term information retention (Yehya, 2020).

Moreover, the increase in the number of Syrian refugees over the last seven years has led to the establishment of 'second shift schools', which provide education to Syrian refugee children, typically in the afternoon.

This increases the load on the education system and hampers its ability to develop in alignment with modern changes, especially the processes of incorporating distance learning and new technological tools into the educational curriculum. Therefore, despite the important role of ICT tools in education, Lebanon's overall educational technology efforts may be considered below the needed level for appropriate implementation (Saad, 2013; Yehya, 2019). Consequently, the level of ICT in Lebanese public and private schools that might enhance the teaching/learning process cannot be attained because of the weak governmental reform policies and the corruption that has led to a lack of sufficient financing and educational reform which increasingly relies on foreign aid.

In a brief look at the chronology of educational technology initiatives in Lebanon, it appears that this country still faces poor-quality educational pedagogies and a lack of modern ICT tools compared to nearby countries (Loo and Magaziner, 2017). The ICT implementation has been sporadic (Zain, 2016: 26). In 2000, the MEHE launched 'school-net' as the first 'ICT in education' project and equipped a few schools with computers. In 2003, the Lebanese government, through the United Nations Development Programme and the Office of the Minister of State for Administrative Reform, completed the development of the 'National e-Strategy' and three years later several initiatives were launched by several US-based companies (Microsoft, Occidental Petroleum, Intel and Cisco) for various technology-related projects in several Lebanese schools (Yehya, Barbar and Abou-Rjeili, 2018: 17). However, it was not until July 2013 that the MEHE started to organise workshops and conferences aimed at adopting an appropriate ICT framework to assess teachers' ICT knowledge, skills and readiness, and to move a step forward on the path of ICT implementation in Lebanese schools (personal communication, head of the ICT department, Centre for Educational Research and Development (CERD), 17 December 2017). Yehya, Barbar and Abou-Rjeili (2018: 31) however investigated that there was hardly any ICT vision or even awareness among school administrators in either sector (private and public) at the time. Moreover, they showed a lack of educational technology resources and time to manage and become familiar with these resources in Lebanese schools (Figure 10.1). The insufficient number of available computers and appropriate software, lack of financial support, insufficient training and technical support and lack of internet connectivity have been identified as the urgent main barriers preventing the implementation of ICT. Thus, very limited technology is in use or is properly integrated into the Lebanese education system. Accordingly, effective ICT implementation in the Lebanese education system is feeble in the absence of a clear ICT vision for schools or real support as well as limited ICT-appropriate tools.

In summary, the Lebanese education system before the COVID-19 pandemic was already facing tough challenges in fulfilling learners' needs to develop the necessary twenty-first-century skills.

Digital learning under COVID-19 159

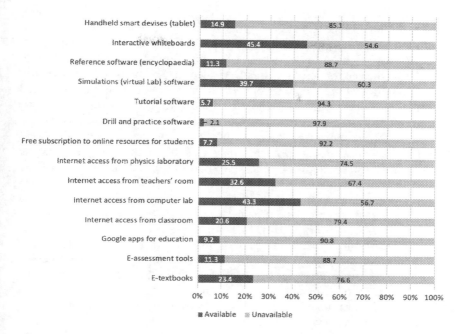

Figure 10.1 Percentage of the availability of information and communications technology (ICT) resources in Lebanese schools in 2017.
Source: Adapted from Yehya, Barbar and Abou-Rjeili, 2018: 23.

10.3 Challenges of implementing distance learning during the COVID-19 pandemic

The COVID-19 pandemic hit Lebanon at an already difficult moment. School closures came at a time when a very large number of schools had already been closed for several weeks because of insecurity and strikes due to youth revolution against the prevailing corruption and the economic crisis that had started on 17 October 2019. Most secondary school and university students were out of educational institutions and participating in the protests and uprisings. This unexpected complex situation played a major role in forcing the educational policymakers to search for alternatives to carry on with the academic year and to keep teaching and learning ongoing. This led to the integration of online courses. Education policymakers had to use a range of resources to support students' learning while they were unable to attend school, including instructional packages (textbooks, worksheets and printouts), educational television and online instructional resources to replace face-to-face learning with distance learning to reach the largest percentage of students possible (Reimers and Schleicher, 2020).

Therefore, educators have had to make adjustments to their classroom delivery, including utilising online platforms for efficient teaching processes, such as Zoom, Google Classroom, Microsoft Teams, Moodle, Blackboard or similar technologies. However, weaknesses of the education system, including poor levels of digitisation, have been brought to light by the COVID-19 pandemic and the economic crisis already virulent in Lebanon. In a fragile education system like the Lebanese one, the transition to online learning posed extreme challenges for teachers and even more so for learners, especially those for whom the conditions for ensuring continuity of learning at home are limited due to technical problems and lack of internet literacy (Abourjeili and Harb, 2020). Consequently, they may miss the stimulating and enriching environment, learning opportunities and social interaction of the classroom.

The literature on the subject claims that the use of online learning in a meaningful way does not occur spontaneously (Yehya, 2020: 19) – malfunctioning hardware and poor internet infrastructure are serious hurdles that cannot be easily overcome (Zain, 2016). Lebanon's internet is not yet transmitted through fibreoptic cables and the current internet infrastructure (copper lines) is old, causing poor internet transmission to homes and businesses. Consequently, this contributes to a lack of possibilities in distance learning.

The majority of Lebanese schools fail to engage learners, teachers, communities and educational policymakers effectively in the implementation of distance learning (Yehya, 2019: 25).

The benefits that distance learning brings cannot benefit the classroom if teachers do not purposefully plan their use of technology (Lassoued, Alhendawi and Bashitialshaaer, 2020). In some schools, while online learning has generally taken place through recorded lectures and online platforms, some institutions have postponed learning and teaching until further notice, due to the lack of ICT infrastructure for both students and teachers (Crawford et al., 2020). Using online learning merely for the sake of using technology does not make for effective teaching. Even with adequate access to online learning, effective professional development remains one reason why it is difficult to increase the level of distance learning. Teachers cannot implement online learning due to the lack of proper training on effective use of the technology inside and outside the classroom, the lack of proper technological tools, inefficient technical support, poor internet infrastructure and the rigid curriculum and lack of professional development (Trisiana, 2020: 69).

Educational technology and the professional development of teachers in the Lebanese learning society are unconnected. Since July 2013, the MEHE has organised workshops and conferences designed to 'adopt an appropriate ICT framework to assess teachers' ICT knowledge, skills and readiness, and to move a step forward on the path of ICT implementation in Lebanese schools' – all the potential has focused on hardware and software and did not address teachers' training and curriculum development (Yehya, Barbar and Abou-Rjeili, 2018). In May 2019, the MEHE and CERD, in partnership with United Nations International Children Emergency Fund (UNICEF), launched Training Professional Development (TPD) workshops, but these TPDs have been ineffective in both private and public schools because they are mostly limited to formal training sessions organised by an external agent. In other words, a TPD is still 'an event'; it has not become 'a process' in schools.

Furthermore, a study that investigated Lebanese secondary school teachers' attitudes towards the use of ICT revealed that most of the teachers in the sample cannot use online techniques effectively. Most of the respondents highlighted a lack of the training necessary to use it to its best advantage. They mentioned that this leads to a lack of confidence among teachers in using the technology and that there is a need to improve skills. They highlighted the need for the government to participate in promoting online learning because the government's dereliction frustrates teachers and reduces their confidence in the importance of technology (Yehya, Barbar and Abou-Rjeili, 2019: 25). Thus, educators need to see the importance of online learning beyond the hardware and the expanded definition of the learning management systems. Online learning should shift away from managing and providing information to opening doors for learners to communicate, interact, explore and create a meaningful learning experience (Yehya, 2020: 13). Thus, the idea of online learning must change from a place where knowledge can be obtained to a place where one can learn actively in an actual learning environment (Tesolin and Tsinakos, 2018). Education policymakers, school administrators and leaders must provide related professional development for distance learning and not leave teachers on their own with the task of choosing the most appropriate online pedagogical strategies and models to support distance teaching and learning.

In an environment where distance learning is no longer a luxury but is becoming a necessity, the training of teachers to integrate so-called active or interactive teaching methods can be done through digital tools. Mastering the use of digital tools (such as Kahoot, Padlet, Zoom, Mindmaster, etc.) does not at all mean mastering distance learning or the active and interactive teaching methods which integrate these digital tools. The General Secretariat of Catholic Schools in Lebanon launched initiatives and organised teacher-training sessions in September 2020. More than 200 schools participated in the online training, reaching a total of 12,000 teachers. These sessions trained the use of Microsoft Teams, Class Notebook, MS Sway and Office 365. However, the identified obstacles are still related to information technology (IT) challenges: teachers' readiness to deal with technology, administrators' (lack of) readiness for the process of distance education, poor infrastructure, scarce devices and the traditional thinking going back to the pre-coronavirus, financial and social outlook of school directors. Thus, teachers are not ready for online learning, and they need to be trained in remote pedagogy to help them integrate active teaching methods in their lesson plans. The following section will recommend interactive teaching strategies with online learning that may facilitate its integration in Lebanese schools.

10.4 Interactive teaching methods and online learning: a needed upgrade for the future

The COVID-19 crisis has forced all school and university teachers to adopt the remote teaching mode, without prior training (particularly in Lebanon and in the Middle East), given the urgent and unpredictable nature of the situation (Yehya, 2020). This experience has unveiled the future world awaiting us: digital, uncertain, on the move and interchangeable. Even teachers who have mastered the use of digital tools have encountered a new difficulty, that of integrating these digital tools into a real remote pedagogy (El Hage, 2020). At the end of the day, platforms and software are mere tools: using them in active teaching methods requires a whole different set of skills.

Many digital tools can be integrated to facilitate the use of active methods in online teaching: Zoom, Microsoft Teams and Webex allow group interactions, such as splitting students into more manageable working groups; Slideshare, PowerPoint and Prezi allow for individual or joint presentations from one computer to another; and platforms such as Canva, Emaze, Slack and Genial.ly are modern teaching environments. Sites for hosting images and videos abound. Google Forms or the less-known learning apps such as Formative or Socrative aid in drafting worksheets and controlling students' learning progress. Padlet, Jamboard and Popplet enable students to submit their group work, and Gitmind, Mindmeister, Mind mapping, Yoa, Milanote, ClickUp, Microsoft Visio, MindGenius, Miro Mind Map and SmartDraw are just some of the many conceptual mapping tools. The list has become very long, if not confusing, and there is literally an application for everything. However, even if all these tools are necessary for distance learning, they remain insufficient for active and online teaching. For this, new skills are required among teachers to learn how to integrate these digital tools into online active teaching methods.

Below are some examples of active teaching methods that already posed a challenge for school and university teachers in Lebanon and in the region prior to the COVID-19 crisis. Teachers are poorly trained and not accustomed to integrating them into course sessions. The COVID-19 crisis has exacerbated this problem, as these teachers are currently being asked not only to master the use of these active methods, but also to use them online with digital tools, as we will illustrate with the following examples:

> **Remote cooperative learning**
>
> Cooperative or collaborative learning, or simply group work, can be done remotely with the appropriate digital tools as breakout rooms via Zoom, for example. This kind of work refers to a group of four to five people interacting with one another to set or accomplish a common

goal. It consists of dividing up tasks and combining the efforts of subgroup members. This method requires students to interact with one another to achieve a common goal: shift from working solo to working within networks (El Hage, 2013, B3-1).

Remote question-based teaching

Several teaching methods are question-based, such as the 'minute paper'. A minute paper is an umbrella term that encompasses a variety of practices aimed at engaging students in the course through very specific micro-activities. In this method, the roles are reversed: students are expected to ask the questions, then to answer them, and it is only at the end that the teacher intervenes. It is worth mentioning that the 'minute paper' technique has many versions. Many platforms can be used (wooclap, Mentimeter, etc.).

Remote flipped classroom

According to Nizet and Meyer (2014), the flipped classroom is a hybrid pedagogical model where the teacher takes advantage of digital technologies (such as video footage) to make concepts and knowledge accessible to students, in a manner that is adapted to their needs and no longer restricted to school hours. In the virtual classroom, the student is placed in active learning situations, where the teacher plays the roles of pedagogical mediator and coach. This teaching method can be implemented in two ways: as an 'in-class flip', with group learning activities focusing on the interaction between peers (Eric Mazur's model) in order to promote co-construction/co-development, or as an 'out-of-class flip', where students acquire the course knowledge individually thanks to the help of ICT. Collectively, small interactive educational projects enable co-development/co-construction work.

Remote project-based learning

Project-based pedagogy is seen in several teaching methods and pedagogical approaches: interdisciplinary projects, POGIL (Process Oriented Guided Inquiry Learning), STEAM (Science, Technology, Engineering, Art and Maths), problem-based learning, etc.

Remote error exploitation-based learning (EEBL)

This method gives a new meaning to errors and puts them at the heart of learning. It consists of drawing up teaching sequences out of the types of errors identified by the teacher: teaching devices are provided to use the errors made by students as learning materials. An error (in the sense of wandering, feeling free to go in all directions) is the product of the learner's intellectual process. EEBL prompts students to analyse their way of thinking, of which the error is only a trace. In this approach, an error is not perceived as a dysfunction, but as inherent in any act of learning. It is even perceived as a driver of learning. Thus, error goes from being a source of guilt to a source of information (El Hage, 2005). EEBL is not an approach of control, but one of regulation. It takes three forms: proactive (at the beginning of learning), interactive (during the sequence) and retroactive (at the end of the sequence). This method can be used entirely remotely (learning by remote error exploitation) (Al-Ahdal, 2020; El Hage and Nahed, 2020).

All these methods employ 'complex tasks'. Complex task teaching is part of a constructivist/socio-constructivist perspective of learning: the development of skills when solving complex tasks, as a process, is conceived of as an individual/team journey of progress. This approach replaces the concept of 'resources' with 'knowledge', which is too limited. Resources can be internal and can belong to different domains (cognitive, affective, attitude, sensorimotor or skills), can take different forms (declarative knowledge and knowledge of action) and has different origins (codified knowledge and experiential knowledge). Resources can also be external (colleagues ask for advice and to share their expertise, scientific databases, reference books, new information technologies, software, etc.; El Hage, 2020).

The big challenge remains how to integrate these active methods into online education. How should the best digital tools be chosen for the steps of each of these methods?

In order to achieve these objectives, several challenges remain:

At university, school and ministry level

A new curriculum design integrating new teaching and assessment methods should be elaborated on. Given the global economic crisis, amplified in Lebanon, sponsorship is needed following the COVID-19 health crisis to ensure that laptops, digital devices and internet connections are available, especially in suffering countries such as Lebanon.

At family level

Better equipment for poorer families, reliable electricity and internet connections are needed. Parental awareness is a must to support the learning of their children at home.

At the teachers' level

A reduction of the workload for teachers in other domains (administrative tasks, for instance) is needed in order not to overburden them structurally, as is professional training on digital tools, remote pedagogy and online assessment (self-organisation of students into smaller learning groups). University students should perhaps be included in school teaching activities in order to support teachers (peer learning).

At the students' level

Students should be introduced to digital tools and techniques. Above all, they must become more autonomous and responsible so that they can take charge of their own learning.

10.5 The humanistic role as a key factor to master distance learning in the digital age

Although it seems fundamental to develop the digital skills of teachers and students, the future world will also require them to continue developing other kinds of skills, such as transversal and psychosocial skills. It is important to remain vigilant against a looming drift: the digital must not reduce the human dimension in any education. If the world of tomorrow, post-COVID, will be a digitalised world based on distance learning, the fact remains that the social sciences and humanities will play a key role in any learning and in the skills required to succeed in complex, interdisciplinary tasks. The more artificial intelligence advances, the more needs will be expressed in terms of philosophy and the humanities (Harari, 2017).

The skills required for the uncertain, digital and complex 'world of tomorrow' can be classified into two categories: those belonging to the field of thought and psychosocial skills – such as complex problem-solving, critical thinking, emotional intelligence, creativity, the capacity to make fair judgements and cognitive flexibility – and those belonging to managerial skills, such as human resources management, coordination, referral to appropriate services and negotiation (Rainie and Anderson, 2017).

Thus, the skills that are more likely to evolve than others are as follows: creativity, which will become an essential quality sought by companies to take advantage of the development of new products, using new technologies and new working methods, and emotional intelligence, which will become the standard of robots and machines that will be, so to speak, closer to the 'human' thought and reactionary structure. This allows us to take into account the complexity of the human being in the learning process.

According to Morin (1999), complex thinking is thought that accepts contradiction; it is thought that connects, that aspires to multidimensional knowledge. Morin explains that this type of thought is not opposed to simplification, but it refuses the disjunction of elements and attempts to bring them together to better understand the links between them. Complexity is therefore not a refusal of simplicity, but rather an openness to the inconceivable. Complexity, by nature, includes the recognition of links between the different entities among which our thought necessarily makes distinctions but must not isolate from each other. This is the closest meaning to the term '*complexus*' (that which is woven together). That being said, complex thinking considers the object of study to be a system in itself, and it proceeds by shuttling between analysis/separation and synthesis/reliance (Morin, 1999). It is constantly animated by a tension between aspiration to unfragmented, non-isolated, non-reductive knowledge and the recognition of the incompleteness of all knowledge. This echoes the ecological approach of Bronfenbrenner's theory, which is based on one central idea: that the environment, in a broader sense, influences the development of the individual (Bronfenbrenner, 1979). As such, the ecological approach considers that the subject constructs their environment which, in return, influences the construction of the subject itself. Development is therefore the result of continual and reciprocal interactions between an organism and its environment. These influence each other constantly, each adapting in response to changes in the other. The ecological approach is therefore a plea to recognise complexity. A characteristic is not a state, but the result of a process. Humans are partially the result of their environments and environments are partially the result of humans (Morin, 1999).

In this context, critical thinking will remain essential to master the content of a theory and to develop psychosocial skills. Critical thinking is important for the workers of tomorrow, for them to be able to make reasonable choices, to carry out ethical reflections that preserve human dignity. Critical thinking focuses on a question, analyses the arguments, elaborates and appreciates conclusions and discusses with other people. All these skills can only be developed via the study of humanities (Goodchild and Janelle, 2010).

The people who will be solicited for the business world of tomorrow are not only the technically competent (for machines and robots will be more sophisticated in terms of results and quality), but those who have successfully integrated and invested in concepts and skills belonging to the worlds of philosophy, psychology, literature, history, education and art.

So, in addition to digital skills, soft skills are gaining traction. Schools and institutions of higher education need to focus on skills that machines lack: collaboration, creation and direction (World Economic Forum, 2015). In this context, it is not knowledge that will make the difference, but the right attitude of the person. Critical thinking, creativity, problem-solving and flexibility are skills that will only become more and more important. Non-technical skills are increasingly the engine of employability.

If digital learning and remote pedagogy are fundamental in teacher training, the humanities remain essential to university education; the methods of teaching in higher education cannot remain traditional, mono-disciplinary, isolated and lecture-based – especially in this digital and robotics age that the COVID-19 pandemic helps to accelerate. Indeed, the different approaches to learning range from the reproduction of information to the transformation of learners through their development as a whole (Marton, Dall'Alba and Beaty, 1993). Learning is now conceived as a process of evolution and personal transformation, and knowledge is therefore seen as an engine of growth and self-actualisation. One who learns is transformed – but they are not isolated from their environment; they have a double entry: a biophysical entry and a psycho-socio-cultural entry, and the two entries flow into and out of each other (Morin, 1999). A learner is a complex being, and education must take this complexity into account.

The standing of the humanities at university will become more and more necessary with the advancement of technology and robotisation. Humanity, emotional intelligence, psychosocial skills and human relations will remain at the heart of recruitment processes in the twenty-first century. However, the pedagogical approach will have to change, referring more to interdisciplinary projects and self-managed, problems-based group learning. Holistic and systemic approaches are nearly the natural declensions of the paradigm of complexity.

These approaches remain unproductive if evaluation does not follow suit; hence the importance of integrating 'authentic evaluation' directed at evaluating skills and remote evaluation, such as Digital Error Based Learning (DEBL) (El Hage and Nahed, 2020). Counterintuitively, the more we see the development of new technologies, IT systems and new scientific discoveries, the more human sciences will be an essential field at university. After hyper-specialisation, humanity will have to return to integrative and interdisciplinary approaches that make sense! Feelings, emotional intelligence, philosophy, literature, education, anthropology, psychology and the art of questioning life will advance in proportion to the fourth industrial revolution, dubbed 'robotic'.

10.6 Conclusion

Online learning shows evident benefits to the education system in expanding learners' learning opportunities beyond the school and university gates by using a variety of distance learning approaches and accessing the curriculum. The COVID-19 pandemic has shown this the hard way, and education policymakers, school leaders, teachers and the community have to cooperate in unconventional ways to make the best out of this emergency situation.

They will however also need to cooperate in future, each in their own field, to provide a conducive and non-threatening environment for teachers to further develop and apply distance learning strategies. They should take stock of the lessons learnt in this crisis and evaluate the learning loss due to the weak and fuzzy e-learning status in their education system – whether in Lebanon or elsewhere.

Several steps can be taken to manage the risks and interchanges for the successful transition of learners into the labour market, and for the deployment of learning in economic recovery.

First of all, it is important to build on the ongoing efforts to develop the infrastructure for online and remote learning and to continue to develop the capacity of learners and teachers to gain competence and confidence in using ICT for teaching and learning. They must convert a positive perception of the role of e-learning into practice for positive-attitude conservation.

Secondly, effective online learning has clearly placed greater demands on learners' autonomy, ability to learn independently, decision-making, self-monitoring and capacity to learn online. Consequently, traditional teaching methods should be replaced and aligned with e-learning potential to lead our school children to become lifelong learners. The most important challenge is to train teachers how to integrate digital tools and platforms in active teaching methods. This goal involves designing new curricula based on remote pedagogy and especially innovative thinking in assessment strategies that integrate distance assessment.

Accordingly, the assessment of learners should focus not just on the extent to which they gained the information and skills intended in the curriculum, but also on what competencies and abilities they established – or failed to establish – during the period of remote learning.

While the COVID-19 crisis has had a terrible impact on a large number of humans, it remains – like any other crisis – an opportunity for development, particularly in education. New curricula and future training programmes for teachers and all stakeholders in education will be based on the integration of digital technology in learning. However, fundamental challenges will lie in the transition from mastering digital tools to mastering digital pedagogy (remote pedagogy). While the importance of integrating active methods in remote education is put into question, the correlating and fundamental question remains as follows: what evaluation system should be designed to support these new pedagogical approaches? In fact, setting up a remote evaluation strategy is necessary. Relevant evaluation tools should be designed to prepare our digital native students for the world of tomorrow while ensuring their humanity is safeguarded in an increasingly robotic, digitalised world.

References

Abourjeili, Suzanne Abdul-Reda / Harb, Seham (2020): *The deteriorated educational reality in Lebanon: towards 'another' critical approach*. Paris: Arab Reform Initiative. www.arab-reform.net/wp-content/uploads/pdf/Arab_Reform_Initiative_en_the-deteriorated-educational-reality-in-lebanon-towards-another-critical-approach_14565.pdf?ver=289fba8adcc6d32a5a5ebf6c78bb9878.

Al-Ahdal, Arif (2020): Using computer software as a tool of error analysis: giving EFL teachers and learners a much-needed impetus. *International Journal of Innovation, Creativity and Change*, 12(2): pp. 418–37, https://ssrn.com/abstract=3570619.

Baytiyeh, Hoda (2017): Has the educational system in Lebanon contributed to the growing sectarian divisions? *Education and Urban Society*, 49(5): pp. 546–59. https://doi.org/10.1177%2F0013124516645163.

Bronfenbrenner, Urie (1979): *The ecology of human development: experiments by nature and design*. Cambridge, MA: Harvard University Press.

Crawford, Joseph / Butler-Henderson, Kerryn / Rudolph, Jürgen / Malkawi, Bashar / Glowatz, Matt / Burton, Rob/ Magni, Paulo / Lam, Sophia (2020): COVID-19: 20 countries' higher education intra-period digital pedagogy responses. *Journal of Applied Learning & Teaching*, 3(1): pp. 1–20. https://doi.org/10.37074/jalt.2020.3.1.7.

El Hage, Fadi (2005): *Le morcellement des connaissances en physiologie: du constat à la remédiation: Intégration du paradigme de la complexité dans l'étude de la construction des liens entre différents concepts enseignés en physiologie, aux niveaux des pratiques enseignantes et des productions des élèves* [The fragmentation of knowledge in physiology: from observation to remediation: integration of the paradigm of complexity in the study of the construction of links between different concepts taught in physiology, at the level of teaching practices and students' productions] (doctoral dissertation). Montpellier: Université de Montpellier. https://tel.archives-ouvertes.fr/tel-00413745.

El Hage, Fadi (2013): *University pedagogy manual*. Beirut: Saint Joseph University. www.usj.edu.lb/intranet/actu/pdf/3211.pdf.

El Hage, Fadi (2019): *University pedagogy manual*. Beirut: Saint Joseph University. www.usj.edu.lb/mpu/manuel/manuel_pu_b3.php.

El Hage, Fadi (2020): *University pedagogy manual*. Beirut: Saint Joseph University. www.usj.edu.lb/mpu/manuel/manuel_pu_d9.php.

El Hage, Fadi / Nahed, Rosette (2020): Apprentissage par exploitation de l'erreur et à distance (AEED). Pour une évaluation formative et un feedback interactif et digital [Learning through error exploitation and at a distance (AEED). For a formative evaluation and an interactive and digital feedback]. *Évaluer. Journal international de recherche en éducation et formation*, Special Issue, 1: pp. 131–42. https://journal.admee.org/index.php/ejiref/article/view/226.

Ghamrawi, Najah A. / Ghamrawi, Norma / Shal, Tarek (2015): Perception of character education: the case of Lebanese school leaders. *Open Journal of Leadership*, 4(4): pp. 129–42. https://doi.org/10.4236/ojl.2015.44012.

Goodchild, Michael F. / Janelle, Donald G. (2010): Toward critical spatial thinking in the social sciences and humanities. *GeoJournal*, 75(1): pp. 3–13. https://doi.org/10.1007%2Fs10708-010-9340-3.

Harari, Yuval Noah (2017): Homo deus: *a brief history of tomorrow*. New York: Harper Collins.

Jabbour, Khayrazad Kari (2013): Issues that restrain teachers from adapting student-centered instruction in Lebanese school. *Tejuelo: Didáctica de la Lengua y la Literatura. Educación*, 17: pp. 85–96.

Lassoued, Zohra / Alhendawi, Mohammed / Bashitialshaaer, Raed (2020): An exploratory study of the obstacles for achieving quality in distance learning during the COVID-19 pandemic. *Education Sciences*, 10(9): pp. 1–13. https://doi.org/10.3390/educsci10090232.

Loo, Bryce / Magaziner, Jessie (2017): Education in Lebanon. *World Education News + Reviews*, 2 May. https://wenr.wes.org/2017/05/education-in-lebanon.

Marton, Ference / Dall'Alba, Gloria / Beaty, Elizabeth (1993): Conceptions of learning. *International Journal of Educational Research*, 19(3): pp. 277–300.

Morin, Edgar (1999): *La tête bien faite. Repenser la réforme. Réformer la pensée* [The head well used. Rethinking reform. Reforming the thinking]. Paris: Edition du Seuil.

Nizet, Isabelle / Meyer, Florian (2014): A flipped classroom design for preservice teacher training in assessment. In: Keengwe, Jared / Onchwari, Grace / Oigara, James N. (eds.): *Promoting active learning through the flipped classroom model.* Hershey, PA: Information Science Reference, pp. 71–90. https://doi.org/10.4018/978-1-4666-4987-3.

Rainie, Lee / Anderson, Janna (2017): *The future of jobs and jobs training.* Washington: Pew Research Center. www.pewresearch.org/internet/wp-content/uploads/sites/9/2017/05/PI_2017.05.03_Future-of-Job-Skills_FINAL.pdf.

Reimers, Fernando / Schleicher, Andreas (2020): *Schooling disrupted, schooling rethought. How the Covid-19 pandemic is changing education.* Paris: Organisation for Economic Cooperation and Development. https://inee.org/system/files/resources/document.pdf.

Saad, M. M. (2013): *Information and communication technology in building prospective teachers' knowledge base: cohort of secondary mathematics pre-service teachers in Lebanon* (doctoral dissertation). Beirut: Saint Joseph University.

Tesolin, Amy / Tsinakos, Avgoustos (2018): Opening real doors: strategies for using mobile augmented reality to create inclusive distance education for learners with different-abilities. In: Yu, Shengquan / Ally, Mohamed / Tsinakos, Avgoustos (eds.) *Mobile and ubiquitous learning.* Singapore: Springer, pp. 59–80. https://doi.org/10.1007/978-981-10-6144-8.

Trisiana, Agustin Dwi (2020): *The use of integrated learning management system (LMS) in EFL classroom: teachers' considerations and challenges* (doctoral dissertation). Jawa Timur: UIN Sunan Ampel Surabaya. http://digilib.uinsby.ac.id/id/eprint/44981.

World Economic Forum (ed.): *Outlook on the Global Agenda 2015.* Geneva: World Economic Forum. http://reports.weforum.org/outlook-global-agenda-2015/wp-content/blogs.dir/59/mp/files/pages/files/outlook-2015-a4-downloadable.pdf.

Yehya, Fouad (2019): *Impact of computer simulation on students' cognitive achievement in physics courses* (doctoral dissertation). Beirut: Saint Joseph University.

Yehya, Fouad (2020): Promoting technology-implementation learning paradigm for online learning in secondary education. *Global Journal of Information Technology: Emerging Technologies*, 10(1): pp. 12–21. https://doi.org/10.18844/gjit.v10i1.4620.

Yehya, Fouad / Barbar, Aziz / Abou-Rjeili, Suzanne (2018): Diagnosing the barriers for integrating educational technology in physics courses in Lebanese secondary schools. *Research in Social Sciences and Technology*, 3(2): pp. 14–39. https://doi.org/10.46303/ressat.03.02.2.

Yehya, Fouad / Barbar, Aziz / Abou-Rjeili, Suzanne (2019): Lebanese secondary physics teachers' attitudes towards the use of ICT. *International Journal of Learning and Teaching*, 11(1): pp. 8–27. https://doi.org/10.18844/ijlt.v11i1.3891.

Zain, Farah (2016): *The potential of technology in education: a case in point of tablets use in a school in Lebanon* (doctoral dissertation). Beirut: Lebanese American University. https://laur.lau.edu.lb:8443/xmlui/bitstream/handle/10725/4401/Farah_Zain_Thesis.pdf?sequence=3&isAllowed=y.

11 Conclusions

The MENA region and COVID-19 – lessons for the future

Zeina Hobaika, Lena-Maria Möller and Jan Claudius Völkel

The contributions to this collective volume have highlighted the numerous challenges that the COVID-19 pandemic has posed for the Middle East and North Africa (MENA) region. In doing so, the articles considered questions of geopolitical relevance, social implications and the relations between political leaders and citizens. As has been the case globally, in the MENA region too, the coronavirus has developed into a systemic risk, a risk that requires systemic responses by both those in power and ordinary citizens (Klinke and Renn, 2019; Schweizer, 2019).

Such systemic responses to the COVID-19 pandemic include the need for technological advancement, for example. Fadi El Hage and Fouad Yehya have analysed how schools in Lebanon were institutionally unprepared for the sudden need for distance learning, just as teachers and pupils were unprepared to be collective agents and clients of education, respectively. Those who live in less affluent environments have a limited ability to work and learn at home; many children do not have sufficient access to the necessary equipment, so following online classes poses a real hardship for them. Teachers have faced difficulties adapting their lessons from (often outdated, teacher-centred) in-class sessions to alternative online-based approaches.

Another example of systemic responses is that of governance. Authoritarianism is gaining ground in many countries around the world, including Morocco. Giulia Cimini and Beatriz Tomé Alonso have illustrated how the kingdom's ruling classes – particularly the royal court around King Mohammed VI – have used the pandemic to further limit the influence of 'secondary elites'. These include parliamentarians and party leaders as well as academics, journalists and civil society representatives, especially if they are critical of the regime's policies. These tendencies have already diminished existing channels for expressing dissent, and public protests have been further criminalised in Morocco, as elsewhere. This form of 'othering', as Carola Richter, Abdulrahman al-Shami, Soheir Osman, Sahar Khalifa Salim and Samuel Mundua empirically prove, is a widespread strategy in many Arab countries: the creation of a patriotic 'us vs them' dichotomy gives people the feeling of belonging to the correct group; potential enemies need to be excluded. Such enemies can be external or internal – in the case of COVID-19,

DOI: 10.4324/9781003240044-14

it might be those who dare to question a regime's authoritarian power grab under the guise of fighting the coronavirus.

The analyses collected in this volume have also shed light on new opportunities. Alexander Lohse expounded on how the political leadership of the United Arab Emirate (UAE) has turned the crisis into a chance to brand their country as a 'savvy, high-tech nation' (p. XXX) and an attractive, reliable partner for other countries in their fight against the pandemic. The increasing use of new technologies, however, also bears the risk that governments might exploit the current health emergency for further surveillance and suppression of their citizens. Thomas Demmelhuber, Julia Gurol and Tobias Zumbrägel documented how 'coronavirus apps' have suddenly become a widely used tool that citizens (and visitors) are often obliged to install and activate these days. This opens up even more sophisticated possibilities for recording citizens' daily habits and behaviour – the risk that these technologies are being used for spying purposes is particularly high in countries where democratic control mechanisms are insufficiently institutionalised (albeit not only there). At the moment it seems highly questionable that the regimes in power will lessen their citizen control via cell phone apps, even once the coronavirus is one day under control. There will potentially be other reasons to oblige citizens and visitors to have such apps installed, which makes control over them frighteningly easier. Thus, in the long run as well, the pandemic has become, as Demmelhuber, Gurol and Zumbrägel put it, 'a silver platter for the ruling dynasties' (p. XX).

The non-transparent involvement of Chinese information technology (IT) companies raises additional questions about the rising influence of China in the MENA region, which was already increasingly visible through the first projects implemented under the Belt and Road Initiative (Kamel, 2018), and is now being further boosted through the COVID-19 action known as the 'Health Silk Road' (Siddiqui, 2020).

From Morocco to Iran, the coronavirus has once again brought the unique importance of functioning public health systems to light. As Michèle Kosremelli Asmar and Joumana Stephan Yeretzian have illustrated, the 'public' in 'public health' is indeed important; however, they identified a 'lack of leadership and trust' as the most important challenge for Lebanon's health governance (p. XXX), so the state needs considerable upgrading if it is to continue to play the role it is supposed to play – providing a sufficient level of care and protection to its citizens. In the case of Lebanon, though, this also opens the door for Iran to re-strengthen its influence in the cedar state through its proxy, Hezbollah. As Nassim AbiGhanem illustrated, Hezbollah discovered that the Ministry of Public Health can be a lucrative institution for managing substantial amounts of state funds, and that international sanctions can be cleverly circumvented when it comes to aid, healthcare and the relief of human suffering.

The advantages of functioning state structures are also an underlying theme in Manara Babiker Hassan's contribution on trafficked women in Khartoum.

She described the 2018 uprisings across Sudan as a 'window of opportunity' for the *samasra* – a transnationally organised group of traffickers – as security forces were 'increasingly busy following the protesters and not them as criminal networks' (p. XXX). COVID-19 has improved their comfortable situation further, since trafficked women depend on their 'services' even more as long as they are stuck in Khartoum without the ability to travel onward to the Arab Gulf monarchies.

The pandemic has also put the relationship between religion, science and politics to a renewed test, including the question of whether to comply with or resist governmental measures on religious grounds. Noël van den Heuvel and Ulrike Freitag showed how religious actors were detrimental in developing and sustaining systemic responses to the current crisis in Iran and Saudi Arabia. It has become clear that for a successful reaction to the systemic health crisis, religious leaders are indeed of particular relevance; one might add representatives of other domains as well, whether it be culture and sports, academia and media, or wherever individuals have the chance to serve as role models for the general public.

An intensified economic malaise and authoritarian suppression might lay the foundation for more political instability in the future. As pointed out at the beginning, the book's geographic focus is on the MENA region, but its message goes well beyond. As such, the individual chapters highlight trends and analytical paradigms that also apply in other world regions. The long-term effects of the crisis will be palpable everywhere, though to different extents, and the risk is high that some of the tendencies shown in this book will be more long-lasting than we might currently hope for.

Mutual trust is a key aspect when systemic responses are developed by both governments and citizens (Siegrist and Zingg, 2014): do the latter trust their government and its advisors? Do citizens believe that governments will take effective and proportional decisions when it comes to limiting self-evident rights and freedoms? Do governments trust that their citizens sufficiently understand and accept the imposed restrictions?

The less trust prevails on either side, the higher the risk that imposed containment measures remain unsuccessful (Margraf, Brailovskaia and Schneider, 2020). If citizens lack trust in their government, they are more likely to suspect ignorance and incompetence behind political decisions; in consequence, they will most likely not comply with any rules imposed. If governments do not trust citizens, they will tend to use disproportionate violence to impose their rules: since the outbreak of the pandemic, violence on the part of police officers in an attempt to enforce the strict isolation and distancing rules has been reported from many countries around the globe (Bowman, 2020).

To a large extent, the MENA region suffers from this double lack of trust. Despite public statements claiming otherwise, authoritarian regimes, after decades of insufficient governance achievements, lack the trust of their people in many MENA countries. And likewise, authoritarian regimes mistrust their people, a mistrust which is shown in harsh prison sentences, manipulated elections, controlled media and illiberal education systems. In the case of the COVID-19 pandemic, this governmental mistrust has become most visible in countries where statistics on infections, deaths and recoveries were kept non-transparent. This is nothing new, by any means: until today, some regimes in the region refuse to provide comprehensive data and information on HIV infections (Wehbe et al., 2021: 3), leading to higher risks of infection because of the lack of awareness among the population and lower research progress due to the lack of reliable sources. This, in the end, lowers the quality of political counselling and eventually of political decisions (Zyoud, 2021: 8).

This lack of reliable statistics and proper empirical data is not limited to the MENA region by any means. Political leaders taking scientific findings into doubt and hindering proper research has also happened in Europe, North America, Brazil, China, Tanzania and elsewhere across the world. The COVID-19 pandemic has taught a simple, but still relevant, lesson: a pandemic cannot be successfully contained with ideologies but must be countered by science-based rationalism. In our introductory chapter to this volume, we argued that governance matters in systemic risk responses. We can now venture one step further and argue that governance is more successful if scientific knowledge is actively promoted and considered. Unfortunately, most MENA countries are still underperforming in this regard: investment in fundamental research is marginal, academic freedoms are limited and political interference at universities is abundant (Kohstall, Richter, Dhouib and Kastner, 2018). Thus, a call for more effective COVID-19 policies must include a call for better acknowledgement and consideration of scientific research.

The coronavirus has drastically shown two implications in this regard. Firstly, medical research is indispensable, but the social sciences and humanities are needed as well to add context and to counter the mutual lack of trust between governments and citizens. Thus, a focus on the 'hard sciences', as has been promoted in authoritarian regimes for decades, is insufficient; higher education and research must be understood as comprehensive and all-encompassing – universities are universal. Secondly, fighting a pandemic requires international cooperation, at both the level of politics and of research cooperation. Cross-border research projects are the dictate of the moment – universities are universal in this regard as well. Promoting sciences in general and getting involved in global science cooperation would lead to better governance in regard to the COVID-19 pandemic as much as many other challenges of our time, be it climate change, human rights, future technologies or fairness in global trade.

References

Bowman, Brett (2020): On the biopolitics of breathing: race, protests, and state violence under the global threat of COVID-19. *South African Journal of Psychology*, 50(3): pp. 312–15. https://doi.org/10.1177/0081246320947856.

Kamel, Maha S. (2018): China's Belt and Road initiative: implications for the Middle East. *Cambridge Review of International Affairs*, 31(1): pp. 76–95. https://doi.org/10.1080/09557571.2018.1480592.

Klinke, Andreas / Renn, Ortwin (2019): The coming of age of risk governance. *Risk Analysis*, online first. https://doi.org/10.1111/risa.13383.

Kohstall, Florian / Richter, Carola / Dhouib, Sarhan / Kastner, Fatima (eds.) (2018): *Academia in transformation. Scholars facing the Arab Spring*. Baden-Baden: Nomos. https://doi.org/10.5771/9783845274348.

Margraf, Jürgen / Brailovskaia, Julia / Schneider, Silvia (2020): Behavioral measures to fight COVID-19: an 8-country study of perceived usefulness, adherence and their predictors. *PLoS ONE*, 15(12): 1–22. https://doi.org/10.1371/journal.pone.0243523.

Schweizer, Pia-Johanna (2019): Systemic risks – concepts and challenges for risk governance. *Journal of Risk Research*, online first: pp. 1–17. https://doi.org/10.1080/13669877.2019.1687574.

Siddiqui, Sabena (2020): COVID-19 diplomacy: mapping China's Health Silk Road in the Middle East. *The New Arab*, 19 May. https://english.alaraby.co.uk/analysis/mapping-chinas-health-silk-road-middle-east.

Siegrist, Michael / Zingg, Alexandra (2014): The role of public trust during pandemics: implications for crisis communication. *European Psychologist*, 19(1): pp. 23–32. https://doi.org/10.1027/1016-9040/a000169.

Wehbe, Sarah / Fahme, Sasha A. / Rizk, Anthony / Mumtaz, Ghina R. / DeJong, Jocelyn / Sibai, Abla M. (2021): COVID-19 in the Middle East and North Africa region: an urgent call for reliable, disaggregated and openly shared data. *BMJ Global Health*, 6: pp. 1–4. https://doi.org/10.1136/bmjgh-2021-005175.

Zyoud, Sa'ed (2021): The Arab region's contribution to global COVID-19 research: bibliometric and visualization analysis. *Globalization and Health*, 17(31): pp. 1–10. https://doi.org/10.1186/s12992-021-00690-8.

Index

4 humanity 97
5G networks 21, 25, 27, 28

Abou Naim, Abdelhamid 82
Abraham Accords 97, 98
Afghanistan 9
African Union (AU) 79, 136
Ahmed, Abiy 136
air pollution 143
air travel 4, 45–7, 66, 109, 144–5
Al-Ahram 62, 63
Al-Ain University 58
Al-Assad, B. *see* Assad, Bashir
Al-Atawneh, Muhammad 113
Al-Bashir, Omar 136, 137
Al-Bayna al-Jadeeda 64, 65
Al-Hariri, Rafik 38
Al-Manar 45, 46
Al-Monitor 95, 98
Al-Mustaqbal al-Iraqi 65
Al Nahan, Tahnoon bin Zayed 24
Al-Otaiba, Youssef 94–5
Al-Quds brigades 42
Al-Sabah 64, 65
Al-Sa'd, Abdullah 113
Al-Sahwa 68–9
Al-Sharq al-Awsat see Asharq al-Awsat
Al-Shorouk 62, 63, 64
Al-Thawrah 60, 62, 67, 68
Al-Wafd 62–3, 64
Aleppo 41–2
Algeria 1, 2, 3, 5, 8
Alibaba Group 27, 28
Al Maktoum, Mohammed bin Rashid 90
Amal Movement 40
Amnesty International 8, 23
anti-Chinese rhetoric 58, 63, 64–5

anti-COVID-19 vaccination campaigns 5
Aoun, Michel 39
apps 8, 23, 24, 27, 29, 162, 172
Arab countries 3, 4, 5, 25, 58
artificial intelligence (AI) 19, 24, 25, 28, 88, 97, 153
Asharq al-Awsat 93
Ashura 108
Assad, Bashir 38, 95
Assad regime 41, 42
authoritarian systems 1, 3, 58–60, 171, 173–4
autocratic collaborations 8, 19–30; China-Gulf ties 20–1; Bahrain 25–6; Oman 28–9; Saudi Arabia 27–8; United Arab Emirates (UAE) 23–5; conceptual roadmap 22; empirical assessments 22–3
Ayatollah 113

Bahrain 2, 5, 8, 9, 22, 25–6
Batelco 25
BBC 82
BeAware Bahrain 26
behavioural immune system 55
Beijing 21, 80, 97
Beirut 39, 45, 46, 47, 131, 142, 143, 144, 145, 146
Beirut International Airport 9, 47
Belt-and-Road Initiative (BRI) 20, 21, 22–3, 30
Benkirane, Abdelilah 74–5
BGI group 24, 26, 28, 29
Bieber, Florian 55, 57–8
Biden, Joe 11
bin Zayed, Abdullah 94, 98
bin Zayed, Mohammed 25, 95, 96
Brinks, Daniel 22
Bronfenbrenner theory 166

Cairo airport 59, 63
Canada 5, 31n5
Casablanca 72, 78, 80
ceremony/ceremonies (religious) 11, 97
China: anti-Chinese rhetoric 58, 63, 64–5; othering 10; partnership with Morocco 79–80; relations with Gulf countries 8, 19–30, 172; Bahrain 25–6; conceptual roadmap 22; deepening of 20–1; empirical assessments 22–3; Oman 28–9; Saudi Arabia 27–8; United Arab Emirates (UAE) 23–5, 94, 95, 96, 97, 99, 100; State Council Information Office 21
China Daily Group 29
Chinese Red Cross 64
churches 107
citizen behaviour 7
closed-circuit television (CCTV) 19, 25–6, 27
communicative strategies 9–11, 148, 150
complex task teaching 164
complex thinking 166
computers 158, 162
cooperative learning 162–3
Copenhagen School 73
Council of Guardians 113
COVID-19 pandemic: communicative strategies 9–11; deaths worldwide 4; economic implications 3–4, 77, 89–91, 151; geopolitical consequences 8–9; infections worldwide 4; social implications 3–4, 11–12; systemic risk and societal resilience 6–8
creativity 165
critical thinking 166

DarkMatter Group 23
data protection 8
Denmark 63
Diab, Hassan 145
digital infrastructure 21
Digital Silk Road 21, 23
digital surveillance *see* surveillance technology
digital technology 27, 153
diplomacy 8, 10, 20–1, 26, 94, 96, 136
distance learning 159–68, 171; humanities' role in 165–7; implementation 159–61; interactive teaching methods 162–5

doctors 1, 4, 43, 45, 66, 78, 115
drugs sales 43–4
Dubai girls 11, 127

e-health 148–9
Ebola 3, 4, 6, 7, 73
ecological approach 166
Economic and Social Commission for Western Asia (ESCWA) 3
economic implications of pandemic 3–4, 77, 89–91, 151
education 12, 144; Lebanon 12, 156, 157–9
  distance learning 159–61, 171
Egypt 1, 2, 5, 9, 59, 62–4, 69
El-Othmani, Saadeddine 75, 77, 81
El-Sisi, Abdel Fattah 59
Emirates 4
emotional intelligence 165, 167
environmental difficulties 143
error exploitation-based learning (EEBL) 163–4
Ethiopian migrants 11–12, 125–38, 172–3; case studies 131–2; effects of COVID-19 132–4; government responses 134–7
Etihad 4
Europe 63
European Union (EU) 1, 136, 137, 138n2
evangelical Christians 107
exclusionary nationalism 57–8

female migrants 11–12, 125–38, 172–3; case studies 131–2; effects of COVID-19 132–4; government responses 134–7
flights *see* air travel
flipped classroom 163
freedom of expression 81–2
functional leadership 6–7; *see also* governance

G42 *see* Group 42
García de Paredes, Marta 78
Gaskell, Jennifer 6
Gaza strip 1
gender equality 93
geopolitical consequences 8–9
Germany 5, 63, 94, 116
Ghebreyesus, Tedros Adhanom 96
Google Play 24, 29
governance 5, 6, 151–2, 171, 174; *see also* authoritarian systems; risk governance

Index

Group 42 (G42) 23, 24, 26, 28, 31n4, 97
Gulf Cooperation Council (GCC) 1, 98–9, 133
Gulf countries, links with China 8, 19–30, 172; Bahrain 25–6; conceptual roadmap 22; deepening of 20–1; empirical assessments 22–3; Oman 28–9; Saudi Arabia 27–8; United Arab Emirates (UAE) 23–5, 94, 95, 96, 97, 99, 100
Gulf monarchies 1, 2

hajj 11, 108, 109, 110, 111, 115
Hamad, Hassan 47
Hanbali (school/scholar) 111, 119n2
haramaininfo 110, 112
health care provision 1–2; Iran 43–4, 116–17; Lebanon 12, 41, 142–4, 172; COVID-19 management 144–7; impact of context, health and governance 151–2; successes and pitfalls 147–50
health security 73
Health Silk Road 20–1, 23, 172
Healthcare Access and Quality Index 2016 2
Hezbollah 9, 12, 36–49, 172; control of Lebanese Ministry of Health 42–4; COVID-19 public health campaign 44–7; as Iranian proxy in Lebanon 39–42, 47–8; political divisions in Lebanon 38–9
HIV 73, 174
Hong Kong 26
Horn of Africa 11
hospitals 2, 4; Egypt 5; Lebanon 142–3, 145, 146, 147, 148, 150, 152, 153; Hezbollah 43, 44, 45, 46, 47; Morocco 10; Tunisia 1
Huawei 21, 25, 27, 28
Human Development Report (UNDP) 73, 78
human security 73
human trafficking 11, 125–38, 172–3; case studies 131–2; effects of COVID-19 132–4; government responses 134–7
humanitarianism 94–6
humanities in distance learning 165–7

Ibn 'Arabi 111
Ibn Taymiyya 111
information and communication technologies (ICT) 156, 158, *159*, 160–1, 168

intensive care beds 1
interactive teaching methods 162–5
Intergovernmental Authority on Development (IGAD) 136
International Humanitarian City (IHC) 94, 95–6
International Monetary Fund (IMF) 77
international organisations 92, 96, 99, 100
international status 92
internet 7, 25, 82, 158, 160, 164
Iran: connections between Hezbollah and 9, 36, 37; COVID-19 public health campaign 44–7; Hezbollah as Iranian proxy 39–42, 47–8; health care provision 43–4; connections between Qatar and 98; COVID-19 cases 44; COVID-19 deaths 44; COVID-19 response 5; healthcare 43–4, 116–17; Healthcare Access and Quality Index 2016 2; media coverage 9; newspapers 62; othering 10, 68; religion 119n3; pilgrimage 108, 109, 110; and state 113–14, 115, 116, 117, 118; religious actors 11; support from UAE 94, 96; US sanctions 42, 65; vaccination campaigns 5
Iranian Revolutionary Guard Corps (IRGC) 40, 41, 42
Iraq 1, 2, 9, 59–60, 64–5
Islam *see* Shi'a Islam; Sunni Islam; Wahhabi Islam
Islamic pilgrimage 108–12, 115–16
Israel: COVID-19 response 5; diplomatic relations with 3; Healthcare Access and Quality Index 2016 2; and Iran 40, 41; and UAE 94, 97–8, 100; ultra-orthodox Jews 107; vaccination campaigns 5

Jabak, Jamal 43–4
Janjaweed 137
John Hopkins University 4, 59
Jordan 2, 5, 8
journalists 81, 82

KAS (Konrad Adenauer Foundation) 8, 10, 13, 152
Khartoum 11, 125–7, 128, 130–2, 133, 172–3
Khartoum Process 135, 136, 137, 145
Khatami, Mohammad 113
Kuwait 2, 5, 8, 9

Index   179

labour migration 129, 135
labour trafficking 134
Lahoud, Émile 38
leadership *see* functional leadership; political leadership
League of Arab States (LAS) 1
Lebanese Red Cross 148
Lebanon 1; civil war 142; COVID-19 cases 145, 146, 147; COVID-19 deaths 145, 146, 147; COVID-19 management 141–2, 144–53; impact of context, health and governance 151–2; successes and pitfalls 147–50; education system 12, 156, 157–9; distance learning 159–61, 171; health care provision 12, 41, 142–4, 172; Healthcare Access and Quality Index 2016 2; Hezbollah's influence in 9, 12, 36–49, 172; control of Ministry of Health 42–4; COVID-19 public health campaign 44–7; H. as Iranian proxy 39–42, 47–8; political divisions 38–9; as Iran's proxy state 9; life expectancy 2; Ministry of Public Health (MoPH) 9, 12; public polls 8; refugees 143, 157; vaccination campaigns 5
legitimacy 19
Libya 1, 2, 5, 8
life expectancies 2

ME3 carriers 4
media 9–10, 28; othering 55–69; cases of investigation 58–61; Egypt 62–4; Iraq 64–5; methodology 61–2; Oman 66–7; theoretical framework 56–8; Yemen 67–9; *see also* journalists
media campaigns 148
Medias24 79, 82
medical care *see* health care provision
medical research 2
medicines, sale of 43–4
Mélenchon, Jean-Luc 80
MENA region 1–2, 3, 5; *see also* Arab countries; Gulf countries, links with China
MERS (Middle Eastern respiratory syndrome) 3, 4, 6, 7, 73, 109, 116
migrant workers 2; *see also* female migrants
Ministry of Public Health (MoPH), Lebanon 9, 12, 42–4, 45, 48, 142, 144, 145–6, 148, 172

Mohamed bin Zayed University of Artificial Intelligence 30n4
Mohammed VI 10, 75, 77, 78, 79, 80–1, 82, 171
Morocco 72–83; COVID-19 cases 72; COVID-19 deaths 72; gross domestic product (GDP) 77; Healthcare Access and Quality Index 2016 2; inequalities 78; othering 10; partnership with China 79–80; public polls 8; respirators 1; securitisation 72–83; freedom of expression 81–2; measures and domains of intervention 77–80; role of the Palace 74–7, 78–9, 81; technocratisation 80–1; vaccination campaigns 5, 79–80
mosques 11, 59, 72, 82, 95, 107, 109, 110, 111, 113, 114
Mourad, Hadi 43, 44, 46
Mousavi, Sayyid Abbas 96
Muharram 110, 118
mujtahids 113
Muscat Airport 24
Muscat Daily 29, 62, 66–7
Muslim World League 117

Nasrallah, Hassan 41, 42, 44
national cohesion 66–7
National Committee for Communicable Diseases, Lebanon 145
nationalism 55, 57–8
Netanyahu, Benjamin 97
Netherlands 5
New York 107
New York Times 24
newspapers 62; Egypt 62–4; Iraq 64–5; Oman 66–7; Yemen 67–9
Norway 8
nurses 45, 144

Obama, Barack 94
Oman: COVID-19 response 60; governance 60; Healthcare Access and Quality Index 2016 2; as Iran's proxy state 9; media 60; media coverage 9; newspapers 62; othering 66–7, 69; relations with China 22, 28–9
Oman Daily Observer 66
online learning *see* distance learning
opinion polls 8
Orbán, Viktor 55
Orient-Le-Jour 146
Orientalism (Said) 56

othering 9–10, 55–69, 171–2; cases of investigation 58–61; Egypt 62–4; Iraq 64–5; methodology 61–2; Oman 66–7; theoretical framework 56–8; Yemen 67–9
Ottoman government 115–16
Oxfam 78

Pakistan 107
Palermo I Protocol 130, 134, 136
Palestine 2, 5
pandemic *see* COVID-19 pandemic
Peng Xiao 23, 30n4
Pentecostal preachers 118
personal protective equipment (PPE) 1, 132, 148
pilgrimage 108–12, 115–16
pilgrims 4, 11, 47
political leadership 5; *see also* functional leadership; governance
political systems 3; *see also* authoritarian systems
private health care 12, 142–4, 146, 152
project-based learning 163
Project Raven 23
Prophet 109, 110, 111, 112
proxy states 9
proxy theory 39–42
psychosocial skills 165, 167
public health systems 4, 12, 142–4; COVID-19 response 144–53; impact of context, health and governance 151–2; successes and pitfalls 147–50
public polls 8

Qatar 2, 5, 9, 63, 93, 98–9
Qatar Airways 4
Qom 45, 47, 109, 110, 111, 114
quarantine rules 31n5
question-based learning 163
Qur'an 109, 111, 112

Rabat 80
Rafik Hariri University Hospital (RHUH) 145–6
Ramadan 5, 95, 107, 110, 127
refugees 143, 157
religion 107–18, 119n3; pilgrimage 108–12; and state 112–17
religious actors 11, 118, 173
remote cooperative learning 162–3
remote error exploitation-based learning (EEBL) 163–4

remote flipped classroom 163
remote question-based learning 163
remoted project-based learning 163
Reporters Without Borders 81
respirators 1, 148
Reuters Staff 108
risk governance 6, 7
Riyadh 27, 62, 68
Russia 41, 94, 97, 100

Safi al-Din, Sayyid Hashem 45–6
Said, Edward W. 56, 57
saints 110–11, 118
samasra 125–31, 132–3, 137–8, 173
Sana'a 60, 67–8
SARS (severe acute respiratory syndrome) 4, 7, 73, 108
Saudi Arabia: COVID-19 response 5, 114; Healthcare Access and Quality Index 2016 2; labour migration 129, 135; medical research 2; Middle Eastern respiratory syndrome (MERS) 3; othering 10, 66, 68; relations with China 22, 27–8; relations with Qatar 98; religion 107, 119n3; pilgrimage 108, 109–10; and state 112–13, 114–15, 116–17, 117–18; religious actors 11; vaccination campaigns 5
Saudi Data and Artificial Intelligence Authority (SDAIA) 28
Saudi Gazette 109
Saudi Media City 27, 31n7
school education *see* education
scientific knowledge 174
secondary elites 171
securitisation, Morocco 72–83; freedom of expression 81–2; measures and domains of intervention 77–80; role of Palace 74–7, 78–9, 81; technocratisation 80–1
sex trafficking 134
Shah, Reza 116
Shbaro, Asrar 46
Shi'a Islam 107, 110–11, 113, 117–18
Singapore 26
Sino-Gulf relations 8, 19–30, 172; Bahrain 25–6; conceptual roadmap 22; deepening ties 20–1; empirical assessments 22–3; Oman 28–9; Saudi Arabia 27–8; United Arab Emirates (UAE) 23–5, 94, 95, 96, 97, 99, 100
Sinopharm 26, 97
Sisi, A. *see* El-Sisi, Abdel Fattah

Index   181

smart cities 27
social implications of pandemic 3–4, 11–12
societal resilience 6–8
socioeconomic potency 6, 7
Soft Power Strategy (UAE, 2017) 94
Somalia 2, 95, 128
South Korea 107
South Sudan 125
Spanish flu 116
speech acts 73–4, 75
Spivak, Gayatri 56
Sputnik V 97
State Council Information Office, China 21
status-seeking 91–3; in a global pandemic 93–9
status signalling 92
status symbols 92
stereotypes 57, 63, 64
Sudan 1; Government of (GoS) 128, 136–7; Healthcare Access and Quality Index 2016 2; human trafficking 11, 125–38, 172–3; case studies 131–2; effects of COVID-19 132–4; government responses 134–7; life expectancy 2; political protesters 3; vaccination campaigns 5
Sunni Islam 107, 110, 111
surveillance / surveillance technology 8; Bahrain 25–6; China 19; Lebanon 148–9; Oman 28–9; Saudi Arabia 28–9; Sudan 137; United Arab Emirates (UAE) 23–5, 90, 97, 172
Syria 1, 2, 5, 38–9, 41–2, 94
Syrian refugees 143, 157
systemic risks 6

Tarrassud app 29
teaching methods 162–5
technocratisation 80–1
Tehran 9, 37, 41, 43, 46, 47, 109
Tehran Times 43–4
Thailand 5
theo-monarchy 113
Tigray 136, 137
Times of Oman 60, 66
ToTok 24
Trump administration 94
Trump, Donald 9, 55, 63, 65, 97–8
trust 6, 7, 13n2, 20–1, 57, 115, 146, 152, 173–4
Trust in Institutions Index, Morocco 79
Tunisia 1, 2, 5, 8
Turkey 5

umrah 108
United Arab Emirates (UAE): COVID-19 response 5; foreign policy 88–9, 172; status-seeking 91–100; Healthcare Access and Quality Index 2016 2; impact of COVID-19 pandemic 89–91; as Iran's proxy state 9; leadership 10; medical research 2; othering 68; relations with China 22, 23–5, 94, 95, 96, 97, 99, 100; relations with Iran 94; relations with Israel 94, 97–8, 100; relations with Qatar 98–9; relations with USA 94, 97–8, 100; vaccination campaigns 5; war in Yemen 98, 100
United Kingdom (UK) 5, 94
United Nations Development Programme (UNDP) 73
United Nations High Commissioner for Refugees (UNHCR) 129, 136
United Nations (UN) 12, 67, 141; Economic and Social Commission for Western Asia (ESCWA) 3
United States of America: Iran sanctions 42, 65; othering 10, 64–5, 67; partnership with Saudi Arabia 27; political leadership 5; religious actors 107, 118; Trump administration 9; and United Arab Emirates (UAE) 94, 97–8, 100

vaccination campaigns 5, 79–80
vaccine 7, 26, 28, 48
vaccine development 97
vaccine trials 26, 28, 80, 97, 99–100
Vietnam 5
Vision 2021 88–9, 90
VIVA (Bahrain) 25

Wahhabi Islam 107, 110, 111–12, 119n2
Wang, Cheng 29
water poverty 143
Wohlforth, William 92, 93
women *see* female migrants
women's participation 93
World Bank 143, 144
World Economic Forum 166
World Health Organisation (WHO) 90, 94, 96, 116, 143, 144, 146, 147
World Health Organization's Eastern Mediterranean Regional Office (WHO-EMRO) 2
Wuhan 28, 65, 81, 88, 109

xenophobia 55, 63
Xinhua 72
Xinhua.net 29

YeeCall 24
Yemen 1; (civil) war 10, 42, 60, 67, 98; COVID-19 response 60; governance 60; Healthcare Access and Quality Index 2016 2; Hezbollah 42; media 9, 60–1; newspapers 62; othering 10, 67–9; UAE's involvement in 98, 100; vaccination campaigns 5

Zain (Saudi Arabia) 27
Zoom 160, 161, 162